Traces of Aerial Bombing in Berlin

A Modern History of Politics and Violence

Series Editors: Paul Jackson *(University of Northampton, UK)* and Raul Carstocea *(University of Leicester, UK)*

Editorial Board:
Roger Griffin *(Oxford Brookes University, UK)*
Leonard Weinberg *(University of Nevada, USA)*
Ramon Spaaij *(La Trobe University, Melbourne, Australia)*
Richard Steigmann-Gall *(Kent State University, USA)*
Aristotle Kallis *(Keele University, UK)*
Matthew Feldman *(University of Teesside, UK)*
Kathleen Blee *(University of Pittsburgh, USA)*

The book series *A Modern History of Politics and Violence* scrutinizes diverse histories of political violence in the modern world, from the French Revolution to the late 20th century. Volumes in the series – comprising both monographs and edited collections – aim to further our understanding of violence as part of the modern experience.

The series has a global scope and seeks to challenge Eurocentric assumptions. Areas of particular interest include: modernization and violence, colonial era violence and acts of aggression accompanying processes of decolonization, political violence associated with communist and fascist movements and regimes, liberal cultures of political violence and the use of violence to achieve emancipatory political ends.

The series aims to explore both violence 'from above', directed by state institutions such as armies or law enforcement agencies, and violence 'from below', developed by a wide range of individuals and groups. Volumes in the series also question the cultural foundations of violence, and how perceptions of gender, race, class, community and memory can be used to legitimate violent acts. In line with its interest in novel methodological approaches, the series encourages volumes that seek to redefine, broaden or challenge extant definitions of violence.

Finally, the series also examines the impact of political violence on its victims, as well as its lasting consequences.

Published:

British Fascist Antisemitism and the Jewish Responses, 1932–40, Daniel Tilles (2014)

A British Fascist in the Second World War, edited by Brendan Fleming and Claudia Baldoli (2014)

Civil Uprisings in Modern Sudan, W. J. Berridge (2015)

Transnational Fascism in the Twentieth Century: Spain, Italy and the Global Neo-Fascist Network, Matteo Albanese and Pablo del Hierro (2016)

Colin Jordan and Britain's Neo-Nazi Social Movement, Paul Jackson (2016)

The Victims of Slavery, Colonization and the Holocaust, Kitty Millet (2017)

Survivor Transitional Narratives of Nazi-Era Destruction: The Second Liberation, Dennis B. Klein (2017)

The Image of the Soldier in German Culture, 1871–1933, Paul Fox (2017)

Nazi Germany, Annexed Poland and Colonial Rule: Resettlement, Germanization and Population Policies in Comparative Perspective, Rachel O'Sullivan (2023)

Traces of Aerial Bombing in Berlin: Entangled Remembering, Eloise Florence (2024)

Forthcoming:

The Comparative History of Fascism in Eastern Europe, Constantin Iordachi

Violence, American Law and the Shaping of Modern Black Masculinity, Seneca Vaught

Traces of Aerial Bombing in Berlin

Entangled Remembering

Authored by Eloise Florence

BLOOMSBURY ACADEMIC
LONDON • NEW YORK • OXFORD • NEW DELHI • SYDNEY

BLOOMSBURY ACADEMIC

Bloomsbury Publishing Plc, 50 Bedford Square, London, WC1B 3DP, UK
Bloomsbury Publishing Inc, 1385 Broadway, New York, NY 10018, USA
Bloomsbury Publishing Ireland, 29 Earlsfort Terrace, Dublin 2, D02 AY28, Ireland

BLOOMSBURY, BLOOMSBURY ACADEMIC and the Diana logo
are trademarks of Bloomsbury Publishing Plc

First published in Great Britain 2024
Paperback publication year is 2025

Copyright © Eloise Florence, 2024

Eloise Florence has asserted her right under the Copyright,
Designs and Patents Act, 1988, to be identified as author of this work.

For legal purposes the Acknowledgements on p. xii constitute an
extension of this copyright page.

Series design by Clare Turner
Cover image: Author's image © Eloise Florence

All rights reserved. No part of this publication may be: i) reproduced or transmitted in any form, electronic or mechanical, including photocopying, recording or by means of any information storage or retrieval system without prior permission in writing from the publishers; or ii) used or reproduced in any way for the training, development or operation of artificial intelligence (AI) technologies, including generative AI technologies. The rights holders expressly reserve this publication from the text and data mining exception as per Article 4(3) of the Digital Single Market Directive (EU) 2019/790.

Bloomsbury Publishing Plc does not have any control over, or responsibility for, any third-party websites referred to or in this book. All internet addresses given in this book were correct at the time of going to press. The author and publisher regret any inconvenience caused if addresses have changed or sites have ceased to exist, but can accept no responsibility for any such changes.

Every effort has been made to trace the copyright holders and obtain permission to reproduce the copyright material. Please do get in touch with any enquiries or any information relating to such material or the rights holder. We would be pleased to rectify any omissions in subsequent editions of this publication should they be drawn to our attention.

A catalogue record for this book is available from the British Library.

A catalog record for this book is available from the Library of Congress.

ISBN:	HB:	978-1-3502-6899-9
	PB:	978-1-3502-6903-3
	ePDF:	978-1-3502-6900-2
	eBook:	978-1-3502-6901-9

Typeset by Integra Software Services Pvt. Ltd.

For product safety related questions contact productsafety@bloomsbury.com.

To find out more about our authors and books visit www.bloomsbury.com
and sign up for our newsletters.

For mum and dad.

Contents

List of illustrations   x
Acknowledgements   xii

Introduction   1

1   A genealogy of remembering area bombing   19
2   A history of remembering through places   47
3   Methods – Gleaning cultural memory from sites in Berlin   71
4   Layers of history   95
5   Vibrant, unruly rubble   125
6   Aerial photography and bodily violence   157
7   Bodies in the stones   185
8   Conclusions   215

Notes   226
References   232
Index   249

List of illustrations

Int.1	Rubble in the forest at Teufelsberg, Berlin	2
Int.2	Teufelsberg, a hill on the outskirts of Berlin made from the resultant rubble from the destruction of Berlin during the Second World War. The former NSA spy station remains on top	3
3.1	Teufelsberg, Berlin	76
4.1	Artwork at the spy station at Teufelsberg, Berlin	96
4.2	The forest at Teufelsberg, Berlin	99
4.3	Rubble entwined in the roots of a tree in the forest at Teufelsberg, Berlin	108
4.4	Rubble in the forest at Teufelsberg, Berlin	109
4.5	The ruins of Anhalter Bahnhof, Berlin	112
4.6	The interior of the abandoned spy station at Teufelsberg, Berlin	115
4.7	The remains of the original platforms at Anhalter Bahnhof, Berlin	117
4.8	The only photograph taken on my research visit to the Jewish memorial cemetery on Grosse Hamburger Strasse in Mitte, Berlin	118
5.1	Rubble in the forest at Teufelsberg, Berlin	128
5.2	Rubble pieces entwined with vines and leaf litter at Volkspark Prenzlauerberg, a *Trümmerberg* in Berlin	138
5.3	Remnants of a metal pipe at Teufelsberg, Berlin	139
5.4	Berliners enjoy the summer in Volkspark Hasenheide, a park built on a *Trümmerberg*	140
5.5	Signage at the Topography of Terror, showing the use of the site as Gestapo headquarters and the damage they suffered under Allied bombs	149
5.6	Anhalter S-Bahn station, showing photos of the overland station that now stands in ruins, Berlin	151
6.1	Forests at Marienhöhe, a *Trümmerberg* in Berlin	158
6.2	Aerial photograph of bomb damage on information boards at the Topography of Terror, Berlin	160
6.3	Open spaces at the Topography of Terror, Berlin	171
6.4	Rubble in the forest at Teufelsberg, Berlin	172

6.5	An elevated view from the top of the spy station on Teufelsberg, Berlin	176
6.6	A path cuts through the rubble that makes up the *Trümmerberg* Insulaner, Berlin	181
7.1	A shard of tile found in the forest at Teufelsberg, Berlin	186
7.2	Rubble in the forest at Teufelsberg, Berlin	188
7.3	A twisted piece of metal in the forest at Teufelsberg, Berlin	190
7.4	The Schwerbelastungskörper in Berlin	193
7.5	Interior of the Schwerbelastungskörper in Berlin	193
7.6	Ground level at the Schwerbelastungskörper, Berlin	194
7.7	Rubble pieces in the forest at Teufelsberg, Berlin	207

Acknowledgements

This book is generously supported by the Australian Academy of the Humanities' Publication Subsidy Scheme 2021. The book was also informed by a postgraduate research project at RMIT University Melbourne, undertaken with support of an Australian Government Research Training Program Scholarship.

The support and insight of all my colleagues at RMIT and Western Sydney University have been invaluable in the development of an idea into a project and then into a book, particularly that of Philip Dearman, Chris Hudson, Glen Donnar and Anna Hickey-Moody at RMIT and Fiona Cameron at Western Sydney. My deepest thanks also to Indigo Holcombe-James at ACMI for her advice, wisdom and encouragement as I worked to turn a research project into a book in the middle of a pandemic, and for all the thoughtful discussions about culture, history and rocks. I am also deeply grateful for the feedback and insights on this project from Robert Saunders at Farmingdale State College (SUNY), Dorota Golanska at the University of Lodz and Shanti Sumartojo at Monash University.

I am grateful to series editors Paul Jackson at University of Northampton and Raul Cârstocea at Maynooth University for their advice and feedback as I developed the concept for the book, as well as the anonymous reviewers who donated their time, provided thoughtful insights on the manuscript and helped improve the book immensely.

I would like to give my warmest thanks to all the friends old and new who helped me in Berlin and the UK when I conducted this research. This book would not have been possible without the help, advice, beds, directions, lifts, beers and breakfasts they provided – thank you.

I am, as always, indebted to the ongoing support of my enduring friends, my wonderful family and my Elliott. Without you all I could not have undertaken, persevered and completed this project. You have always cheered me on and kept me going, and I can never thank you enough.

Introduction

Teufelsberg

On the outskirts of Berlin stands a small, green hill. It is not, by any standard, particularly tall or impressive – rising only about 80 meters – but it nonetheless stands out significantly from the otherwise flat Teltow Plateau on which Berlin sits. The hill is Teufelsberg, or 'devil's mountain', and it was named after the nearby lake Teufelssee (devil's lake). It is covered in the trees of the Grunewald, a large, sprawling forest that stretches northwest of the city, thick with deciduous trees and wildlife. In the winter, small tracts of cleared forest are perfect for sledding, and were once used as ski slopes. In the summer, the greenery, birdlife, and nearby lake make it nigh on idyllic, and it is a popular place for hiking, mountain-bike riding and parties that pump techno music and driving bass lines through the trees at night.

In the hot Berlin summers, walking Teufelsberg can be like walking through a fairy tale forest, weaving one's way between trees and basking in the dappled sunlight that falls on the criss-crossing pathways. Look closer at the paths, however, and one will see a scattering of small stone objects. Some are quite innocuous rocks, but others are more curious, cut at irregular angles. Some are made up of dramatically different colours and materials; some have strange markings on them; some are unmistakably man-made: tiles, glass, bricks, and pavers.

Teufelsberg is a *Trümmerberg*, a 'rubble mountain'. It is a hill made up of the 55 million tonnes of rubble that resulted from the hugely destructive aerial bombing raids the Allies visited on Berlin during the Second World War. Berlin's buildings, its houses, schools, shops, city halls, museums, train stations, hospitals, factories, Gestapo headquarters, cemeteries and monuments were reduced by Allied explosives and incendiaries to rubble, much of which was cleared, sorted, cleaned and carted into seven small hills – *Trümmerberge* – across the city. At 80 meters, Teufelsberg is the highest.

Today, Teufelsberg remains as a testament to Berlin's violent history. This, of course, is nothing short of commonplace in the capital: one can't throw an irregularly shaped stone without striking a memorial, museum, monument, plaque, or *Stolpersteine* detailing, acknowledging, 'working through' the city's history as the centre of the Second World War, the Cold War and, most importantly, as the linchpin the Nazis' terror and genocide machine. But as a huge amassment of rubble caused by Allied violence and destruction on a civilian setting, Teufelsberg's looming mass and the plethora of rubble on its paths also speak to a particular episode of Berlin's history that has more often than not been excluded from the story of the Second World War, a story that has been obsessively told and retold for decades for and by English-speakers.

✶✶✶

Allied bombing of German cities during the Second World War was unprecedented in scale and severity. Over a million tonnes of ordnance fell on German cities and towns. Recent research has found that the campaigns were so violent they damaged the earth's outer-most layer of atmosphere, the ionosphere (Scott & Major 2018), where the International Space Station orbits and where auroras are made. Each raid had on average the energy of 300 lightning strikes.

Figure Int.1 Rubble in the forest at Teufelsberg, Berlin. Photograph by Eloise Florence, 2017.

Figure Int.2 Teufelsberg, a hill on the outskirts of Berlin made from the resultant rubble from the destruction of Berlin during the Second World War. The former NSA spy station remains on top. Photograph by Eloise Florence, 2017.

This mass bombing marked the culmination of a phenomenon that became known as 'area bombing': rather than targeting military facilities or supporting the advance of ground troops, area bombing aimed to break the morale of the enemy through large-scale attacks on built-up civilian areas. German civilians living in cities were subject to raids by the American air force (USAAF) by day and the British Royal Air Force (RAF) at night,[1] leaving what one British author (Bielenberg 1984[1968]) called 'the few hours left for living' in between (p. 242). The target was enemy civilians' 'will to resist', earning the campaigns other monikers like 'terror bombing' and 'morale bombing'.

The total number of civilian casualties of air bombing across Germany is the subject of ongoing and often vitriolic debate.[2] National numbers vary greatly across historical accounts, from around 300,000 (Arnold 2011; Moeller 2006; Overy 2014) to almost a million (Connelly 2002; Friedrich 2006). For Berlin alone, total civilian causalities due to bombing have been recorded as high as 25,000 (Rigden 2020; Schaffer 1980) and as low as 3,000 (Davis 1991; Groehler 1992). Moeller (2006) adds 'all casualty counts are estimates because local officials were kept so busy tending to the living that they could not accurately count the dead' (p. 108).

This book emerged from a certain discomfiture caused by the knowledge of the scale and severity of the bombings that is evidenced by places like Teufelsberg. It began in 2015, when I read W. G. Sebald's lecture 'On air war and literature', published in English in 2004 with several other works of Sebald's literary criticism under the translated title *On the Natural History of Destruction* (2004). An authoritative examination of what Sebald sees as a notable lack of literature that offers German perspectives of the experience of aerial bombing during the Second World War, the book addressed what Sebald saw as a taboo amongst German writers against properly acknowledging and depicting the suffering many Germans underwent during the war under the Allies' bombs. The book had an immense impact on still ongoing debates about German memory cultures surrounding its wartime and Holocaust past (see Childers 2005; Friedrich 2006; Grayling 2007; Kettenacker 2010; Moeller 2005; 2006; Overy 2013; Schmitz 2007; Taberner and Berger 2009).

But despite being focused on and having huge resonances in German literary, academic, and political circles, the book also spoke to something closer to home. It was, at first, inexplicably uncomfortable to read. It uses words like 'annihilation' (p. 11), 'liquidation' (p. 7), and 'destruction on a scale without historical precedent' (p. 4) to describe the deaths of thousands of civilians and the destruction of hundreds of thousands of buildings. But my discomfiture did not stem from these descriptions *per se*, but from the fact they were made of events that were in relation to, but with very little mention of, the context of the Nazis and the Holocaust. At the time I was researching Hollywood depictions of German resistance to the Nazis, and I imagined I was well-versed in the cultural impacts of the Second World War in the West, and aware of similar debates about those of Germany. But what was becoming evident on reading Sebald was not so much the *reality* of the bombings and their effects, although that was itself shocking enough. What was so discomfiting, it seemed, was the increasing awareness that I had so far read the history of the bombings through a particular lens, through a cultural memory of the Second World War that was by and large told from a perspective that can still be characterized as that of 'the victors'. My reaction towards Sebald's study of *German* wartime experience revealed the cultural frames through which I had come to understand the *Allies'* role in the war.

The purpose of this book is not to contest the historical guilt of German victims of area bombing, or the vagaries of the German victimhood debate. Rather, this book turns to the systems of telling and retelling the story of the war that causes events like area bombing to cause such discomfiture in Anglophone audiences. What has become clear is that this particular episode of wartime history lies outside of more dominant cultural memories of the Second World War. Telling and retelling the story of the Second World War has been habitually structured around specific narratives, narratives that remain significant cultural touchstones of many national cultures, not the least of Britain and America. These narrative structures position the Allies as the heroes of a 'good war' against a 'bad empire', 'winning' against a tyrannical and genocidal regime. In such narrative structures, there is little room for the suffering of Berliners under the bombs, for the exploding walls of school buildings, for entire neighbourhoods being reduced to rubble that was swept into a hill on the outskirts of the city. Teufelsberg therefore speaks to an episode of the war that is, in the very least, uncomfortable for English-language visitors to Berlin to consider in the wider context of Germany's difficult past.

Whilst forming an essential barrier against the ever-present (and by some accounts rising) threat of historical revisionism, moral relativism and outright Holocaust denial, the contentiousness of the effects of Allied aerial bombing has *also* prevented the former Allies from facing direct questions over their moral responsibility and historical accountability for mass civilian deaths and destruction in many expressions of cultural memory. In an environment in which questions about deaths or destruction caused by the bombings easily devolve to questions of the veracity of the guilt and responsibility of modern Germany for Nazi atrocities, former-Allied countries have therefore had little cause to critically examine the morality, necessity, and justification of Allied area bombing campaigns in their cultural memory. While Germany has relentlessly (and rightly) wrestled with its past for nearly eighty years (and will likely continue to do so for some time), the mainstream cultural representations of the former-Allied combatants on both sides of the Atlantic have continued to mostly exclude any Allied culpability in civilian deaths and the destruction of non-military targets from their national stories. This book aims to continue already occurring processes of addressing this, looking to more experiential encounters with the material traces of the bombings that Anglophone visitors can find in Berlin as a way to engender a more complex and nuanced cultural memory, one in which the memory of the air war becomes entangled with that of the Allies' victory over a genocidal regime, and in which the Allies might be held more accountable for mass civilian deaths and destruction.

Historical stories: Colston and Hiroshima

In the American summer of 2020, the Black Lives Matter movement swelled after the murder of George Floyd, an African American man, by white Minniapolis police officer Dick Chauvin. The movement ran alongside a wider protest against white supremacy in America and often found expression in the vandalism, destruction, and removal of statues of Confederate leaders from the American Civil War and profiteers of the trans-Atlantic slave trade from the sixteenth to the nineteenth century. This accompanying movement was by no means restricted to America; protests against many statues of chief instigators and profiteers of the British slave trade took place across the UK. An exceptional display of this revisiting of public British history occurred on 7 June 2020, when protestors removed the statue of sixteenth-century merchant Edward Colston from the city centre of Bristol, dragged it through the streets, and threw it into the water of Bristol Harbour, the very water that played a significant role in the trans-Atlantic network of slavery and from which Colston profited off human enslavement.

Colston plunging into the Bristol harbour and the similar fate of other statues across the UK and the United States was seen by many as more than a challenge of the commemoration of the trans-Atlantic slave trade. In allowing 'the activist event of the toppling of the Colston statue to speak for itself in its performance of history', protestors were challenging the 'ubiquitous veneration' (Branscome 2021) of colonialism that underpinned British national identity, the too long-accepted narrative that underpinned Britain's national sense of self. Days after Colston's fall, protestors and counter-protestors amassed in central London. Opponents to the Black Lives Matter movement were seen actively 'protecting' the statue of Winston Churchill in Parliament Square, 'so-called patriots who were there to promote the idea that British history consists only of white culture and white identity' (Branscome 2021, p. 7). These counter-protests were in a sense not against the Black Lives Matter protestors themselves, but were acting against the challenge they posed to the assuredness of Britain's historical foundations, which have been built in no small part upon heroes of the British Empire. This was evidenced by then British Prime Minister Boris Johnson's discomfiture not with the vandalism of public property but with what he saw as the cultural upheaval surrounding the Black Lives Matter movement and the accompanying removal of statues. 'Let's fight racism', Johnson argued, 'but leave our heritage broadly in peace' (BBC News 2020, p. np). The fear of destabilizing the underlying narratives of British heritage was Johnson's primary concern, and is further evidenced by counter protestors 'protecting' Winston Churchill's statue after Colston fell into the harbour. Toppling statues poses a threat in the fact it entails facing up to the ongoing potency of Britain's history of colonialism long after the Empire has crumbled. This evidences both the nature and the strength of this history, and, in a Foucauldian sense, the need to disrupt it.

The discomfiture at disrupting these established narratives of the past has been shown to apply to narratives of the Second World War too. In 1994, the Smithsonian National Air and Space Museum in Washington DC encountered considerable controversy when Enola Gay – the plane that dropped an atomic bomb on Hiroshima – was set to be displayed alongside photographs that included images and accounts of the impact of the bombs on Japanese civilians. Critics comprised mainly of veterans' groups objected to the inclusion of images of Japanese victims and so-called 'survivor objects' (Neiman 2015). 'Mostly', Neiman (2015) identifies in an analysis of the controversy, 'the critics complained that only Japanese not American victims were depicted' (p. 16). The museum's director Martin Harwit was called before Congress and asked to severely alter the exhibit. Media outlets stated Harwit 'obviously hate[d] this country and shouldn't be working [at the Smithsonian]' (Neiman 2015, p. 16). In the end, Harwit eventually resigned his post, and the exhibition was cancelled, with only the plane remaining on display.

The Colston saga belongs to the same class as the uproar over the Smithsonian exhibition about the Enola Gay: not only uproar over the *content* of historical displays or statues, but also over the underlying threat of disrupting deep-seated and long-held assurances about national stories that are so often grounded in history. Like in the Enola Gay controversy, the outrage over toppling, defacing or vandalizing Confederate and slave-trader statues seems to stem from the implication that there are more perspectives than those that have been cemented quite literally into our streets and museums, the perspectives that dominate our histories and cultural memory. After Colston fell into the water and the statues of Nelson Mandela and Mahatma Ghandi were boarded up in London (ostensibly to protect them from the right-wing counter-protestors), many commentators called for 'the need for continued dialogue to take place, on the basis that there has to be an understanding of a more complex and inclusive narrative in British history' (Branscome 2021, p. 7). Branscome points out that although they took place in the direct context of the removal of Confederate statues in the United States, the events in Britain were 'expressing something far more specific to the British situation', in which attacks on the ubiquity of colonial proponents in British history were also framed as an attack on the supposedly unshakeable certainties of the nation's stories. As the Enola Gay controversy shows, the stories surrounding the Second World War are similarly central and considered unshakeable on both sides of the Atlantic. In fact, Noakes and Pattison (2013) argue that 'One of the key functions of the cultural memory of the Second World War in post-war Britain is to mask the decline of Empire and the economic and political decline of Britain as a world power' (p. 12), demonstrating how the storying of the years 1939–45 continues to form a large part of the country's cultural memory and national identity. The widespread renegotiations of both British and American history that occurred in the summer of 2020 demonstrate the unfinished business surrounding formative histories of both colonial conquest and quite modern wartime victories. Deeply entrenched historical narratives continue to shape not only our urban landscapes but the trans-Atlantic climates of Euro-scepticism, deeply divided cultural politics and rising far-right violence, and these climates have roots in common narratives surrounding the Second World War. And yet these historical narratives, for so long concreted as the founding stories of both national identities, continue to be disrupted and challenged, demonstrating the need for a more complex and nuanced framework, with multiple voices.

Entangling cultural memory

Into this context enters the cultural memory of area bombing, a theatre of the Second World War so often positioned outside of the dominant Anglo-American articulations of cultural memory of the war. This book looks to the city of Berlin to explore the ways the violence caused by Allied wartime bombing can be remembered, and how encountering the material traces of this violence might complicate some of the underlying assumptions of the former Allies' national and historical guilt and responsibility, which, as I've demonstrated, continue to lie beneath some extremely contemporary debates. The book is structured around Teufelsberg, a hill made of the rubble created by Allied bombing, and draws on encounters with other material traces of the bombs scattered across the city. I posit that Anglo-American visitors to these sites are able to form complex counter-narratives about the Allies' area bombing that can disrupt the narratives that continue to regulate who can and cannot be held accountable for mass destruction and civilian casualties during the war. Using a walking, self-reflexive method, I look to Teufelsberg as an assemblage of various ways one can both approach and disrupt the cultural and material memory of destruction through ruins, rubble piles, forests, archaeological digs, Nazi remnants and burial grounds. This book examines how we record and read violent histories in urban landscapes, and how the history of the bombings as it is found in Berlin might disrupt the cultural memory of the war, making more space for a more complex and inclusive cultural memory to emerge.

Perpetrators: The case for complication

The Enola Gay controversy most prominently demonstrates how, in the context of the Second World War, English-speaking critics remain uncomfortable with the idea of perspectives holding space in the memory of the war that are those of the *perpetrator*. Below, I will demonstrate how this has particular potency in relation to area bombing and what became known as the German victimhood debate. The debate, largely occurring in German and in the German cultural sphere, stemmed from attempts in the post-war era to shift attention to the experience of Germans during the war that fell outside those of the Holocaust, such as victims of area bombing.[3] The vagaries of the debate are explored in more detail in Chapter 1, but the most prominent tension at the heart of the debate was a concern about the incompatibility of these victim narratives with the role of perpetrator that had been so assuredly and non-negotiably assigned to Germans in the post-war decades (Judt 1992). Given the horrors of the Nazi regime and the exceptional trauma of the Holocaust, German perspectives, particularly in English-language texts, were necessarily designated perpetrator perspectives. Kettenacker (2010) argues that the German victimhood debate stemmed from an Anglo-American fear that 'all of a sudden, the Germans tend to see themselves as victims of the war, tacitly insinuating that they wish to set the record straight' (p. 216). This uneasiness is also layered with a well-founded fear of moral equivalency, revisionism and outright neo-fascism explored below, which cannot be dismissed as simple tribalism or a fear of challenges to the status quo. But it does indicate the disruptive potential of exploring the possibility that there can be more than one perspective of a conflict, as in the case of Enola Gay and the victim perspectives of Japanese citizens under the atomic bombs.

In the next chapter, I will explore how cultural memory, particularly that surrounding the war and the Holocaust, is traditionally – and necessarily – grounded in a duty to victims of trauma. The very real risk of the far right and very real challenges to the hegemony of the memory of the Holocaust as the dominant frame through which to remember the war means this focus on the victims remains necessary. In mainstream Anglo-American depictions of the Second World War, 'German perspectives' are mostly considered *perpetrator* perspectives, and therefore including the perspectives of the people living under falling Allied bombs comes uncomfortably close to including the perspectives of perpetrators of Nazi crimes and atrocities (indeed these are often not mutually exclusive), something which should by most ethical and moral codes be avoided. Continuing dualistic and national notions of victim and perpetrator, good and evil, Allied and German, in a way assists the memory of the effects of Allied area bombing to remain in the realm of the memory of guilty perpetrators.

But I agree with Maja Zehfuss (2007), among others, when she argues that 'the possibility of German self-pity is a poor reason to shy away from scrutinising Second World War memories [as distinct from the Holocaust]; this accusation prevents engagement with the political and ethical issues involved' (p. 27). The possibility of considering Germans as victims should not prevent proper interrogation of the historical guilt and accountability of the Allies for mass civilian deaths and destruction of cities. Properly engaging with the ethical issues involved in other Second World War memories entails a complication of this dualistic frame of morality that continues to divide accountability for historical death and violence along the lines of 'Nazi Germany' vs. 'the Allies'.

As in the case of challenges to British and American public history that emerged in 2020, complicating more homogenous Anglo-American memory discourses might simply entail entertaining the fact that the events of the Second World War can have more than one meaning – the area bombing campaigns can be *both* a necessity to end a genocidal war *and also* the use of technology and the military to kill civilians on a large scale. In the case of the German victimhood debate, the reverse might also be true: wartime Germans could be considered as witnesses to, complicit in or perpetrators of genocide *and also* victims of indiscriminate attacks on civilian areas. But the German victimhood debate, although related, falls outside the scope of the book, as are ongoing investigations of German memory cultures and debates about the motivations and techniques of the Allied air forces. This book is limited to the implications such a framework of cultural memory might have for the ongoing Anglo-American deification of war narratives and their place in national histories and memory cultures. Boris Johnson's discomfiture with the cultural upheaval of the summer of 2020 shows that suspicions of 'German perspectives' in the German victimhood debate might *also* stem from a simple discomfort with multiplicity, the possibility of multiple perspectives of the war, multiple stories, multiple truths.

It is important to make clear that whilst I am examining the possibility of a broader range of perspectives of the war that might circulate through the sites in Berlin explored within, these perspectives should not in the slightest be heard at the expense of or as a replacement for the histories and memories of Holocaust victims and survivors, nor of the considerable and ongoing intricacies of German memory negotiations. This research is part of a shift in cultural memory work that is beginning to allow room for multiple perspectives that are not restricted by national or victim identity but remains profoundly aware of them. It is an approach that moves beyond seeing memory cultures as a zero-sum game: remembering one event more doesn't have to mean remembering another event less. Taberner and Berger (2009) have identified instead 'the emergence of a more fluid, less monolithic and often more fragmented discourse on the years 1933 to 1945' (p. 1). In this new turn, they argue, there is room for complexity and 'gaps' in cultural memory, including the uncomfortable idea that 'Germans could be both guilty and also victims simultaneously' (p. 1). Again, in relation to the German victimhood debate, Assmann (2006) similarly suggests an alternative to the binary of victim and perpetrator, pushing beyond the zero-sum conceptualization of memory frameworks. Assmann argues:

> [the Holocaust] is the normative framework into which all the other memories have to be integrated. It is not a question of either/or; of this memory of German guilt over that memory of German suffering. One memory does not have to challenge and eliminate the other, as long they are not in a competition for the master-narrative.
>
> (p. 198)

To do this, I have developed an approach to cultural memory (outlined in Chapter 2) that levels the hierarchization of different actors of cultural remembering – governments, media, artists, German, Allied, victim, perpetrator – without levelling the hierarchy at the top of which is the importance of bearing witness to the Holocaust.

Such a view of cultural memory is overdue regarding that of the former Allies. The cultural upheaval that both caused and followed Colston's topple into the water of Bristol Harbour, and the huge uproar following the simple inclusion of images of victims of American atomic warfare in Japan, shows us that at least *additional* – not necessarily counter- – perspectives of cultural memory are still sorely needed. I seek to apply these additional and complicating perspectives of both the bombings and approaches to studying the bombings to continue the long over-due disruption of the foundational mythologies of the former-Allies that draw on a restrictive understanding of guilt and responsibility and prevent true historical accountability.

Book structure

In short, there is unfinished business in Anglo-American cultural memory of the violence visited on German cities during the Second World War. This book aims to provide a history of this violence in response to the fact that most cultural articulations of this history – its cultural memory – remain diffuse with gaps, omissions, and outright denial of some elements.

I begin by detailing the history of the cultural memory of area bombing. As a military technique, a lived, violent reality for so many, as the seeding point for a discussion on historical revisionism, moral relativism, and Holocaust denial, as the conceptual pre-runner to modern-day drone and 'shock and awe' campaigns: area bombing has a deep and complex history. Using a genealogical approach from Foucault, I outline how this history has played out within the context of the ongoing reverence of particular narratives of the Second World War in trans-Atlantic and international cultural memory. In films, politics, news, video games, art, literature, statues, Tweets, TikToks and protest signs, the story of the Second World War continues to be told along particular narrative lines, foundational to Britain, America and their cultural and political allies' sense of self and national mythologies. These narratives, I will show, above all structure and regulate who can and cannot be held accountable for mass death and destruction during the war, and often do so along dichotomous, either-or lines.

This dichotomous understanding is allowed not only by such restrictive understandings of 'victim' and 'perpetrator' but also by the normative ways in which we approach cultural memory being done. In Chapter 2 I show how many traditional approaches to cultural memory see it as a site of contest, control or manipulation, a 'battleground' over which actors fight for influence. In this context the Anglo-American memory of area bombing is often framed as a threat to the cultural memory of the Holocaust in the zero-sum memory game of Second World War historical memory. The approach I outline in Chapter 2 draws on cultural studies, communications studies, cultural geography and new materialist and posthuman theory, to offer a way of remedying this impasse through bringing additional, not counter-, memory narratives to the memory of the war. Such an approach similarly allows room, in a theoretical and methodological sense, for *both* memories of the Holocaust and of area bombing to co-exist simultaneously, rather than in competition with one another. This approach frames the findings of my analysis as adding to, rather than countering, the normative cultural memory structures of the war, entangling these structures with more experiential encounters with material traces of the bombings in Berlin.

Finding traces of the air war in Berlin means an Anglo-American visitor will bring the material impacts of the bombs into direct contact with the normative cultural memory framings to which she is so accustomed. Chapter 3 therefore details the methodology I developed to enact the nuanced and complicated cultural memory of the bombings I argue for in Chapter 1. By making room for both the ethnographic encounter of the sites in Berlin and the discursive understanding of the bombings that accompanies me to these sites, I can entangle the two and potentially offer an expanded and more comprehensive form of cultural memory. Chapter 3 outlines the nuts and bolts of my fieldwork and analysis method, before introducing the phenomenon of *Trümmerberge* ('rubble hills'), and outlining how Teufelsberg forms both a fieldwork site and a conceptual framework for analysis. The chapter also introduces the other sites whose visits I draw on in my analysis in the following four chapters: the Topography of Terror, the Schwebelastungskörper, Anhalter Bahnhof, the Gleis 17 memorial, the Jewish memorial cemetery on Grosse Hamburger Strasse and, briefly, the other seven *Trümmerberge* across Berlin. This methods chapter acts as a guide for the following four analysis chapters, in which the findings of my study emerge through a palimpsest of ethnographic observations, photographs and encounters with the sites, framed through the more discursive cultural-political understandings of the bombings outlined in Chapter 1.

The first of these chapters (Chapter 4) explores the possibility of considering Teufelsberg as layers of Berlin's history, built upon and over one another like geological strata. To understand the commemorative impact of this stratigraphical way of understanding Berlin's past at Teufelsberg, this chapter examines semantic and rhetorical uses of burial, digging and archaeology as ways of disrupting the 'established order' of remembering and forgetting, found at other sites in Berlin – the Topography of Terror and the Jewish memorial cemetery. The chapter also explores the possibility of finding Teufelsberg as haunted ruins, which Gordon (2011) argues 'alters the experience of being in linear time, alters the way we normally separate and sequence the past, the present and the future' (p. 2). Considering Teufelsberg and other ruinous sites like Anhalter Bahnhof and the Jewish memorial cemetery might disrupt some of the linearity at the heart of dominant Anglo-American frames of cultural memory of the air war explored in Chapter 1 and embodied in the verticality of geological strata. Together, these elements of burial and haunting provide an opportunity to explore more variegated, complicated ways of understanding Berlin's past, in which the memory of the bombing might be included.

Such a complicated cultural memory comes to the fore at Teufelsberg when one considers the unruly and inherently active materiality of the hill. Chapter 5 therefore draws on posthuman and new materialist frameworks to explore the materiality of urban sites as vibrant, or agentic. I frame the encounter with Teufelsberg as an interaction between two *actants* – the hill and the walker – and consider both the hill and the bombings through Jane Bennett's networked model of accountability (2010). The bombings, as a cultural, political and technological phenomenon, can be remembered as an assemblage of many *actants* that are both human and non-human. If we consider these non-human actors, as Bennett does, as possessing a kind of agency, this spreads accountability and responsibility for death and destruction across this assemblage. In the context of the other sites of memory considered in this chapter – Anhalter Bahnhof, the Topography of Terror and the Schwerbelastungskörper – blurring distinctions between human and non-human *actants* also reveals conceptual gaps between the humans and machines involved in networked systems of violence. Chapter 5 engages the chains of command, technology, bureaucracy, intelligence networks and policy of area bombing that worked to lengthen the emotional, psychological, moral, causal and conceptual distance between deaths on the ground and the individuals responsible. The encounters with Teufelsberg's unruly materiality offer potential to disrupt this distance and capture more actors – human and non-human – in the accountability network.

The conceptual and objective distance from which material violence of the bombings is often conducted and understood can be typified by aerial photography, instances of which continue to inform normative structures of Second World War historical memory. Chapter 6 explores how walking Teufelsberg might reintroduce the bodily and sensory violence of the bombings 'on the ground' that are so often missing from these pictures and from many structures of memory. Remembering through and with Teufelsberg includes tripping and sliding over pathways, scratching knees and hands, covering the skin with dirt, and toiling up steep slopes – in other words, encountering the site bodily. This offers potential for walking urban sites of violence to evoke the bodily and subjective nature of this violence, thereby reintroducing violence as a lived experience into its cultural memory. Crucially, however, the continued presence of aerial imagery and objective, sanitized, military-technological language at both sites in Berlin – that is, the Topography of Terror – and in the dominant memory structures that accompany Anglo-American visitors to these sites means that the bodily and subjective violence of the bombings is always layered with this detached perspective. The military language and aerial viewpoints that have so characterized normative Anglo-American cultural memories of the air war, and which have held the responsibility of the Allies at a distance from the corporal effects of their actions, are thus complicated, rather than countered, and a more nuanced account of area bombing becomes possible.

Taken seriously as traces of material and bodily violence, the pieces of stone, metal, ceramics, brick, glass and wood that make up Teufelsberg and the other *Trümmerberge* can also be read as forensic records of this violence. The Topography of Terror, Anhalter Bahnhof and the Schwerbelastungskörper offer remnants of Berlin as representational devices for framing cultural memory, using the remnants' status as material witnesses to violence to legitimize particular historical narratives. Chapter 7 therefore examines Teufelsberg and the other *Trümmerberge* as collections of forensic records, of both the Allies' destruction and the political and cultural undertaking entwined with Berlin's post-war remembering and forgetting. Such a forensic approach to the *Trümmerberge* also introduces the disturbing possibility of human remains entangled with the dirt, rubble, rocks and tree roots of the hills, and by extension entangled with the very materiality of Berlin's urban landscape. This not only further implicates bodies and bodily violence into potential articulations of the cultural memory of the air war, but it also offers the opportunity to explore the *Trümmerberge*, and Teufelsberg in particular, as a site of the Anthropocene. The blurred lines between humans' and 'nature's' effects on the planet hold implications for the cultural memory of the air war. Teufelsberg can be thought of as an assemblage of the nature, culture, architecture and history of Berlin, much of which is inherently violent. This final analysis chapter considers what it means to remember the bombings and the effects they had on human bodies, culture and the earth's crust and atmosphere in the age of the Anthropocene.

The sensory subjective encounters with the urban fabric of Berlin detailed in the analysis chapters reveal some of the characteristics and contradictions of the normative framings through which Anglo-American populations form and reform cultural memory of the Second World War. The final chapter draws together the threads of analysis to outline how these encounters can entangle these normative frameworks with the sensory and experiential realities that the bombings left behind and reveal how dominant productions of the cultural memory of the war are underpinned by particular assurances of the former Allies' historical identities and senses of self. I explore three significant elements upon which underlying assumptions of the former Allies' current memory structures of national and historical guilt and responsibility regarding the war are built: a linear model of cause and effect, in which area bombing is accepted to have occurred in direct response to (and was thus indirectly caused by) Nazi war atrocities; a dichotomous moral framework that is incapable of identifying a person, group or nation as simultaneously a victim and a perpetrator; and the objective distance of the perpetrators of the bombers from their material impacts and violence, most often epitomized in the aerial perspective of the bomber and aerial reconnaissance photograph. By offering an additional perspective, this book demonstrates how sensory subjective encounters with the urban fabric of Berlin can reveal some of the characteristics and contradictions of the normative framings through which Anglo-American populations form and reform cultural memory of area bombing. This is possible because Anglo-American visitor can encounter the more sensory, visceral and embodied effects of the bombing *through* these very normative framings that accompany them.

A note on the term 'Anglo-American'

Throughout this book, I use the term 'Anglo-American' to describe the dominant frames through which stories of the war are habitually told and re-told to and with particular audiences and populations (which are explored in detail in Chapter 1); in short, cultural memory. But rather than a particular national or ethnic identity of an individual visitor to Berlin, I use the term to refer to both the narrative frameworks and the audiences who have come to understand the war through the continuous recirculation of these frameworks.

The discourses about the war with which I am concerned repeatedly draw on particular perspectives, tropes, themes, characters and conventions that are continually created, disseminated, consumed and reinforced in and by the victorious English-speaking Allies following the war. This is not to say, however, that these frameworks are restricted to these two countries or their cultural and political outputs, nor are they set in stone; to do so would be a gross simplification of the global cultural media landscape, both during and since the war, not to mention the omission of a diversity of perspectives that are more often than not ignored along racial and gender lines. Nevertheless, there remain entrenched patterns beneath the fluid circulation and negotiation of these accounts of the war in English-language cultural texts (defined in the broadest sense, see Chapter 2) that ensures the predominance of certain stories, perspectives, themes and motifs.

My use of the term 'Anglo-American' therefore focuses on the patterns of cultural memory frameworks that are implicit in and reinforced by certain global media cultural practices. This means that it encompasses negotiations and re-negotiations of the meaning of the Second World War through cinema, literature, family history, national days of mourning and celebration, political rhetoric, television, news cycles, social media, museum openings and mediated tourism – a myriad of texts, representations and images produced and reproduced across the latter half of the twentieth century and into the twenty-first. The patterns of production and consumption of these texts have become a kind of canonical framework that regulates possible meanings of the war for former Allies and English-speakers. Audiences don't *only* engage with this canon when remembering the war, but particular tropes, themes, perspectives and stories maintain a hegemony that aligns with the cultural and political capital of certain institutions: Hollywood and the mainstream entertainment and information industry, global media conglomerates and international politics (that remained mostly dominated by America and Britain and the rest of Europe for much of the post-war era in which these practices took root).

The term 'Anglo-American', as it is used in this book, speaks therefore of a social, cultural, political and historical position from which the memory of the war is habitually engaged, rather than identifying a population or group of people. This position can be broadly defined as that of 'the victors', and continues to frame transnational cultural and political trends, but nonetheless follows the vagaries of global flows and changes in history, geopolitics and cultural shifts. My use of the term therefore acknowledges the accepted cultural and political influence of the United States and Britain on particular post-war narratives without privileging the nationality or ethnicity of the individuals that make up these populations or produce the cultural texts in question. The term therefore acts as a kind of shorthand for the continuing (if somewhat outdated) potency of the dominant storying of the Second World War in transnational cultural memory practices. It is the term that best describes the cultural landscape in which particular visitor populations in Berlin are entrenched and from which they have gleaned significant facets of their understandings of the Second World War. Entrenched cultural communicative practices continue to provide common ways of making sense of the war for visitors to Berlin, and frame cultural remembering that can be done at and through the sites explored below. Chapter 1 explores some of the intricacies and entrenched patterns of these practices, and Chapter 2 details the theoretical approaches to culture, communication and memory that underpin such a stance.

1

A genealogy of remembering area bombing

Introduction

In 2006, German author Jörg Friedrich released an English version of his 2002 book *Der Brand*, in which he depicted in great and often graphic detail the effects of the Allied bombing campaigns on German cities and German civilians. The translated edition, released under the English title *The Fire*, contained a special 'Afterword for American and English readers', in which he addressed (or perhaps pre-empted) a common response from Anglo-American audiences: that the bombings were fair retribution for the devastation delivered upon Europe by Hitler's Germany. 'No interview with the English-language press', wrote Friedrich (2006) in this afterword, 'failed to ask if it was not Hitler who started both the war and the bombing of cities. "They that sow the wind shall reap the whirlwind"' (p. 484). The question of 'did they not start it?' revealed a common and, as we shall see below, persistent framing of area bombing in Anglo-American audiences: the bombings, however violent they may have been, were justifiable, necessary, even morally correct, when considered in light of the horrors of Nazism that would soon be revealed at the end of the war. But as well as revealing a common Anglo-American response to the memory of the bombings, Friedrich's afterword hinted at a truth that remains at the heart of Anglo-American historical memory of the Second World War: we were, and still are, the 'good guys'. Italian historian Alessandro Portelli identified a similar sentiment in 2006 in his essay 'So much depends on a red bus, or, innocent victims of the liberating gun':

> ... a short circuit of memory: if we blame the Fascists for the disaster, it is logical to surmise that they and their allies were the perpetrators; the more we identify Fascism and Nazism with evil, the more logical it is to expect that this evil was their doing. This way, we are no longer forced to deal with the fact it was the 'good guys', 'our side', those with reason and humanity on their side, that

destroyed your house and killed your family. How can the gun that kills us be 'liberating'?

(Portelli 2006, p. 36)

This chapter explores how the Anglo-American cultural memory of area bombing was formed in relation to wider debates about the Allies' historical role in the Second World War and other, more recent conflicts. After introducing and exploring area bombing and its military, cultural and political history, and specifying its history as a focal point of the German victimhood debate, I then explore the characteristics of the most common tools Anglo-American populations use to make sense of the area bombing during the Second World War. The bombings are by and large represented in these memory cultures as necessary, morally and militarily justified, reasonable in scale, and against an absolute evil Other. Underpinning these characteristics of the cultural memory of area bombing are particular assurances about the belligerents' historical roles and behaviour during the war. I therefore explore these assurances in light of recent debates about the historical foundations of the United States and the UK, and how these characteristics continue to frame modern Western notions of sacrifice, victimhood, justice and historical responsibility.

This chapter largely finds that *in addition* to the very real risk German victimhood narratives pose to the primacy of Holocaust victim narratives, refusing to question the *absolute* historical guilt of Germany has also meant that the absolute righteousness of the Allies' cause and actions has remained similarly unquestioned. As Zehfuss (2007) argues, '[t]he suffering [of German civilians from aerial bombardment] does not cease to exist, become less painful to remember or indeed less relevant to situations of war today because it occurred in response to a war of aggression or because the German people at the same time committed unimaginable atrocities' (p. 28). The inverse implications of this statement are also true: the responsibility for damage and deaths caused by the Allies does not diminish or become less relevant because it was carried out against a nation responsible for mass atrocities. This chapter outlines how the cultural memory of area bombing continues in English language spheres to regulate who can and cannot be held accountable for mass deaths and destruction, not only during the Second World War, but in more recent conflicts and political turmoil. It is for this reason, I will show, that a more nuanced, complicated and disruptive form of cultural memory of the air war is required, to disrupt these ongoing cultural memory frames, and create space for a more comprehensive cultural history of the violence of area bombing.

As covered in the Introduction, this book does not specifically engage or seek to cover new ground regarding the extensive and ongoing debates about German national identities in relation to the cultural memory of the Second World War. The Anglo-American memory cultures regarding the bombings are of course not wholly separate or distinct from that of Germany, and in fact scholarship and literature on post-war German memory cultures inform the debates explored below significantly, and these are examined where they intersect with those of the former Allies. However, the cultural memory of the Allies' conduct in area bombing in Anglo-American spheres remains the focus of this book, as it is an area that requires significant disruption and nuance, and which has been so far under-examined.

Area bombing and the German victimhood debate

In mass and severity, the Allies' bombing of German cities and towns would be succeeded only by the two atomic bombs dropped on Japan and the carpet bombing campaigns during the Korean and Vietnam wars[1] (Hastings 2013; Grant 2012, p. 55). The bombing raids were widespread, violent, destructive, did not often discriminate between military and civilian targets, and were focused largely on cities and towns (Overy 2013). Sebald (2004) called the campaigns 'a battle of annihilation' (p. 10). One journalist called the effects of one raid on Cologne 'a model of destruction' (Flanner 1945, p. 58). In one raid over Dresden in 1945, incendiaries caused firestorms in which temperatures reached a thousand degrees centigrade: 'the asphalt on the streets turned to molten lava' (Crew 2007, p. 127). The bombs killed thousands and rendered millions homeless (Overy 2013). They destroyed valuable infrastructure such as gas, water, public transport, communication lines and housing. They destroyed many of the medieval Old Town centres of German cities, as well as countless archives, libraries, works of art and architecture. Australian journalist Alan Moorhead (1968[1946]) followed the British Army into Berlin in the final weeks of the war:

> The Germany in which we found ourselves travelling at the end of April presented a scene that was almost beyond human comprehension. Her capital lost and almost razed, and nothing to give that ash-heap significance beyond a name, a history and the presence of a lunatic who was about to make his last gesture to a colossal vanity – his death.
>
> (p. 230)

In area bombing – also called strategic bombing, morale bombing, or terror bombing – built-up areas were targeted, which differentiates the method from targeting solely military or strategic targets. The strategy was born out of the concept of 'total war' wherein any act that contributed to a country's capacity to wage war is considered a legitimate target. A British decree in 1943 states the campaigns were designed to 'destroy the morale of the enemy civilian population and, in particular, of the industrial workers' (in Sebald 2004, p. 17). Debate continues today over the morality of both the intent and effect of the campaigns (Childers 2005; Connelly 2001; 2004; Davis 1991; Friedrich 2006; Grayling 2007; Gregory 2011; Hansen 2008; Hastings 2013; Kettenacker 2010; Lowe 2012; Maier 1988; Overy 2013).

The task of estimating civilian casualties of the bombing campaigns is immensely difficult, not the least because the task remains entwined in complex memory debates and historical controversies of post-war Germany and former Allied countries. A footnote by Hoelscher (2012) summarizes the political and cultural potency of the wildly variable numbers that circulate in reference the wartime air raids on Dresden:

> Numbers as high as 250,000 have been offered, and strategically utilised by Germany's far-right, to relativise atrocity. Kurt Vonnegut, in *Slaughterhouse Five*, cited 130,000 dead, using the notorious Holocaust denier David Irving's calculations. In 2008, a multidisciplinary team of some of Germany's most distinguished historians and forensic anthropologists produced the results of a four-year scientific investigation [(Müller, Schonherr, & Widera 2010)] into this issue … the scientists estimated the likely death toll at approximately 25,000. Importantly, this long awaited and extremely important report, although convincing in its triangulating scientific methodologies, has not resolved but only added to an extremely controversial matter. The massive-scale 2009 far-right protests were launched after the book's publication.
>
> (Hoelscher 2012, pp. 293–4)

What is of concern to this volume is less the actual figures of casualties from the bombings and more that which the difficulty in estimating and agreeing on these figures points to. Such debate over even basic historical facts of civilian causality figures demonstrates the ongoing political potency of area bombing in the context of post-war memory cultures and structures of historical responsibility, much of which has come to be labelled 'the German victimhood debate'.

Because of its disproportionate effect on civilian lives and major cities, the campaigns have become embroiled in a continuing debate about ideas of wartime victimhood and responsibility. Allied bombing in Germany comprises the central part of both the German victimhood debate and the related German Historian's Debate ('der Historikerstreit').[2] The German victimhood debate spans decades, and involves academics, politicians, writers, artists and commentators, in both Germany and in the UK, America and the rest of Europe. The debate often concerns how the bombings have been remembered as much as it does the tonnes of bombs dropped, the number of lives lost, or the intents and purposes of the campaigns, and centres on the possibility of considering non-Jewish Germans as anything other than perpetrators, that is, as victims.

German victimhood has been and continues to be used in sinister circles for dangerous projects. Germans being afforded the status of victims, many argue, would exculpate German civilians' guilt for their complicity in the Nazi regime and the Holocaust (Taberner & Berger 2009). Much of the debate has therefore been defined by a perceived 'taboo' in German culture on the depictions of the suffering of German civilians. German civilians, the taboo doctrine argues, have not been permitted to share their civilian experience of the war, either due to fears of detracting from memories of Holocaust victims, survivors and witnesses, or by the enduring narrative of the Allies' actions as wholly righteous and acceptable. This 'taboo' argument has been offered predominately by far-right and neo-Nazi groups hoping to minimize the significance of the Holocaust to allow narratives of German, non-Jewish and non-Holocaust victimhood to emerge. On the relationship between victimhood and historical responsibility for Nazi crimes, Sebald (2004) wrote:

> [T]he question of whether and how [the area bombing of cities] could be justified was never the subject of open debate in Germany after 1945, no doubt mainly because a nation which had murdered and worked to death millions of people in its camps could hardly call on the victorious powers to explain the military and political logic that dictated the destruction of German cities.
>
> (p. 13)

Sebald argued that representations of the widespread destruction of Germany's cities were never allowed to exist in the German collective consciousness for the greater part of the post-war period. Moeller (2006) has countered that the 'taboo' was 'not one on speaking; rather, it was on listening' (p. 116); German authors and civilians had long since attempted to share their wartime experiences, but there had been no audience willing to hear them, and no room for them in the enduring narratives of the Second World War that figure the German as a clear perpetrator, not a victim. This problem remains at the heart of the German victimhood debate, and signals how it remains a dangerous act to engage the cultural memory of area bombing in both Anglo-American and German cultural areas.

The German victimhood debate is, at least in Anglo-American cultural memory debates, most concerned with what many see as the danger of moral equivalency. Renowned scholar on, advocate against and subject of Holocaust denial and anti-Semitism, Deborah Lipstadt (1993) calls it 'immoral equivalency' (p. 212). The potential to equate or at least compare the suffering of Germany's bombed civilians with the suffering of the victims and survivors of the Nazis' genocidal regime remains the ultimate and ever-present danger in all articulations of the debate. A touchstone of this concern is the German author Jörg Friedrich's 2002 book *Der Brand* discussed above, published in English in 2006 as *The Fire*. Seemingly taking up Sebald's call for more representations of the bombings and their impact, *The Fire* documented the destruction of German cities from victims' perspectives. Friedrich (2006) worked to create what he called an 'alternative history' of the bombings to a typical Anglo-American one that he argued 'stops when the bombs hit the ground' (p. 12). Notably, a predominant criticism of Friedrich's work gained traction when it was translated into English in 2006. When he described the destruction of the bombings, Friedrich used language that proved to be traditionally reserved for describing the Holocaust, like 'mass extermination', 'annihilation' and 'war crime', as well as imagery of 'ovens' and 'crematoria' to describe the conditions of air raid shelters in which many German citizens perished. For drawing on imagery that his Anglo-American audience was already familiar with, many charged Friedrich with deliberately drawing parallels between the millions of gas-chamber deaths that made up the Holocaust, implicitly comparing them with the deaths caused by the bombing raids. In a review of *The Fire*, American critic Fischel (2007) provides an example of this kind of critique:

> [Friedrich's] argument for moral equivalency suggests a trend in Germany's political culture that portends a retreat for its responsibility for the Holocaust. It may only be a question of time, therefore, before memorials for the victims of Allied bombings will find their place alongside the victims of the Holocaust; and future generations of Germans will comfort themselves with the condition that the crime of their fathers was no worse than that of their enemies.
>
> (p. 294)

Fischel and other English-language critics (Childers 2005; Preußer 2007; Primoratz 2010) argued Friedrich was using the thousands of deaths caused by the Allies to absolve Germany of responsibility for murdering millions.

This is no over-anxious fear. Remembering the suffering of German civilians under Allied bombs has often been used to downplay the cultural memory of the Nazi genocide by far-right groups, revisionist historians and Holocaust deniers. These groups utilize the shared memory of suffering under Allied bombs to equate the suffering of German civilians with that of the Holocaust and to exculpate some of Germany's historical responsibility for the Holocaust. The cultural memory of the bombings and the related concept of Germans as victims is therefore inherently linked with the rise of the 'alt-right' in Germany and elsewhere, which makes remembering the bombings a potentially dangerous evocation of the past. Any investigation into the memory of area bombing must be fully aware of this danger. The debate remains politically and morally fraught.

A history of the present of war memory

So far the memory of the air war has been discussed largely in relation to German historical memory and responsibility in relation to the war. However, the movement of cultural memory across national borders and cultures (detailed in Chapter 2) means substantial parts of the German victimhood debate are no longer concerned solely with *Germany's* self-image. The debate also includes how changes to that self-image might affect the self-image of the former Allies, and it is with these aspects of the debate this book is concerned. The mobility of people, communicative texts and cultures means remembering area bombing in relation to German historical responsibility remains heavily entwined with remembering area bombing in relation to dominant Anglosphere discourses. In America, leaders of 'alt-right' groups continue to draw on Nazi maxims in their speeches and rallies, where crowds of attendees raise their right arms in salute (Levi & Rothberg 2018). American fraternity men chanted 'Blood and soil!' and 'Jews will not replace us!' as they carried tiki torches through the streets of Charlottesville, Virginia in 2017 (Rosenberg 2017; Wagner 2017). The past remains a volatile force in contemporary negotiations of Anglo-American culture and politics, all too often through the language of Nazi fascism. But despite these dangers of anachronism, interrogating the consistent re-telling of history of area bombing (through specific narrative tropes, themes and perspectives) remains necessary, because it might allow us to explore whether and how any responsibility for mass civilian deaths and destruction can be attributed to the former-Allies.

We turn now to how the bombings' cultural memory, including the German victimhood debate and the ongoing wariness of revisionism and denialism, has shaped and been shaped by the retelling of histories of the Second World War for and by Allied audiences. I do this using Foucault's genealogical approach, providing a 'history of the present' of former-Allied cultural memory of area bombing.

Drawing out the facets of the Anglo-American cultural memory of area bombing cannot be simply an attempt to 'go back in time to restore an unbroken continuity that operates beyond the dispersion of forgotten things … to demonstrate that the past actively exists in the present, having imposed a predetermined form to all its vicissitudes' (Foucault 1977, p. 146). An analysis that simply draws links between Allied bombing of German cities and contemporary expressions of neo-Nazism would not, Foucault might argue, go far enough. Instead, Foucault's (1977) history of the present can interrogate the continued presence of the memory of area bombing in the circulation of cultural texts, and, importantly, expand the analysis to include the pre-existing conditions upon which many of these debates are framed, such as the continued dominance of particular narratives.

Foucault examines the term 'genealogy' in Friedrich Nietzsche's essays, taking particular notice when Nietzsche used the German word '*Herkunft*' (1977, p. 145). This term Foucault establishes, has particular connotations of descent or ancestry. These connotations view the subject – a concept or idea – less as a single point of origin and more as 'an unstable assemblage of faults, fissures, and heterogeneous layers that threaten the fragile interior from within or from underneath' (p. 146), like the entanglement of actors, forces and events that form a person's family tree. Foucault is keen to stress that Nietzsche's genealogy is not the search for 'origins' (p. 140), because 'the historical beginning of things is not the inviolable identity of their origin: it is the dissension of other things. It is disparity' (p. 142). When applied to the concepts of truth or morality, for example, as Foucault does, there is no whole truth of these concepts that lies beneath the noise of discourse, politics, society. A history of the present in a genealogical framework, as opposed to search for 'origins', will 'cultivate the details and accidents that accompany every beginning' (Foucault 1977, p. 144). The idea of descent or ancestry permits the discovery of the myriad of events through which these concepts were formed, but does not suppose these events have a singular point of origin.

A history of the present always begins with a diagnosis of present problems and conditions, born from 'a certain puzzlement or discomfiture about practices or institutions that others take for granted' (Garland 2014, p. 379). The genealogist problematizes the present by revealing the power relations upon which it depends, as well as the network of contingent events and processes that have brought it into being (Garland 2014). A history of the present is not simply trying to discover or describe past events through the concerns of the present. Genealogists instead aim to 'interrogate the present, to undermine the self-evidence, necessity, and universality of its ruling forms, to eventalize and defamiliarize them, and open up the possibility of changing them' (Falzon 2013, p. 293). A history of the present attempts to draw out the underlying preconditions of a set of problems in the present.

This study therefore emerged from a discomfiture with the present framing of the relationship between German victimhood and the memory of the air war as it is articulated in Anglo-America cultural memory. It is my hope to complicate such a framing to reveal the faults, fissures and heterogeneous layers upon which the severely limited critical eye that the former Allies take to their own wartime behaviour has been constructed.

Questioning the historical responsibility of Germany's government and citizenry during the war, decades of German post-war memory, or the threat that victimhood might pose to historical responsibility for Nazi crimes, therefore, lies outside the scope of this book. Rather, I use Foucault's genealogical method to disturb what was previously considered immobile and fragment what was thought unified in Anglo-American memory cultures: the *absolute* righteousness of the Allies' wartime actions. I therefore examine the entrenched practices of cultural memory that have by and large restricted depictions of wartime responsibility. These practices – enacted by authors, artists, filmmakers, leaders, historians, politicians and protestors – have co-constituted foundational characteristics of Anglo-American national mythologies that are characterized by a deeply ingrained refusal to confront the wrongs of the past.

Anglo-America and area bombing memories

Beyond the German victimhood debate and German post-war cultural memory, the exploits of the Allied air forces during the war have been subject to a smaller but ongoing debate in British commemorative culture and historical memory for decades (Hughes 2021), which has followed the contours of post-war memory cultures. The cultural memory of the air war has often been used as a way to critique the Allies' wartime activities. This is in line with a recognized turn in Western European transnational memory cultures in the decades since the end of the Cold War, which has allowed space for depictions of the effects of the war on Germany. There were well-documented protests, for example, against the erection of an Arthur 'Bomber' Harris statue in London in 1992 (Connelly 2004). In the later decades of the twentieth century, discussions around the morality of the bombing grew stronger, and were often framed as direct attacks on the memory of the bravery and sacrifice of air force veterans (Hughes 2021). Discussion of the bombing campaigns thus remains a contested issue, but nonetheless often follows a certain set of rhetorical and narrative trends.

The history of area bombing has therefore often found expression not only in official histories, commemorative celebrations and days of mourning, and statues and memorials, but in the films, television programs, books, games and advertising that form the cultural texts through which cultural memory can be formed (see Chapter 2). Military-scientific objectivity, a focus on bravery and sacrifice (particularly that of the air crews), a sense of horizontal comradery, and an absolute evil Other against which any war is wholly just and justified, form just some of the ongoing frames through which the war has been remembered in the post-war cultures of the Allies (see Florence 2016). These characteristics and others form the post-war mythologies that continue to shape and reshape the former-Allied nations' sense of themselves and their historical role in the conflict, which will be explored below, and within which the cultural memory of area bombing must be positioned.

Distant, visually purified

The cultural memory of the air war is most commonly characterized by a notable lack of area bombing victims. This is in line with wider trends in conflict cinema. Cora Sol Goldstein (2017) found glaring omissions of civilian deaths in films that were set in or in the context of the Second World War between 1945 and 2017.[3] This omission was particularly noticeable when examining possible depictions of area bombing or the nuclear destruction from the air in Japan:

> There have been no modern American feature films made about the bombing of Tokyo, or Berlin, or Hiroshima, or Nagasaki. Therefore, it has been possible to make the issue of large civilian casualties disappear from the cinematic record, and from the way viewers imagine World War II. A war that is increasingly distant has been visually reconfigured and purified.
>
> (Goldstein 2017, p. 25)

Goldstein argues that in the 1300 Hollywood films set in the context of the Second World War during this period, 'bombings were repeatedly shown, but victims – even when their existence was implied or even commented upon – were not seen' (p. 16). As Goldstein demonstrates, these distant, visually purified forms of violence linger and are aligned with broader trends in representations of American forces killing civilians in film. Goldstein argues that depictions of American soldiers killing civilians virtually disappear after 1955, particularly in relation to concerted efforts to depict the Second World War as a 'clean war'. Later, as the depictions of the violence of war in film shifted, many films did depict the violence and brutality of war through the suffering of soldiers. But the death of civilians remained severely limited, if admitted at all. Goldstein points out that in many war films of the late twentieth century and into the twenty-first the killing of civilians remained individualized, often moral quandaries faced by individual American infantry men, rather than systemic and widespread annihilation of hundreds of thousands of people: 'The violence that is highlighted … is targeted, concrete, bounded, explainable and just. Killing, even when the victim is a non-traditional combatant, is depicted as necessary, controlled, calculated and precise' (p. 31). With area bombing, the destruction and death inflicted by the bombs tend to remain similarly controlled and calculated, distanced from the viewer either by the physical and conceptual distance afforded by the elevated viewpoint of the bomber, or the abstracted, military-scientific language of 'mission', 'target', 'success rates' and 'impact zones'. Across the Atlantic in the British wartime press, Connelly (2001) found that many depictions of German cities were 'largely devoid of descriptions of the targets, or the effects on the ground … the British people did not want to be bothered with this aspect and the government was keen to avoid it too' (p. 148). In Chapter 6 I explore how popular perspectives of aerial attacks on Germany are habitually positioned through the lens of objectivity, either embodied in the critical distance of an aerial viewpoint from the windows of Allied planes, or in the military-scientific rationality through which the effects of bombing are often understood and represented. Many stories of the air war focus on the technology of the planes, the strategy and decision-making of the generals or the scientific brilliance behind the design, creation, testing and delivery of bombs. Depictions of the *effects* of the bombings on the ground, either on cities or on humans' bodies, are therefore rare.

The fact there is little place for the effects of the bombings in Anglo-American cultural memory is further evidenced by the fact many authors – especially German ones – have been accused of revisionism or self-pity because they featured vivid descriptions of the material effects of the bombings on humans and cities. Jörg Friedrich's book *The Fire,* for example, was controversial (in part) because it detailed the bodily effects of the bombings. This mostly took the form of graphic depictions of the bodily harm and injury the bombs caused. Friedrich drew criticism for descriptions such as this one of a night raid on Hamburg:

> Little blood flows in a fire or nuclear war. Emergency physicians in Hamburg reported that hundreds of people were caught in typhoon-like drafts of hot air and later found lying naked in the streets. Their skin was a brownish texture, their hair was well preserved. The facial mucous membranes were dried out and crusted.
>
> (p. 166)

At other times Freidrich provides a grounded perspective simply through personal stories of individuals and their emotions, thoughts and actions. Freidrich's book was notable because it provided a perspective of the bombings 'from below', but *The Fire* also diverged from the objectivity of military history that is customarily used to describe this facet of history. 'The book delivers one visceral emotional shock after another', Childers (2005) argues in a review, 'the reader finds no antiseptic military language here' (p. 77). Against these grounded perspectives of victims, Friedrich contrasts how the British military employed scientists who specialized in anatomy, physics and explosives to study the effects of blasts on the human body and residential architecture to inform a strategy of mass bombing of urban areas (Gregory 2011). The Research and Experiments Department of the Ministry of Home Security was a department of the RAF's Bombing Analysis Unit, and the US air force conducted a similar United States Strategic Bombing Survey to quantify and analyse the impacts of their campaigns as a matter of scientific research. Both Allies systematically documented the effects of the bombing campaigns on the bodies of victims and the materials of cities while remaining at a safe scientific distance from the visceral trauma of them enabled by the distance of military and technological objectivity. The dichotomy between the visceral, bodily impacts of aerial bombing and the objective safety of an aircraft from which the bombs were dropped or the military history perspective through which the campaigns have been commonly digested continues to characterize the cultural memory of the air war. This will be explored in greater detail in Chapters 5 and 6, but for now it is worth noting how the controversy of Friedrich's book, much like that over the Enola Gay exhibition at the Smithsonian discussed in the Introduction, suggests a dissonance between the scientific objectivity of military language commonly used to describe bombing campaigns' planning and implementation and the *effects* of the bombs on the ground.

Veterans' perspectives

This focus on military-objective history language is also related to the focus of post-war Allied narratives that centred on the bravery and sacrifice of air force veterans. This is particularly noticeable in Britain, where the exploits of Bomber Command were initially excluded from many post-war memory cultures, particularly after questions of the morality of area bombing were raised in the 1980s (Hughes 2021). The air crew veterans and their families argued they had been 'denied their place among the nation's war heroes' (Connelly 2004, p. 6). This was despite the disproportionately high casualty rates of Bomber Command crews – 64,000 people, more than all the British officers lost in the First World War (Werrell 1986, p. 708). As the Enola Gay controversy discussed in the Introduction demonstrates, the omission of Bomber Command from these immediate post-war memory cultures in Britain makes it clear why paying attention to the effects of the bombing raids on the ground might be framed as taking attention *away* from the already under-represented stories of air crews.

However, owing in part to the limited access that British and American populations had to physical or visual evidence of the Allies' conduct overseas, much of the early post-war narratives did in fact draw on veteran accounts of the air war. For example, mainstream British cinema of the immediate post-war era depicted the war years as re-living the air force's glories of the war. Most films that featured aerial warfare during this decade unswervingly buttressed the idea of the 'People's War' that was developed during the conflict (Connelly 2004). The most prominent example of this was the film *The Dam Busters* (1955), one of the only films that depict the exploits of British Bomber Command to become an enduring cultural artefact in British culture. The film tells the story of RAF No. 617 Squadron, who launched a daring attack against the Möhne and Edersee Dams in Germany in 1943. *The Dam Busters* depicted the RAF as a rag-tag team of mismatched underdogs, defying the odds and a technologically advanced enemy to win a strategically minor but morale-boosting victory. These were slightly different heroes to those that came to make regular appearances in Hollywood war films, often modelled after the hero of Westerns and other hero's journey mono-myths. The 'bomber boys', as they came to be known, were modelled after the American bomber hero, 'not a rogue figure, but rather a thoughtful and intelligent man who ponders the moral consequences of aerial warfare, always reaching the conclusion that bombing, although destructive, will shorten the war, save American lives and help the US defeat its enemies'

(Goldstein 2017 p. 19). Furthermore, the squadron's hero status was achieved by a targeted, bounded attack on a specific target; a dam, not a vaguely defined target of Germany's 'will to war' or the indiscriminate 'built up areas' that formed the target of area bombing. The film was evidently largely early post-war propaganda, but these themes have also been deliberately perpetuated for varying political objectives over the post-war decades.

Necessary retribution

As *The Dam Busters* demonstrates, the bombings do feature in the dominant post-war historical narratives, but they are largely framed as a necessary and even justified response to Nazi brutality and expansionism. In Britain in particular, press photography and military reports during the war often characterized the destruction as punitive, a kind of retribution for the actions of Germany's people. The images of German cities in ruins in the British and American wartime press were framed as the just rewards for those who allowed an evil regime to take power and murder millions (Connelly 2002). No sooner was Dresden mentioned than was Rotterdam, Lidice, Coventry or Stalingrad presented as justification for the RAF and USAAF's bombings. Investigating wartime representations of the air war in the British press, Connelly (2004) argues that British citizens 'were led to believe that the [bombing] campaign was the just scourge of all Germans, the terrible and terrifying retribution of the righteous against the wicked' (p. np) because of the frames through which they were depicted. Connelly refers to depictions of the RAF such as this one from a poem titled 'The glory on their wings' that appeared in *Illustrated London News* in 1943: 'for they go to avenge the innocent, to break the tyrant, to release a continent from slavery … *to save mankind*' (p. 2, original emphasis). Framing the RAF's exploits as revenge also gave reason and meaning to the suffering experienced by British civilians during the darkest parts of the war – one report in 1944 called an RAF attack on Essen a 'bigger and better blitz' (*The Times* 1944, p. 5). Descriptions of the bombing that foreground revenge, reckoning and punishment continued after the end of the war, in film, television and literature (Parker 2013). In 2015, several newspapers ran stories online to mark the seventieth anniversary of the firebombing of Dresden in February 1943 (Gallup 2015; *The Telegraph* 2015). Many of these articles showed 'before and after' images of the city. In the comment sections of these articles, readers expressed sadness at the pointlessness of the destruction, or remarked that Germany once again 'rules over Europe', referring explicitly to the EU and evidencing the need for Britain to leave the Union. Specifically, many of the comments epitomized these themes of retribution and punishment. On a story from *The Guardian* (Gallup 2015), one user stated 'And they started it, you[sic] fight fire with fire', whilst another simply asked 'What about the London blitz?'. The bombings are still, in many instances, remembered as the punishment and retribution of Germany for their war of aggression and the murder of millions.

Scale: 'A little like Coventry'

The rhetoric of necessity in Anglo-American war mythologies also underpins the diminished scale of the bombings as represented in the mainstream Anglo-American imagination. One of the things that distinguish the Allied aerial bombing campaigns from those of the *Luftwaffe* over Britain is scale. Even in terms of the volume of bombs dropped, across the entirety of the Second World War, Allied air forces dropped an estimated 1,415,745 tonnes of bombs over Germany, whilst the *Luftwaffe* dropped an estimated 45,000 on British soil (Hastings 2013, p. 333).

But significant Anglo-American populations have difficulty understanding the true scale of the Allied bombing campaigns. A 2016 study found that British collective memory of the bombings is characterized by an inability to fully comprehend or articulate the scale of the destruction caused by Allied air forces (Ryan & Hewer 2016). Ryan and Hewer's study found that 65 per cent of their participants underestimated how many Allied sorties flew on bombing missions over the continent per day. Seventy-five per cent of respondents were unable to detail or understand the extent of the destruction in numerical terms, and only 6.5 per cent were able to accurately estimate the amount of German civilian casualties. Lowe (2012) argues that most Britons still think that in terms of scale and severity, Allied raids on German soil were 'a little like Coventry, or perhaps slightly worse' (p. xii). In dominant Anglo-American discourses, representations of the scale of the bombings have remained firmly within what was considered reasonable, proportionate and necessary to defeat the Nazis and end the war.

This gap between the actual and the imagined scale of the bombings indicates that the mainstream Second World War discourse sees Bomber Command and the USAAF's campaigns as a necessary, and therefore proportionate, response to Nazi warmongering (Kelsey 2013). This also shows how the Allies saw themselves in opposition to the war-hungry Nazis. The British Blitz Myth signifies 'muddling through' and 'carrying on'. In the American context this takes the form of what Williamson (2010) calls 'Yankee ingenuity': 'a near religious faith in the power of science and technology to transcend nature, to overcome our enemies, and, in general, to surmount all obstacles put in the way of our fulfilment of "our dream"' (p. 226). Williamson found dominant accounts of the war reflected an understanding of American military action – especially the bombing of civilian targets – as 'used only when necessary', an idea mirrored in the reduced scale of destruction from Ryan and Hewer's (2016) British respondents and their comprehension of the scale of the campaigns. The reduced scale of the campaigns in mainstream representations of the Allies' war efforts indicates an underlying belief in the Allies' moral superiority and military restraint.

War stories

The cultural memory of the bombings reflects restrictions regarding historical accountability that persist in dominant cultural memory of the war more broadly. These ongoing restrictions and emphases in the way the bombing war is represented, negotiated and remembered are entwined with the wider "continued reification of World War II" (Goldstein 2017, pp. 17–18) in the national and transnational cultures of Britain and the United States, mostly aligning with but occasionally contesting normative narratives of the war.

Looking closely at the cultural memory of the bombings therefore reveals some of the underlying preconditions of the wider Anglo-American cultural memory of the Second World War, and therefore the related senses of self and national identities of the former Allies that continue to be built in relation to this memory. Cultural memory both draws on and helps to reproduce embedded assumptions about the Allies' role and actions during the war and throughout history. Particular cultural works that retell the story of the Second World War have helped produce a foundational mythology for English-speaking Allied nations, and these are inextricable from America and Britain's historical senses of self. This section outlines what the cultural framings of the area bombing campaigns can tell us about this foundational mythology, and points to some contemporary instances that demonstrate the ongoing potency of these narratives as foundational stories.

Reluctant defenders of freedom

Discourses on the war on both sides of the Atlantic tend to reaffirm the Allies only intervened in the war as a necessary response to a dangerous threat to the safety, rights and freedoms of Europe and its citizens (Connelly 2001, p. 2). It is what Goldstein (2017) calls 'a truism that, if anything, has become more believable with time: the Allies had to win the war to prevent the Axis from doing so' (p. 21). The storying of wartime Britons as stoic, reluctant defenders of freedom mentioned above echoes what Williamson (2010) argues was the 'American variant of just war rhetoric', casting Americans as 'the reluctant defenders of freedom who make war only as a last resort' (p. 221). And yet most descriptions of the *effects* of area bombing appear far from necessary. Friedrich positioned his account of the bombings from the victims' perspectives as a move against what he considered to be 'the interpretation of mass annihilation as a military necessity' (p. 485). Friedrich's book was controversial when translated into English, in part because it painted the objectives behind the mass death and destruction of the bombings as mostly punitive, which contradicts the idea that the Allies' bombings sought *only* to end a war that nobody on the 'good' side had wanted in the first place.

Characterizing the war as an unfortunate necessity is reflected in popular representations that depict Allied citizens as peace-loving citizens, willing to fight but only when necessary (Hedetoft 1993). During the war, the British press worked in close tandem with its government and American propagandists to cultivate a careful self-image of the Allies (Calder 1995) that one could argue remains effective to this day. For instance, Calder (1995) identified a particular self-image of Britain that has prevailed and has prevented the interrogation of any 'unpleasant' memories of the war:

> The British internalised an Anglo-American view of themselves at war, incorporating with the 'finest hour' notions of volunteer improvisation and 'muddling through', which in effect stood in the way of realistic representation, or hard questioning, of their wartime activities for about three decades.
>
> (p. 60)

The way the war is often remembered through the frame of the Blitz Myth, for example, suggests an underlying (and now very familiar) characterization of British society in the 'story' of the war I have written about elsewhere: 'a small, dispersed power structure; solidarity and horizontal camaraderie between all classes; a dedication to democracy and the personal freedoms associated with it;

and a reverence for military discipline, hierarchy, and authority (diffuse through civilian life)' (Florence 2016, p. 125). 'The British people remained entranced by the image of themselves as defenders of world democracy in their "finest hour"', writes Calder (1995, p. 57). 'They alone had kept the beacon of European democracy burning in the dark period between the fall of France and US entry into the war' (Calder 1995, pp. 56–7). The Allied war mythology privileges moments like the Blitz and Dunkirk, identifying both Britain and America as a small, tough force that defeated a large and technologically superior empire, but only because it was necessary. This self-view of the Allies as defenders of democracy continues to underpin many depictions of the Allies in the conflict (see, for example, the box office and critical success of Christopher Nolan's patriotic *Dunkirk* (2017) or Mel Gibson's *Hacksaw Ridge* (2016)) and, as we shall see below, continues to shape their views of themselves in more contemporary political and military conflicts.

'A good story'

Such a reading of the roles of the Allies in the war is supported by the narrative of the war itself. Reynolds (2017) delineates the historical event of the war as a 'good story': 'a struggle that had a dramatic and heroic start, a clear turning point in the middle, and an utterly decisive ending' (p. 217). This narrative has found plentiful expression in the transnational culture that has stretched across both sides of the Atlantic. Binns (2017) argues that the historical reality of the war enabled the predominance of certain narratives in Hollywood war films:

> It was a tidy war, with reasonably clear battlefields and areas of engagement ... There were two sides, the Allies and the axis: one that was ostensibly 'good', the other apparently evil. Further, the victory of the Allies was absolute in a strategic sense. This is arguably the most important point – the 'good guys' won.
>
> (p. 147)

This tidy, clean war, with a strong narrative structure, has made it possible to seamlessly co-opt the strong mythology to many contemporary issues and debates, particularly those that are notably lacking in narrative clarity: from the Cold War, the post-Cold War realignment of global order, to the two Gulf Wars, the so-called War on Terror, the cultural and political upheaval surrounding Donald Trump's election and the Brexit referendum, and possibly even Russia's 2022 invasion of Ukraine.

The 'good story' retold: Brexit

Some have noted how the debates and fervour surrounding Britain's exit from the European Union have leant itself to the mythology of the Second World War with ease, and this was done in no small part through this satisfying narrative arch that the war provided. 'In the wake of Brexit', Franklin (2019) argues, 'war commemoration has – almost inevitably – become the most prominent source of national celebration to fill the vacuum left by the idea of being either global citizens or European' (p. np). Through both the Leave and Remain campaigns, in both popular culture and in Parliament, Brexit has been viewed and depicted as kind of modern day play on the narrative of Britain's role in the Second World War (Franklin 2019). Korte (2019) writes that most films about the Second World War that were released after the referendum in 2016 were inherently linked to Brexit by commentators, particularly the Dunkirk evacuations, the Blitz and the Battle of Britain:

> … historical events which, in mythified and heroised shapes, evoke the idea of Britain standing alone against the enemy and its people standing together, enduring the war both at the front and at home.
>
> (Korte 2019, p. 2)

The story of Dunkirk in particular feeds well into the 'good story' of a Brexit narrative: a heroic retreat, isolationist strength in the face of a multi-national, empire-like force and the emphasis on horizontal camaraderie across classes (Florence 2016). There is even a literal escape from Europe, as Korte (2019) points out, across 'the symbolically charged topography of the English Channel, a geographical border that seems to "naturally" separate Britain and the Continent' (p. 3). The 'plot points' of the Dunkirk story fit so well into the narrative pillars of Britains war memory that they were easily co-opted into the Brexit narrative.

There have also been more insidious uses of the Second World War to frame Brexit. An example of this counter-discourse occurred in 2016, when the then former-Mayor of London and Leave campaigner Boris Johnson drew parallels between the Nazi empire and the European Union, speaking of those who try to bring about the:

> golden age of peace and prosperity under the Romans, by trying to unify [Europe]. Napoleon, Hitler, various people tried this out, and it ends tragically … The EU is an attempt to do this by different methods.
>
> (in Ross 2016, pars. 14–15)

A similar invocation can again be found in Johnson's first speech to Parliament as Prime Minister in July 2019:

> No one in the last few centuries has succeeded in betting against the pluck and nerve and ambition of this country ... They will not succeed today.
>
> (in BBC News 2019)

The post-war anti-fascist consensus that once stabilized Europe collapsed at the end of the Cold War, resulting in 'the frequently observed globalisation of holocaust memory' becoming 'shadowed by a more insidious counter-discourse characterized by resentment and the embrace of (defeated) projects of conquest' (Levi & Rothberg 2018, p. 359). The 'good story' of the war, aided in a way by the globalization of Holocaust memory cultures, means there is ample opportunity to use the narrative to bolster a range of political and cultural projects.

Moral righteousness

Another element of the mythology that underpins Anglo-American cultural memory of the war is a narrative of moral righteousness. This storying of the war emphasizes the strength and heroism of the victorious nations, and elides the more-questionable actions during the war. And this self-image is outright challenged by the possibility, such as that posed by the violent realities of the air war over Europe, that the British military was not absolutely righteous in their cause during the war. '[A] distinction was [therefore] made', argues Connelly (2001), in relation to the exploits of the RAF during the war in particular, 'between the war the British fought and the war the Nazis fought. The British can express regrets for deaths, but the righteousness of the cause means that the British do not, and should not, apologise' (p. 139). Because the Allies' cause was righteous, so too were any of their actions in pursuit of this cause, including bombing civilians.

Goldstein (2017) points out how the 'silence' surrounding American (and by extension, Allied) troops killing civilians (explored above) is due in no small part to the fashioning of the war as a morally just war, and how this was enabled again by the moral reality of the war:

> The extent and the depravity of the Nazi crimes against humanity, and the unconditional defeat of the Third Reich, have made this silence possible.
>
> (Goldstein 2017, p. 17)

Reynolds (2017) found this sense of moral righteousness reaffirmed a certain 'grand war narrative' in Hollywood and mainstream British war movies from the two decades following the war, again supported by the reality of the situation in Europe: 'In most movies, the Germans and Japanese were clearly "baddies"' (p. 217). The very real horrors of the war that emerged after the Nazis' surrender proved that on some level, aside from or despite political rhetoric, the Allies really were fighting a 'good war' (Calder 1995, p. 59). Thus, as Goldstein (2017) argues, 'the Nazi crimes against humanity were so grave, and the Holocaust so monstrous, that any attempt to discuss American (and British) aerial bombardment seems revisionist and dangerous' (p. 31). It is within this context that the area bombings of German cities are remembered by the former Allies, and which continue to shape the dominant ways of making sense of the war today.

Nostalgic moral certainty

The moral clarity of the conflict has meant the Second World War can act as a kind of proto-war, the war against which all others are modelled, including those that might otherwise be morally murky. 'Of all the modern American wars', Noon (2004) argues, 'the Second World War represents the default symbol of national virtue, the "good war" to which all other wars (metaphoric or actual) are supposed to refer' (p. 343). The stories of the Second World War as a proto-conflict have become sacred in mainstream expressions of American national identity, in no small part because of communicative practices like literature, television and Hollywood war movies. Stuckey (1992) identifies the homogenizing effect of this mythology:

> In memory and Saturday afternoon movies, World War II has been emptied of potentially controversial content and moral ambiguity; it stands as a national symbol of a 'good' war, when all the villains were on the other side, and Americans fought a clearly delineated foreign enemy, not one another. The American military cooperated with their equally moral allies, and ensured the triumph of freedom and justice.
>
> (p. 246)

Because of this moral clarity, this historical experience has continued to guide the way the former Allied audiences digest and negotiate post-war conflicts and more contemporary times of moral ambiguity, such as the Gulf wars (Williamson 2010).

As I've established above, Britain and America's moral superiority during the war was established in contrast to the immorality of Nazi Germany. The righteousness of the Allied cause only strengthened as the guilt of the Nazis deepened. The full horrors of the Nazi regime that were revealed after the war only further justified any violence carried out against Germany during the war. 'Nazi criminality', Goldstein (2017) argues, 'particularly the German extermination campaign against the European Jews, has become, *ex post facto*, sufficient justification for any American military policy during the war itself' (p. 17). Reynolds furthers this argument. 'Here were atrocities on a scale and character that dwarfed anything from Belgium in 1914', argues Reynolds (2017) 'endowing the war of 1939–45 with a moral clarity that the British did not perceive in 1914–18' (p. 214). As more camps were liberated, and more images of emaciated survivors and mass graves began to circulate through Anglosphere media, the more they evidenced the righteousness and necessity of the Allies' victory, and the more moral clarity was afforded to the conflict. 'With victory came vindication', argues Reynolds (2017), 'as the advancing Allies exposed the horrors of the German death camps' (p. 213). Within the context of area bombing, the existence and horror of the camps only reaffirmed the monstrous qualities of the Nazis, and a monster that grew almost immediately to encompass every German citizen, including those who died in bombing raids. In fact, the full scale and horror of the Holocaust was not revealed until after 1945, and was not once mentioned in the British or American governments' documents as a motivation for an area bombing campaign (Hansen 2008).

The cultural memory of the Second World War, with its solid narrative structure and clear winners and losers, therefore also provides a helpful, but notably dichotomous, moral framework within which the former Allied countries can position themselves in more contemporary morally ambiguous conflicts, and an absolutely evil Other against which they can construct their absolutely righteous cause:

> Our narratives about World War II repeat familiar dualisms that bifurcate the world into mutually exclusive, opposing forces (for example, 'civilization' versus 'barbarism,' 'East' versus 'West,' or 'democracy' versus 'totalitarianism'); these 'prophetic dualisms,' as Philip Wander has described them, externalize 'evil'.
> (Noon 2004, p. 345)

Noakes and Pattison (2013) have pointed out how 'the cultural memory of the "good war" against European fascism and Japanese imperialism [was] mobilized in support of a simplifying rhetoric that places the West as "good" and its enemies as "bad"' (p. 9). The debates about area bombing in the former Allied nations demonstrate the need for this 'other' well. The mere mention of the bombings is often assumed to be an attempt to garner sympathy for German victims, as Hitchens (2003) pointed out: 'those non-Germans who have drawn attention to the … devastation are suspected of a courting sympathy for the other side' (p. 186). During and after the war, constructions of 'British', 'American' and 'Allied' were built in opposition to a foreign threat – 'German', 'Japanese' or 'Axis'. Mainstream Anglo-American cultural memory therefore constructs Allied identity and morality as mirroring that of Nazi Germany.

A central tenet of Anglo-American war discourse is thus the Nazis' wartime atrocities. Whilst this is certainly not new – Bell (2003) argues that collective memories are more than anything a way to distinguish the 'national self from the foreign alien "Other"' (p. 94) – it is still important to note the centrality of the Holocaust to the narratives that the former Allies told about themselves. This further indicates the inherently dichotomous frame of cultural memory that formed after the Second World War, and which continues to structure models of historical guilt and victimhood to this day.

The evil Other

The 'good story' (Binns 2017) of the Second World War has a clearly identifiable and comprehensively defeated enemy: the Nazi. On both sides of the Atlantic, the unequivocal villainy of Nazi Germany was a central component of the frame through which Allied civilians came to understand their place in the conflict. In the very least, the absolute evil of the Nazi provides justification for any action against him, thus bolstering the moral righteousness of the Allies' cause explored above. 'The motif of the Nazis as the ultimate adversaries simply legitimizes even the hardest level of aggression to fight them', argues Widdman (2020, p. np). What's more, if the Allies' moral wartime identity was forged in opposition to the Nazis, the worse the Nazis became, the better the Allies looked.

Many have identified 'The Nazi' as a character, a ready-made, simple and easy villain against which a wholly good hero can be constructed. The titular hero of the *Captain America* comics, for example, has often been investigated as co-constitutive of American geopolitical power and national identity as he fights enemies often specifically within a Second World War context. 'Cap', as he is known, was initially an anti-Nazi hero launched during the Second World War, until he was frozen in ice and resurrected to fight America's 'modern' enemies during the Cold War and in the post-reunification period (Dittmer 2013). Crucially, Cap was crafted in the frame of the Second World War in explicit opposition to Hitler as the ultimate supervillain (Dittmer 2013). The Nazis were brought in as the main villains in the *Captain America* comics in the 1960s precisely because they were 'uncomplicatedly evil', even 'iconically evil' (McClancy 2017 p. 9), which proved helpful in the morally ambiguous times of the Cold War.

This depiction of Nazis as the moral opposite to the West has not remained confined to wartime or Cold War texts but has continued to shape mainstream and dominant depictions of the Second World War in popular culture, which in turn continue to shape national and international mythologies for many nation states. Kelsey (2013), for example, found the terrorists of the London 7/7 bombings in 2005 were characterized as equivalents of the *Luftwaffe* of 1940 in the British press. These moral frameworks have proven to be all the more appealing in morally uncertain times, such as in the post-Cold War 90s when Communism declined as the anti-democratic threat. When the Iron Curtain lifted and the threat of Communism receded, the post-Cold War era was defined by a distinct 'nostalgia for the politics of clear enemies' (Hake 2012, p. 25). The Nazi emerged as a readily available, clearly defined and *shared* enemy for the world, providing what Brian (2020) calls 'the simple equation of ultimate evil represented by Nazis' (p. 367). Many films, television programs and literature continued to bolster war mythologies centred around the Nazi as the ultimate villain. Brian (2020) writes how the post-race, Obama-era America similarly required a 'clearly identified, unquestionably evil, and ultimately defeated enemy' (p. 364), which then resulted in a continuing 'obsession' of Hollywood with Hitler and Nazi imaginaries. The 2011 adaption film of *Captain America*, (*Captain American: The First Avenger* (2011)) for example, is set during the Second World War, and uses Nazis as two-dimensional villains against which the titular hero can exhibit his heroism; 'less characters than they are dummies in an obstacle course', as one review of the film stated (Snyder 2011). Nazis are also instantly recognizable, instantly feared, and 'effortlessly impersonated' (Brian 2020). This role of the ultimate evil other is also often rather faceless; the German pilots shooting at stranded Allied troops and British spitfire pilots in *Dunkirk* (2017) remain identifiable only as a source of plot pressure on the main characters.[4] As the ultimate villain, found across the texts that make up cultural memory to this day, the Nazi as a character perhaps communicates more about the Allies' historical memory of themselves than it does about their view of the Nazis.

The not so 'other' evil Other

There are exceptions and nuance to this of course: as long as there have been Hollywood films that reinforce British and American morality as existing in opposition to that of Nazi Germany or Communist Russia, there have also been Hollywood films that challenge this absolutist stance. What's more, while maintaining this 'good war' narrative has meant that accounts of the complexities of German wartime experience have been scarce in English-speaking popular culture, this has begun to be amended. For example, there has been a spate of hugely popular films in the last two decades that portray the diversity of German experience under (or as part of) Nazi rule: *Der Untergang (Downfall)* (2004), *The Reader* (2008), *The Boy in the Striped Pyjamas* (2008), *Valkyrie* (2008), *The Book Thief* (2013), *Where Hands Touch* (2018), *The Keeper* (2019) and *Jojo Rabbit* (2019). Furthermore, the flow of cultural and media materials across national boundaries enabled by globalization has increased the circulation of texts that involve less traditional depictions of wartime Germany, particularly media content made by and for primarily German populations. For example, Han's Fallada's 1947 book *Jeder stirbt für sich allein* (Every man dies alone) was published in English in 2009 and adapted into an English-language film in 2016 under the title *Alone in Berlin* (2016). *Alone in Berlin* depicts, in English, wartime Germans with complexity and nuance, even reluctant sympathy.

It is also important to briefly look to how this assured 'otherness' of the Nazi is perhaps more complicated outside of Hollywood and in real life, particularly in the face of the developments in America during and after Donald Trump's presidency. When neo-Nazis marched on Charlottesville in 2017, and far-right extremists attempted to invade the Capitol building in Washington DC in 2021, both brandishing neo-Nazi symbols and paraphernalia, the 'evil other' enemy of Nazism reared its ugly head in the mainstream American public life, and appeared to be somewhat less than 'other'. Whilst neo-Nazism has been a threat to American culture since the end of the war (Jackson 2020), it has more or less appeared to remain on the fringes of civic and political life. The Charlottesville protests and the Capitol attack showed nothing if not how these ideologies are becoming increasingly mainstream (Cammaerts 2020; Giroux 2016; Mondon & Winter 2020; Stanley 2020). The assured 'otherness' of the ultimate 'evil other' that is embodied in the figure of the Nazi seemed to be less assured as Nazi symbols, chants and ideology returned with great volume to American streets and politics. Hake (2012) argues that a certain 'fascist imaginary' in Hollywood 'thrives on an endlessly repeated process of demarcation and externalization' (p. 5) wherein the threat is always 'other'. By continuing to have the Nazi as othered in mainstream depictions of the Second World War, it is perhaps understandable that many democratic nations are struggling to comprehend the emergence of fascist threats from within.

Thus there is sufficient evidence to at least entertain the argument that the continued 'othering' of the Nazi in Hollywood and other dominant digestions of the Second World War serves only to obscure the long tradition of racialized politics in the United States. Recent events in the United States explored above also suggest that 'extreme forms of far-right ideological beliefs have never been historically at the fringes of culture and society but at their core' (Lee 2020, p. 139). Whether this is the case or not lies outside the remit of this book, but it is worth noting that strict, us vs. them, good vs. evil frameworks of not only morality but also history and historical accountability continue to restrict cultural negotiations about the underlying characteristics of national and transnational cultures. Pushing beyond these restrictions where they relate explicitly or tangentially to the Second World War is part of the aim of this book. Complicating this framing might therefore allow for a more nuanced understanding of ongoing negotiations of former-Allied identities as they are formed in relation to concepts of wartime morality, justice and accountability.

Conclusions

Foucault's (1977) genealogy encourages us to disturb and interrogate underlying assumptions and power relations that we take for granted and consider immobile. This chapter has brought to light some of the underlying preconditions of very contemporary debates of national and international identity, history and cultural memory, and has shown that these are often conducted in explicit and implicit relation to entrenched retellings of the story of the Second World War. The fact that the war remains entwined with contemporary negotiations of a myriad of issues – from immigration, the Brexit referendum and Donald Trump's presidency to debates over free speech and the Black Lives Matter movement – reaffirms the need for a more nuanced, complicated and disruptive form of cultural memory of the war, in which there is room for multiple truths and multiple perspectives.

Rather than interrogating the basis of far right and neo-fascist exploitations of the cultural memory of area bombing or the vagaries of the German victim debate and German post-war cultural memory, this chapter has sought to investigate the underlying conditions that continue to entrench particular Anglo-American perspectives of the war and exclude others. Of most importance, beneath the rhetoric that characterizes area bombing during the war as moral, necessary, justified, strategic and against 'an evil Other', I have shown that normative practices of remembering the Second World War posit the Allies as the heroes and the Nazis as the villains. The cemented historical guilt of Germany for the post-war fate of Europe cements the absolute righteousness of the Allies in comparison, thus negating the need for – and perhaps even actively preventing – Anglo-American discursive practices to scrutinize Allied historical culpability in civilian deaths and civic destruction.

The use of the cultural memory of area bombing by the far right and for historical revisionism, whilst a genuine and serious concern, should not therefore completely allow the former Allies to elide historical responsibility for mass deaths and destructions during the war in their cultural memory structures. The fact that the Allies were morally righteous in their cause against a truly evil regime does not necessarily absolve them of perpetrating mass destruction on civilian populations. This restrictive, 'either/or' dichotomy of historical morality heavily colours normative Anglo-American memory discourses. This chapter therefore presents the need for a plurality of perspectives, subjectivities, identities and moralities regarding the cultural memory of area bombing, which has been advocated by several other authors and scholars and the need for which is only intensifying. But a revised approach to the cultural memory of area bombing requires a revised approach to memory, which is outlined in Chapter 2. In that approach, I examine the act of visiting tourism sites in Berlin as a way to generate the multiple temporalities, actors, politics, events, forces and accidents that make up the bombings and how they can be remembered, as a way of disrupting these restrictive frameworks, and providing a more comprehensive cultural memory of area bombing in Berlin for Anglo-American visitors.

2

A history of remembering through places

Introduction

In 2020, the Black Lives Matter movement was enacted not only through protest, politics, speeches and Instagram posts, but in no small part through vandalism, destruction and removal of statues. The movement became occupied, in part, with memory. When the protestors began destroying or defacing statues of slave owners and Confederate generals, they were effectively re-inscribing – some argued re-writing – the memory of nations through the actual material of the streets. Rather than simply destroying the nations' cultural heritage – and aside from the question of whether that colonial heritage deserves to be destroyed – these protestors were creating their nations' cultural heritage, enacting the negotiations of both British and American history that occurred in the summer of 2020.

Destruction itself therefore became an act of memory, both a way of challenging the ubiquitous veneration of racism and colonialism that remains at the heart of these nations and a form of civic and anti-racist resistance. Toppling statues is a communicative act that is part of a wider process of forming and shaping new cultural and political states of play. Destruction, vandalism, graffiti, these things that are often seen as existing outside the realm of memorialization, are part of the process of cultural memory.

****

The contemporary debates and negotiations of cultural memory explored in Chapter 1 indicate the need for an interdisciplinary approach to how we remember through places. This book is interdisciplinary, situated at the intersection of memory studies, communication studies and cultural geography, and with some minor but significant contributions from new materialist and posthuman theories and methodologies. The intersection of culture, memory, place and these latter two philosophies is explored in more detail in later chapters, but in this chapter I outline my approach to cultural memory that is capable of accounting for the productive layering of different narratives, perspectives and temporalities of encounters with the places presented in Chapters 4–7 and how they are caught up in the Anglo-American cultural memory of area bombing.

After a brief introduction of the very loose 'field' of memory studies, I begin by outlining what I see as intersecting limitations in some approaches to memory and place that have arisen out of the field's history as a form of resistance against genocide, as well as legitimate fears of perpetrators controlling narratives of trauma and victimhood. The context of interrogating the cultural memory of area bombing as co-created by Anglo-American audiences outlined in Chapter 1 necessitates an approach that takes seriously threats to the primacy of the Holocaust and victim narratives in Second World War memory cultures. I argue that many of these concerns stem from a restrictive understanding of the relationship between memory and culture, wherein memory is seen as a 'zero-sum' game, or an ideological battleground, over which varying groups, voices and narratives must vie for 'control'. In the context of these concerns I build on existing approaches to memory that propose ways to formulate the relationship between memory and culture, focusing on the 'cultural' in cultural memory. Rather than as a form of control over information or influence, these approaches look to cultural memory as the outcome of ongoing communicative practices. I position memory texts such as the places studied in this volume as tools with which visitors continually imagine and re-imagine their place within certain social and cultural contexts, making sense of and continually forming, reforming, negotiating, contesting and imagining the past. Such an approach pays attention to the flow of power through social relations that are enacted through communicative texts, rather than figuring these sites as tools that one party can 'use' to control the other.

The tensions I identify above are particularly evident when applied to memory and place, necessitating an interdisciplinary approach to how we remember through places. Rather than considering places as inert matter onto which cultural memory is simply projected, I again build on approaches that interrogate the practical activities of visitors as they engage with and make sense of these sites and produce cultural memory. Such an approach is informed in no small part by cultural geography, but also draws on new materialist models of experience, the materiality of the sites and the bodily and sensory interactions between the site and the visitor.

Building on Golanska's (2020) 'collision approach', I propose that the intersection of bodily, sensory interactions with the discursive-cultural currents of dominant cultural memory of the war in Anglo-American spheres has the potential to complicate normative readings of historical responsibility and accountability. By fully interrogating *both* the sensory and bodily interactions between visitors and the sites *and* the more representational understandings of the war that accompany them, a more complex and nuanced memory of the war can emerge.

The entanglement of both the bodily and discursive readings of the war at these sites necessitates a method that takes the cultural and sensorial subjectivity of myself as a visitor-researcher into account. I therefore briefly introduce my method at the end of this chapter as a way of accounting for myself as a researcher interacting with the sites' materialities *and* the cultural and political frames that I outlined in Chapter 1 that I as an English-language native and cultural participant 'bring with me'. The 'history of the present' (Foucault 1977) approach I have adopted understands the specific spatial and temporal position of the researcher as well as their cultural political position to be an integral part of analyses. The subsequent method chapter (Chapter 3) further explores the implications arising from being a member of the Anglo-American population being studies, as well as implications of the subjective body as a tool of research.

Memory studies and cultural studies

A short history of memory studies

Situated amongst existing literature attempting to understand how and why we remember and forget, this book draws on memory studies. Memory studies is less a 'field' of study per se, more a recurrent preoccupation, stretching across disciplines, with the ways that the past manifests in the present. 'Memory, it seems', argue Tota and Hagen (2015), 'is almost everywhere. From *lieux* to oblivion, cells to museums, text messages to dementia – memory as an object of study is perpetually elusive and evolving' (p. 1). As an object of study, memory 'continually refocuses and reinvents itself, searching for moments, events and places in an effort to locate the multitude of ways that memory makes its way into lives, or in fact is life' (Tota & Hagen 2015, p. 1). Approaches to memory vary across disciplines, but the foundations for studying traces of the past in the present are often attributed to Maurice Halbwachs (1992) and Pierre Nora (1989). Some scholars look at memory as personal, subjective articulations of the past, which are often framed as a counter to 'official history' (Ebdenshade 1995). Political and sociological disciplines often focus on the ways that memory can be 'used', examining how past experiences shared by groups are then formed into political and cultural tools and used by (often national) institutions of power (Lowenthal 1985). The past, in these studies, is seen as a tool that can be used 'in service of the present' (Schwartz 1982, p. 374), contingent on the aims and methods of the groups who 'control' expressions of memory. Other studies look at the commodification of memory (Landsberg 2003), and the rise of what many call the 'memory industry'.

Memory studies has evolved in conjunction with shifting social, cultural and political circumstances as well as techno-social developments in mediation and communication. Beyond individual and psychological memory or memoir, memory in a more collective sense has almost always been approached where it is mediated, and has therefore been examined as it relates to more traditional mediations of literature (Assmann 2006; Fussel 2009), film (Eley 2001; Erll 2008; Landsberg 2003; Winter 2006) and art (Saunders 2020), as well as more recent examinations of digital memory (Frith & Kalin 2016; Hoskins 2017; Kansteiner 2017; Reading 2014), games and gamification (Chapman 2016; Miller 2020; Widmann 2020), and virtual and augmented reality (Hassapopoulou 2018; Kysela & Štorková 2015). The rise of social movements through social and digital media has also entailed an examination of how these social movements use historical narratives and mnemonic devices to mobilize populations, particularly of how this has played out in digital and social-digital spaces (Berger, Scalmer, & Wicke 2021; Eyerman 2015; Merrill, Keightly, & Daphi 2020).

In light of the Anthropocene, memory studies scholarship has also begun to turn to the 'more than human' (Craps et al. 2018; Golanska 2020), decoupling memory from the purely socio-political realm (methodologies born from such approaches are explored in more detail in Chapter 3). Memory is now being considered where it is mediated through substances such as earth (Pastor & Kent 2020), ruins (Bennett 2020), human remains (Sturken 2020) and even bio-feedback data (Osborne 2019). Memory has been examined beyond the confines of 'the human' and on more expansive temporal scales, including that of deep geological time and archaeological traces (Tien & Florence 2022). Crownshaw (2017) pushes memory from the past into the future, investigating the applications and implications of 'speculative' or 'anticipatory' memory in literature and fiction. From this perspective memory emerges somewhere in the 'space in-between' the discursive and the material (Golanska 2020), ever reliant on the intersecting threads of mediation and experience of audience, author and matter. Such an approach to memory is discussed further below as a means of broadening some limitations in the study of the cultural memory of area bombing. Taking matter seriously, I will argue, means interrogating the practical activities of visitors as they engage with and make sense of the matter of sites with which they can produce cultural memory, as well as more ephemeral cultural political processes.

Memory and mass trauma

Closely tied with history and historiography, memory studies found fertile ground in the post-war cultural and political landscape of Europe and North America. The so-called 'memory boom' of the early 1990s, for example, was part of a global response to the dramatically changing dynamics of the world following the collapse of the Iron Curtain and nearly four decades of international politics and society divided along Cold War lines (Olick, Vinitzky-Seroussi, & Levy 2011). But the memory of the Second World War and the Holocaust is largely agreed to be the most formative nexus of memory studies as we understand it today. The monstrosity of the Holocaust has meant that what can only loosely be called the 'field' of memory studies has developed in no small part in direct relation to the task of healing from, remembering, and 'dealing with' – the famous *Vergangeheitswebelantung* – the Holocaust. Much of the characteristics of memory studies have therefore been forged in the decades in which the cultural, political and philosophical impact of the Second World War and the Holocaust were being reckoned with. Pierre Nora famously declared 'whoever says memory, says Shoah' (in Olick, Vinitzky-Seroussi, & Levy 2011, p. 9), and the cultural and metaphysical weight of the Holocaust has guided the development of studies of memory on a collective level. Beyond the Holocaust, memory studies have also looked to the politics and forms of dealing with other mass traumas such as forced expulsion (e.g. Demshuk 2012), ethnic cleansing (e.g. Volčič 2007), slavery (e.g. Eyerman 2001) and more.

Memories of the Holocaust and the Second World War therefore remain at the centre of many studies of memory on a collective scale, and this has resulted in the field's necessary preoccupation with themes of justice, preservation and victim testimony. Preserving victims' accounts of mass trauma has emerged as an enduring goal of what Darian-Smith and Hamilton (2013) call 'memory work' (p. 371). The Holocaust, Olick, Vinitzky-Seroussi and Levy (2011) argue, 'has placed the image of the victim at the core of contemporary culture as a whole' (p. 10). Darian-Smith and Hamilton (2013) point out that early post-war memory work first 'aimed to fend off forgetfulness, especially as the generations who lived through the First and Second World wars were dying out' (p. 373). This was later replaced by an 'obsession' (Darian-Smith & Hamilton 2013) with remembering on a collective level as a direct response to trauma and violence, bringing about the 'era of the witness', where 'the testimony of survivors [became] central to the meanings of war and other traumatic experiences' (p. 373). Olick, Vinitzky-Seroussi, and Levy (2011) argue victimhood has particular currency in the wake of the Holocaust and other histories of genocide and ethnic cleansing, and this currency has only strengthened in the face of the threat of Holocaust denial, anti-Semitism, neo-Nazism, the rise and legitimization of the far-right and intersecting trends of Islamophobia and racial violence.

The testimonial function of victim and survivor memory is more than symbolic or philosophical: survivor accounts and records are central in holding perpetrators legally, morally, politically and culturally accountable, and resisting very contemporary and very real threats of violence. The 1961 trial of Adolf Eichmann in Israel, for example, became a locus of a shift in understandings of the Holocaust and the potential testimonial function of survivor, victim and witness memory (Wievorka 2000). The Eichmann trial linked the memories of victims and survivors of the Holocaust with international justice and helped bring this justice to the centre of Holocaust cultural memory and therefore the study of cultural memory. This also indicates the preoccupation of 'memory work' with an almost psycho-biological concern of fading memories, wherein the lessons and wisdom of the past are seen as at risk from neurological decay or the loss of repositories of knowledge, be they archives or dying generations. Listening to survivor accounts became an act of repair against the institutional erasure that is often carried out in conjunction with mass trauma events. Post-war projects of truth-finding and justice thus afforded memory political and ethical potency.

Memory is thus framed as a source of evidence, of both the existence and the deliberate annihilation of millions of lives. The anxiety I identified in Chapter 1 about the memory of German victimhood stems from the threat the cultural memory of area bombing might pose to remembering Holocaust victims and survivors and preserving their narratives. This is no abstract or over-anxious fear, as I've shown in Chapter 1: Holocaust denial is on the rise, and the new far-right movements sweeping across Europe and America – which often make use of area bombing in their rhetoric as a source of victimhood for non-Jewish German citizens – have deep roots in and frequently frame their messages using historical relativism, revisionism and outright anti-Semitism. Preserving the memory of victims and survivors thus remains an essential task of 'memory work', and any work on the memory of area bombing must be carried out within the specific context of these direct attacks on the testimonial and justice function of victims' and survivors' memory.

Making space for area bombing memories

Documenting the cultural memory of area bombing takes place within this landscape of memory focused on preserving victim and survivor accounts of Nazi atrocities. The politically and ethically fraught task of remembering area bombings also reveals some of the limitations of particular approaches to memory on a cultural scale. As I outlined in Chapter 1, memories of area bombing are often assumed – often correctly – to be used as a weapon against the vital work of preserving the memory of survivors, victims and witnesses of Nazi atrocities. Attempts to form a cultural memory of area bombing are regularly cast as a move to undermine the particular status that Holocaust victim and survivor accounts now have as foundational stories of Second World War memory. The need to document and preserve the cultural memory of the exceptional trauma of the Holocaust fuels concerns that some parties (particularly perpetrator parties) might dominate the available space for retelling the story of the past, or might encroach on the space left for accounts of victims. The politics of remembering area bombing, as outlined in Chapter 1, are a typical example of these concerns. The fear that the perpetrators (depicted as Germany) might seize the narrative at the expense of voices of victims of German war crimes is, again, legitimate.

However, I join Aleida Assmann (2006) in arguing that the ethical necessity of preserving Holocaust memories has also caused a certain impasse in the post-war cultural memory landscape in relation to German victimhood. This impasse is caused by the fact that Second World War memory is generally considered to operate in the form of a hierarchy, at the top of which sits the Holocaust or in a zero-sum game, wherein there is only so much space for memory allowed, and space for the Holocaust must therefore be carefully and vigilantly guarded. Many debates (including the one over German victimhood) have been sparked by acts that are taken as attempts to at least level this hierarchy of memory, if not invert it, or to take up precious memory real estate:

> On the one side there is German suffering, which is claimed to make possible the acquittal of the perpetrators; on the other side is German guilt, which excludes all consideration of suffering. The debate re-establishes the contradictory categories of victims and perpetrators with an accuracy that rules out any possibility of overlap.
>
> (Assmann 2006, p. 189)

As I demonstrated in Chapter 1, such a hierarchical, zero-sum game of cultural memory has resulted in there being no room for investigating the historical responsibility of the Allies in mass deaths during the war on a cultural level. Assmann argues that there *is* room for other kinds of accounts in the lexicon of Second World War memory and I agree, but such a model of the cultural memory of the Second World War can only be formed if other accounts, like those of Allied culpability in German suffering, are not modelled as vying for the primacy of the Holocaust, but are allowed to exist *alongside* them, and even become entangled with them.

In terms of scholarly approach, Assmann argues that the 'normative framework' of the European and trans-Atlantic Holocaust memory culture must remain, but argues that the ways and places cultural memory is seen to operate continue to dictate the structure of this framework. To allow room for other memories to surround it, Assmann suggests, a wider variety of stories from a wider variety of perspectives must be included in a broader scope of analysis. Assmann specifically calls for the inclusion of more heterogeneous *forms* of memory:

> The heterogeneous memories that exist side by side on the social level are integrated and contained in the normative framework of memory on the national level [the Holocaust]. As long as this framework remains in place, the diverse memories of suffering, guilt and resistance can co-exist side by side without necessarily cancelling each other out.
>
> (p. 198)

These diverse memories could find expression in museums, film and television, public days of mourning and celebration, historical fiction and more. In order to 'allow room' for accounts of area bombing, we need to shift the way we understand how and where memory is performed outside of individual recollection, to avoid viewing heterogeneous memories as existing within a zero-sum framework, or as memories in competition with one another. To do so requires a revised approach to the relationship between memory and cultural texts, as the sites where memory is formed, reformed, negotiated and even contested.

In light of this call for a new way of 'doing' cultural memory, the subject has therefore also been approached as a form of disruption, resistance or 'counter-memory'. Many scholars have investigated expressions of 'counter-memory', 'counter-memorials' or 'counter-memory texts' relating to the Second World War (see Forest, Johnson, & Till 2004; Gould & Silverman 2013; Young 1992). The cultural memory of the bombings and German victimhood has often been studied as a form of these counter-memory texts. Narratives that highlight German victimhood are often characterized as an example of 'dormant' memory narratives, which directly oppose 'dominant' ones (Langenbacher 2010, p. 35).

However, often these studies of counter-memory only reify the distinctions between 'official' and 'vernacular' constructions of memory and history, focus too heavily on the 'source' or 'author' of memory texts and articulations, and in fact ignore the fluid and complex processes in which cultural memory is formed and reformed by populations. More recently, Tello (2022) has offered a conceptualization of counter-memory that moves 'beyond thinking of counter-memory as simply a means to maintain or register erased and/or contested histories, or as a dialectical mnemonic system' (p. 390). To effectively open up the zero-sum framework of memory cultures, I propose reconsidering cultural memory as productions and renegotiations of cultural and communicative practices. I therefore join Tello and others in approaches (outlined below) that, combined with new materialist approaches to matter and the interdisciplinary inclusion of theory from cultural geography, investigate the complex assemblage of narratives, experiences, matter and texts that become imbricated in ongoing processes of cultural communication, an outcome of which is 'cultural memory'. The approach developed below might allow room for a cultural memory of area bombing to form alongside, but not in competition with, that of the Holocaust and Nazi atrocities. Furthermore, it allows for a form of cultural memory that disrupts the assumed total righteousness of the Allies' actions during the war.

The 'culture' in cultural memory

Normative practices of remembering the war discussed in Chapter 1 – what McRae would call 'the official order' (2002, p. 2) – are never complete or total. Whilst they may follow persistent patterns, their various elements are constantly disputed, contested and contradicted. It is the various means through which memory on a cultural scale is produced and reproduced that prevents these normative practices from ever being wholly confined to either 'dominant' or 'counter' memory.

A 'third wave' of memory studies is decoupling cultural or collective memory from pre-defined groups or 'collectives' altogether (Erll 2011). Memory is now seen as a continuous, fluid, unpredictable phenomenon. Memory studies as a field is defining itself as thoroughly 'transcultural, transgenerational, transmedial, and transdisciplinary' (Bond, Craps, & Vermeulen 2016, p. 2). 'Memory has, in the last few years, increasingly been considered a fluid and flexible affair' argued Bond, Craps, and Vermeulen in 2016 (p. 21). Landsberg's (2003) 'prosthetic memory', for example, is able to move across borders because of the mobility afforded to globalized media texts, artefacts and practices. Erll's (2011) 'travelling memory' consists of 'the incessant wandering of carriers, media contents, forms, and practices of memory, their continual "travels" and ongoing transformations through time and space, across social, linguistic and political boundaries' (Erll 2011, p. 11). Erll (2022) has since proposed the concept of 'implicit collective memory', an 'invisible world' of memory that includes 'narrative schemata, stereotypes, patterns of framing, or world models, which are usually not explicitly known or addressed, but get passed on from generation to generation – in order to shape perception and action in new situations' (p. 1). Rothberg's (2009) 'multidirectional memory' recognizes the connectedness between events that are hubs of memory and those that are less so across the boundaries of nation, ethnicity or religion. Also moving beyond the normal boundaries of nations, Levy and Sznaider (2002) developed the idea of 'cosmopolitan memory', 'a process of "internal globalization" through which global concerns become part of local experiences of an increasing number of people' (p. 88). Memory, in these approaches, is not defined by the source or author of particular memory regimes, nor by the media in which it is produced, nor by the particular groups that have utilized it. Memory is unpredictable and mobile, yet thoroughly entwined with its form of mediation, and the specific conditions in which it is produced and circulated.

Building on these approaches, I contend that remembering a shared past on a collective scale is a cultural communicative practice – the 'cultural' in 'cultural memory'. What I define as cultural memory is an outcome of ongoing productions and reproductions of the past through cultural texts. Culture is continually formed, reformed, developed and negotiated by these acts of communication, and so too is cultural memory.

The debates over the place of the cultural memory of area bombing are often reliant on more reductive analyses of the relationship between memory, culture and texts. The fears I identified above of the memory of the war being controlled or manipulated by German perpetrators' perspectives are underpinned by the assumptions implicit in what Landsberg (2003) calls 'the brainwashing model' of communicative texts, or what in communications theory might be called an 'idealist' or 'transmission' model of communication. Landsberg formulates her theory of 'prosthetic memory' to address this brainwashing model in which 'mass culture is seen solely as a site of domination and deception' (p. 149). But rather than a neutral site over which groups or actors can exercise control, texts are the materials with which audiences can construct cultural memory. Texts are, Landsberg argues, 'not capsules of meaning that spectators swallow whole, but rather the grounds upon which social meanings are negotiated, contested, and sometimes constructed' (p. 149). Far from fears of manipulation, bias or propaganda, the relationship between texts and memory should instead be approached as co-constitutive. Communicative texts are a site of negotiation and formulation; not sites of manipulation or control, but the tools with which populations can construct cultural memory. Under such understandings, questions evolve not as to who has 'control' over their meaning, but over the possibilities surrounding what audiences can *do* with these texts when continually constructing their cultural memory.

This approach to media as spaces where cultural memory is produced becomes more evident where communication and media studies intersect with memory studies. Hoelscher (2012) identifies texts (specifically images) as 'technologies of remembrance through which people construct the past and give memory its texture' (p. 291). Sturken (1997) best articulates the lively nature of memory texts and audiences with her description of textual objects like photographs as 'the technologies of memory, not vessels of memory in which memory passively resides, but the objects through which memories are shared, produced, and given meaning' (p. 9). Building on these studies, cultural memory becomes less an imprint of experience – whether of an individual or 'a culture' – and more an outcome of constant communicative work.

Importantly, these constructive, cultural process are inherently shared and collaborative: 'Culture as communication', Grossberg et al. (2006) argue, 'is the process of producing new shared meaning out of the interaction of historically given shared meanings and individually created meanings' (p. 22). The shared nature of these processes means engaging with the political and power dynamics of these negotiations. A cultural approach to memory remains cognizant that political actors can and do utilize certain iterations of the past to achieve their objectives. As Bond, Craps, and Vermeulen (2016) warn, we cannot ignore the political volatility of the past completely. We must 'remain sensitive to the inequitable distribution of power and resources and the role that memorative discourses may play in ongoing struggles for justice, equality and varying forms of (political, cultural, or juridical) representation' (Bond, Craps, & Vermeulen 2016, p. 21). Detaching the study of cultural memory from the nation-state and social bodies does not mean ignoring institutions and power centres completely. Bond, Craps, and Vermeulen argue that we must acknowledge 'the complexity and plurality of mnemonic movement', but strongly warn against 'the temptation to elide the role that hegemonic institutions, such as the nation-state, continue to place in contemporary memorative practice' (p. 21). As Forest, Johnson, and Till (2004) point out, 'power cannot be conceived merely as a directional flow of ruler to ruled, or described simply as repression and domination' (p. 361), but there remain 'uneven topographies of power' (Bennett 2010, p. 23) distribution in cultural memory work.

Such a view aligns with Foucault's formulations of power and discourse, and sees cultural memory as inherently imbricated in dynamic but often entrenched topographies of power relations. Foucault best articulates his approach to power in *A History of Sexuality* (1979):

> Power is everywhere; not because it embraces everything, but because it comes from everywhere ... power is not an institution, and not a structure; neither is it a certain strength we are endowed with; it is the name that one attributes to a complex strategical situation in a particular society.
>
> (p. 93)

Foucualt looks to the complex networks of relations across which power is dispersed, albeit often unevenly and in entrenched patterns. Foucault (in Fornet-Betancourt et al. 1987) calls these entrenched patterns 'states of domination': cases where 'the relations of power are fixed in such a way that they are perpetually asymmetrical, and the margin of liberty is extremely limited' (p. 123). Political and posthuman theorist Jane Bennett (2010) similarly identifies particular assemblages of power relations 'with uneven topographies' (p. 23), patterns of power relations that appear permanent and difficult to shift. For example, the entrenched cultural and political frames through which Anglo-American populations habitually produce cultural memory of the war (outlined in Chapter 1) render some points on the topography of power relations in which cultural memory can be formed more influential than others, and some patterns of sense-making more likely to occur than others. A cultural approach to memory remains aware of these entrenched social and political patterns through which memory is habitually communicated and around which it is frequently structured. My analysis therefore focuses on the set of social power relations in which the sites in Berlin are continually reproduced and circulated. The authors, audiences and texts are all involved in networked relations of politics, power and meaning-making, and this set of relations is bound up with the production of what I identify as 'cultural memory'.

Memory and place

It is amongst this productive topography of power relations and negotiations of cultural memory that I position the sites in Berlin, viewing these places as some of the cultural texts through which cultural memory is produced, reproduced, negotiated and continually reformed. The limitations underpinning studies of collective memory identified above are most evident when applied to analyses of memory places. Places of memory – memorials, monuments, tourist attractions – are often seen as malleable media upon which institutions can impose their official narrative of the past. Ingold (1993) articulated a 'sterile opposition' between commonly held views of landscapes: 'the naturalistic view of the landscape as a neutral, external backdrop to human activities, and the culturalist view that every landscape is a particular cognitive or symbolic ordering of space' (p. 152). Common approaches to the relationship between memory and places often begin from the latter view. Monuments and memorials, in particular, are often seen to solidify state-sanctioned narratives of the past. Some studies characterize monuments as sites of singular, solid and prescribed retellings of the past that are seldom open to question. Dellenbaugh-Losse (2020), for example, explores the relationship between memory and architecture in Berlin and asserts 'choices about architecture and symbolism in capital cities are attempts at concretizing the values and identity of that country's residents (or at least the dominant group)' (p. 1). Ware (2004) describes public memorials as 'highly formal, and prescrib[ing] a certain form of interaction', providing a past that is 'fixed and singular to a passive audience' (p. 121). Edensor (2005b) argues that monuments present only 'publicly sanctioned narratives and institutional rhetoric', and heritage sites often 'banish ambiguity and the multiplicity of the past' (p. 831). Like with other memory texts, places can be approached as passive 'containers' of memory.

Importantly, this kind of thinking is prevalent in analyses of post-war and post-Soviet cities like Berlin, where 'the importance of Berlin's urban and cultural landscape as a physical expression of power and political posturing during the Cold War ... cannot be overstated' (Dellenbaugh-Losse 2020, p. 2). The influence of state-sponsored narratives on public space takes on particular congruence in a city that suffered two authoritarian regimes over the space of five decades, regimes that are well known for controlling historical memory by controlling public space:

> The public landscape of the capital is lined with monuments and memorials advertised to tourists, many who specifically travel to witness a past that cannot be glorified. Urban planners, city officials and citizens have spent decades negotiating the details of the memorialisation of Germany's past and they use the urban landscape as an expression of both remembering and forgetting.
>
> (Gould & Silverman 2013, p. 792)

In opposition to the rigid and prescribed spaces of memorial and monuments, ruins, archaeology or more temporary and transient forms of memorialization are offered and approached as largely 'free' from these attempts to prescribe forms of interaction and meaning. Edensor (2005b) identifies ruins in particular as 'the spatialisation of memory' (p. 834) because they are free of narratives of the past that might not fit with an 'official' view. These ruinous sites of memory are therefore seen as more 'authentic' encounters with the past, material witnesses to the events of history, 'free' from narrative framing.

While it is important in this context to remain cognizant of the very real attempts to order public memory in Berlin through ordering public space on both sides of the Wall (Dellenbaugh-Losse 2020), much of this distinction lies with who or what is perceived as the 'author' of a place-based memory text: 'official' memorials, and monuments are often approached as the expression of static state-sanctioned narratives because they are made by 'the state', whilst community or artist-led commemoration projects are often approached as the 'social', 'vernacular' or everyday expressions of memory because they were made by unofficial, vernacular authors. Like the idealist or 'brainwashing' approach to communication mentioned above, approaches like this assume a coherent group that 'impose[s] their ideological understandings onto seemingly passive subjects through grandiose public displays and monumental spaces' (Forest, Johnson, & Till 2004, p. 361), or else a separate group of counter-memory makers. The focus, in both approaches, is on the 'author' of a site.

Such distinctions can be fraught, however. As Fullbrook (2009) demonstrates below and as we shall see at the Topography of Terror in Chapters 5 and 7, the guiding distinction between 'designed memory sites' and 'authentic traces' falls away when authentic traces of the past are mobilized by state-sponsored actors to legitimize particular narratives. Fullbrook (2009) explains in relation to Berlin:

> Each 'authentic' but in fact constructed and re-presented 'site of memory', each specially designed memorial, however intrinsically bound to a historical referent in the past, is at the same time a situated construct of a later present: those commanding resources and power over space thus also contribute to new forms of collective identity through public representations of selected features of the past.
>
> (p. 126)

Authenticity can be used as a narrative device, and so too can assumptions of a memorial being 'vernacular', community-based, 'bottom-up'. Rather than define an analysis of a memory place based on whether it is 'official' or 'vernacular', we should instead expand analyses to examine the cultural communicative processes in which a place becomes imbricated and is an actor. This also entails a radical embracing of the inherent agency of the sites, both in their capacity to shape and influence cultural memory and their material potential to create change (as explored below). Engaging the cultural role and function of memory places demands an interpretation that goes further than understanding the sites based on their physical and cultural forms, as simply either the epitome of state-sponsored memorials and monuments, or as counter-memorials aimed to subvert the established order, or as ruins and remnants supposedly 'free' from either. Places of memory are not merely reflections, symbols or forensic evidence of abstract processes such as remembering. Meaning is not self-evident in these place-texts through their forms, and understanding the cultural meaning of these memory places also requires an investigation of both the materiality of the site and the audience's reading practices.

Cultural geography

To this end I draw on cultural geography to consider how traces of violence are engaged when forming cultural memory in Berlin. Built environments tie us to our past beyond symbolism or state-sponsored memorialization. Environments that have been shaped by materially destructive or violent processes like bombs and bullets and demolition crews have also been shaped by political and cultural processes of healing, remembering, forgetting or 'dealing with' the past. The plethora of crumbling ruins, demolished buildings and vacant lots across Berlin, for example, are marks of eight decades of remembering the war as much as the memorials, monuments and commemorative places. They evidence a myriad of narratives, themes, processes, actors, politics, histories, presents and more, coalesced on concrete and stone along with rust, mould, decay, bullet holes and graffiti.

Cultural geographer Till (2004) approaches sites from the position that physical worlds and abstract worlds are co-constitutive. Places, Till (2004) writes, are 'always in the process of becoming ... fluid mosaics and moments of memory and metaphor, scene and experience, dream and matter that create and mediate social spaces and temporalities' (p. 75). While the materiality of our surroundings shapes our social, cultural and political practices, so too do our cultural contexts shape our material environment and our interactions with it. Marschall (2015) argues 'memory and meaning are never inherently attached to objects or lodged in spaces; they are inscribed and maintained through communication and performative action' (p. 345). Built environments remain bound up with the ongoing sense-making practices of audiences imagining their past, and this extends beyond the narratives 'solidified' in state-sponsored monuments.

Within the specific context of this research, Confino (2000) set a precedent when he used 'the social and symbolic practice of tourism as a methodological vehicle to illuminate post-war values and beliefs concerning National Socialism' (p. 92). An analysis that ignored these social and cultural reading practices, Confino argued, would be an analysis devoid of the social conditions in which these place-texts exist and are made sense with. 'People make places of memory' argues Till (2004), 'to work emotionally, socially, culturally, and politically for their needs and in the process, search for meaning about them – selves, their worlds and times' (p. 79). Furthermore, Sumartojo (2015) argues that 'commemoration activates landscape through practice, but landscape also enables and encourages forms and articulations of commemoration; in other words, they are co-constitutive' (p. 8).

A similar approach is taken in the field of dark tourism or 'thanatourism' (Foley & Lennon 1996), wherein sites of genocide, torture, holocaust, crime or incarceration are preserved and subsequently become museums, memorials, monuments or other sites specifically designed to invite visitors – in short, tourism destinations. The study of dark tourism shares many theoretical and methodological similarities with cultural memory and geography, not in the least the 'questions of authenticity and fact [that]are sometimes juxtaposed with the operation of tourism facilities' (Lennon 2017, p. np). With the exception of the Topography of Terror, the sites studied herein aren't specifically designed as visitor tourism destinations, although this of course does not exclude them from being encountered as such, as we shall see, and I explore the commemorative politics surrounding such sites (both in brief in Chapters 4–7 and in more detail elsewhere (see Florence 2019; 2021)). Whilst not explicitly engaged with in this book's methodology, dark tourism's focus on the sense-making practices of visitors to sites of memory, history, violence and trauma, particularly my own practices as a researcher-tourist, aligns with the approaches outlined below.

Cultural memory and cultural geography

Building on these scholars, studies at the intersections of cultural geography and memory studies investigate how both narratives and the materiality of sites are drawn into complex processes of cultural memory (Azaryahu 2011; Cook & van Riemsdijk 2014; Drozdzewski, De Nardi, & Waterton 2016; Vuolteenaho 2017). One way of approaching this is attuning the interactions of visitors with these sites. Drozdzewski and colleagues (2019) do this through the lens of 'experience', arguing that monuments are 'normative materialities of memory' (p. 253) in that they are frequently used in commonplace processes of forming both individual and national identities. They argue that these processes are never straight forward or unilateral, but that 'through attentiveness to individual experience we can better understand how cultural memory is enveloped into constructions of identity and critique such constructions alongside official narratives' (p. 252). Drozdzewski and colleagues (2019) suggest attuning to individuals' experiences as they 'make sense of state narratives', processes in which they incorporate, challenge, contest, digest, negotiate and ultimately form new cultural memory that will in turn be similarly negotiated. The mundanity of these processes should also not be ignored: 'such narratives are actually taken up in complex ways that do not somehow sit apart from other aspects of our lives' (Drozdzewski et al. 2019, p. 272). Cultural memory in relation to places is an inherently 'lived in' process, entangled with both the political and cultural currents surrounding negotiations of national and international memory and the material, sensory and embodied negotiation of these urban spaces in the everyday.

Materials with agency

Alongside and often overlapping with cultural geography, memory scholars also draw on new materialism to consider the role of material elements of sites in making cultural memory. Drozdzewski and colleagues (2019) and others

(Azaryahu 2011; Cook & van Riemsdijk 2014; Vuolteenaho 2017) shift their focus to materiality as part of the turn in memory studies to new materialism. With its roots in Latour (2004) and his actor network theory, new materialism at its heart seeks to embrace the inherent agency of matter, and to position humans within a network of actors of which they are not the only ones with the ability to create and affect change (see Bennett (2010) below). The materials that are bound up with memory have the potential to be understood as more than merely tools that humans use to remember. What might occur if we introduce agency to seemingly inert matter such as bricks and mortar that are involved in remembering at places? What is the agency of trees, animals, rain, rust and gravity, in shaping the ways in which the past can be imagined? What does this entail for the reading of and remembering through, with, and at a place? If we consider rust or decay as part of a memory text, who is the author who has put this text to work?

Vibrant materiality

Embracing the inherent agency of matter in my approach stems in no small part from political theorist Jane Bennett's theory of vibrant materiality (2010). Matter is vibrant, Bennett argues, in that it can act and counter-act. Bennett's vibrant materiality (guided by Foucault's (1979) ideas on power and Latour's (2004) actor network theory) charges material objects with agency, or the ability to affect change. Bennett argues that 'impersonal affect', or the power to change things and other bodies, is inherent in the materiality of objects (p. xiii). This 'material vibrancy' can be found in what Bennett calls 'thing power': 'the strange ability of ordinary, man-made items to exceed their status as objects and to manifest traces of independence or aliveness' (p. xvi). Bennett poses the political provocation of understanding a range of everyday events as 'encounter[s] between various and variegated bodies, some of them mine, most of them not, and none of which always gets the upper hand' (p. viii). The vibrancy, vitality and agency that Bennett affords matter are an expansion of Latour's (2004) term *actant*. An *actant* is simply, but radically, a 'source of action that can be either human or nonhuman' (Bennett 2010, p. viii). An *actant* 'is that which has efficacy, can do things, has sufficient coherences to make a difference, produce effects, alter the course of events' (Bennett 2010, p. viii). The agency of an *actant*, Bennett argues, is not defined by its human/non-human status, which Bennett argues is too often bound up with 'fantasies of a human uniqueness in the eyes of God' (p. ix). Instead, agency is defined by the capacity to act. I therefore draw on

Bennett's vibrant matter to figure the imagined past as inherently bound up with and constituted by the non-human matter of the sites in my study, not simply as an outcome of human interactions.

Memory and new materialism

The turn to new materialism in memory studies runs parallel to the above interest in the liveliness and vibrant materiality of memory objects and materials. Knittel and Driscoll (2017) look at how materials of memory act and act *back*:

> If Pierre Nora's monumental *lieux de mémoire* project was inscribed within a narrative of entropy and loss, in the face of which the cultural memory of the nation must be 'preserved', subsequent work has moved to a conception of memory as dynamic and mutable. In other words, the critical attention of the field has increasingly shifted towards observing and documenting the behaviour and continuing evolution of these media of memory 'in the wild'.
>
> (pp. 380–1)

Freeman, Nienass, and Daniell (2015) call for a way to understand memory objects like photographs as 'more than merely repositories of memory, separate from the human and activated by human desires to pour memory into their material form for retrieval, reminiscence, or forgetting' (p. 5). Like Bennett's (2010) concern that traditional concepts of the human are 'fantasies of a human uniqueness in the eyes of God' (p. ix), Freeman, Nienass, and Daniell (2015) argue that 'this dream of mastery' of memory 'objects' as simple containers of memory 'is full of a particular kind of human hubris that ignores the agency of things and denies the complex dynamics of remembering' (p. 5). To go beyond this view of materials as passive containers for memory we might also look to other historical memory scholars like Ladd (1997), who infuses the urban environment of Berlin with a kind of political agency by stating 'many (if not all) pre-1933 structures in Berlin are indelibly marked as witnesses to or *participants in* the events of the Third Reich' (p. 5, emphasis added). As memory objects, Ladd understands the buildings of Berlin as actors in the events being remembered. If buildings are able to participate in history, they must also be figured as participants in remembering that history. Through a new materialist lens, we can expand what we consider as the objects and actors of memory to include more things such as trees, sunlight, rain, rust, masonry. These objects might then be afforded the same capacity to act in cultural remembering.

Posthuman memory studies

The new materialist turn in memory studies is couched in a parallel embracing of ideas of the posthuman, which are particularly noticeable in the engagement of the non-human elements involved in remembering. A posthuman notion of memory, Wiel (2017) argues, means turning to memory that exists in archives that aren't typically thought of as archives; bodily archives, or those inscribed with other kinds of writing, including archives of 'other animals as subjects whose bodily and gestural memories have been overlooked, if not forgotten' (Wiel 2017, p. 399). Pushing beyond the human in studies of memory means taking seriously the capacity of non-human agents not only to act but to enact cultural memory.

Posthumanism decentres the human from analysis, and Vermuelen (2017) joins memory studies scholars turning to posthumanism and new materialist thinking, 'attuning cultural memory studies to the creatureliness that marks the Anthropocene' (p. 386). Through posthumanism, we might therefore see memory studies itself as a form of memory *after* humanism. Memory studies was born of the post-war period, from the culmination of modernism in genocide, eugenics, colonial exploitation (Knittel & Driscoll 2017). Engaged as it is with justice, preservation and witness (as explored above), memory studies is a response to the rampart humanism of genocide, war, eugenics, ethnic cleansing and culturecide that characterized the twentieth century:

> These historical atrocities have been part and parcel of humanism. There is a straight line[1] running from the humanist commitment to the principle of human perfectibility and progress to the eugenics movement, the Nazi euthanasia program and right up to contemporary techno-utopian fantasies of genetic engineering and prosthetic enhancement.
>
> (Knittel & Driscoll 2017, p. 381)

In Chapter 7 I look to the specific political and ethical implications of this decentering of the human from issues of historical responsibility and victimhood in the specific context of these modernist, humanist culminations of the twentieth century.

My analysis therefore begins from the assumption that the sites' materiality has been transformed both by acts of non-human and human material transformation and of design and communication, and both material and discursive processes are involved in the subsequent processes of remembering the bombings. As an example of this, Sturken (2016) looks to the material transformation of objects involved in the 9/11 attacks on the Twin Towers of the

World Trade Centre in New York. In particular Sturken examines the 'survivor objects' (p. 25) at the 9/11 Memorial and Museum in Manhattan, which have been transformed, rather than destroyed, by the material violence of the attacks: the keys, clothing, ID cards, watches, wallets, bags, fire engines, antenna, floor number signs and steel beams. Sturken sees these objects as both transformed by the tragedy and transformative of the memory of the tragedy. 'One could argue', states Sturken, 'that things that are transformed through violence offer a particular kind of aliveness through their evoking of survival' (p. 21). Engaging their material transformation in this way engages these objects as vibrant, as active in the processes of both their destruction and remembering the destruction. As both material traces of violence and textual objects, the 'survivor objects' are afforded lives of their own, the capacity to affect other matter and humans:

> These material objects produce intangible, sensory experiences. They operate as agents, making demands on us, shaping affect, exuding vitality and vibrancy, asking of us that we think beyond the binary of matter and life.
>
> (Sturken 2016, p. 25)

An approach to memory places couched in posthuman and new materialist approaches entails taking seriously the assemblage of actors involved in the cultural *and* material process of remembering: the rust and bullet holes and bricks and grass and trees as much as the signs and photographs and tourist maps. When afforded agency, matter becomes constitutive of new states of play, driving the force of history, not only recording its marks – it is, like cultural texts, productive. When considered vibrant, matter is inherently entwined with processes of meaning-making. The wind that whips the trees around Teufelsberg, for example, acts upon the kinds of remembering that can occur there in much the same way (if not to the same extent) as the concerted memorializing efforts of the Berlin Senate like signs, tourism material and fences. Oxidization and gravity play a part in imagining the bombings at and through Anhalter Bahnhof in the same way a plaque added by a local historical association describing the wartime deportations of Berlin's Jewish community does. And yet while neither the wind nor the trees nor oxidizing metal nor gravity can be said to be human, nonetheless, they act. If 'act' is defined as having an effect or an impact upon other elements of the world, then the wind and rust and gravity act, and act specifically on the ways that we might remember the bombings though site encounters.

It is important to remain cognizant that Latour (2004), Bennett (2010), and Foucault's (1979) theories are based around a network with varying and inconsistent topographies of power. The *actants* – human and non-human, individual and institutional – are not equal in terms of their capacity to act. 'In emphasizing the ensemble nature of action and the interconnections between persons and things', argues Bennett (2005), 'a theory of vibrant materialism presents individuals incapable of bearing *full* responsibility for their effects' (p. 463, original emphasis), but this does not mean removing *any* responsibility for the effects of one *actant's* actions. As explored above in relation to Foucault's 'states of domination', the topographies of power across an assemblage are uneven and ever-changing, but often follow long-entrenched patterns: distributions of power relations across this network mean some *actants* have more agency and responsibility than others. The new materialist streams I bring to this method therefore do not make claims that the wind in the trees at Teufelsberg has the *same* representational influence on cultural memory of the bombing as signs and tourism material. But I maintain these non-human elements of these sites still must be investigated for their role in remembering the destruction. Visitors engage not only with the historical markers of the bombings, but also with various matters of current social concern (resurgent far-right nationalism, Holocaust denial and so on), as well as the texts on signs, films about the bombings or Instagram posts. These must *all* be kept in mind in order to gain a more complete picture of the dynamics of remembering that are possible at and through these sites.

Entangled memory

Whilst drawing on new materialism and posthumanism to properly engage the materiality of memory sites, new materialist approaches to memory also engage the cognitive, discursive and cultural influences that accompany us to the sites (Allen & Brown 2011; Dittmer & Waterton 2019; Sumartojo 2019). It is not so much the materiality of the sites *alone* that is the focus of these approaches, but the interactions between the materials and the political and cultural subjectivity of the visitor. Golanska (2020) argues the political potential of this approach in the specific context of traumatic memory cultures is palpable:

> Contingent on always unstable assemblages, the effects of the encounters with the memorials bear potentials for disturbing, subverting, or transcending the well-established institutionalized frameworks for cultural remembrance, opening them to more singular negotiations as well as exposing numerous vulnerabilities and susceptibilities of mnemonic processes.
>
> (p. 85)

My approach therefore takes both the cultural and sensorial subjectivity of the researcher into account. I pair Bennett's (2005) agentic assemblages with Foucault's (1977) history of the present to interrogate the inherent situatedness of the researcher – myself. My method and primary sources of photographs and auto-ethnographic observations are explored in the following chapter as a way of accounting for myself interacting with both the sites' materialities and their cultural meanings, including the cultural meanings that accompany me as an individual thoroughly entrenched in Anglo-American cultural memory. Using a genealogical approach untangles the mess of threads that intersect in the specific times and places that the visitor-researcher encounters these sites. As Roth (1981) argues: 'Writing a history of the present means writing a history *in* the present' (p. 43, original emphasis), and that present entails the current state of play regarding the cultural-political situation in Europe *as well as* the specific moments of encountering the sites, such as when I step off a train and onto Teufelsberg, in the sun, at 3:34pm on a Tuesday afternoon. Appraising specific commemorative temporalities, or the time and place through which we remember, is vital to ethical memory studies methodologies (Guggenheim 2009). As such, the following chapter details the method I have employed to account for the highly specific temporality of my encounters with these sites as well as the multiple other temporalities that intersect with my encounters.

Conclusion

The restrictive, either/or frameworks of memory that were explored in Chapter 1 show the need for a revised approach to cultural memory, particularly where it relates to place. This chapter has sought to outline a way of approaching cultural memory that addresses some of these limitations, and allows for a cultural memory of area bombing to emerge that is layered, messy and complicated, and that allows multiple events, narratives, perspectives and histories to emerge. Through an interdisciplinary approach that draws on memory studies, communication and cultural studies, cultural geography, and new materialist and posthuman theories and methodologies, I therefore look to memory sites as texts through which visitors can form and reform cultural memory of area bombing. As the outcome of ongoing communicative practices, these sites are imbricated in many overlapping and intersecting social and political contexts, and a cultural studies, communications studies and cultural geography approach works to pay attention to and incorporate these contexts. I also draw on cultural geography to properly incorporate the sense-making activities of visitors to memory sites in their formulation, negotiation and re-formulation of cultural memory at and through these sites. Finally, I draw on new materialist and posthuman studies of memory to account for the materiality of memory sites as well as the sensory and embodied experiences of visitors. Rather than considering places as inert matter onto which cultural memory is simply projected, this approach interrogates both the sites' vibrant materiality and the practical activities of visitors as they engage with and make sense of the sites as texts that produce cultural memory.

To fully capture the mnemonic potential of sites of urban destruction, rubble and accumulation in Berlin, we require a method that takes the cultural and sensorial subjectivity of the researcher into account as well as the materiality of the sites of study. This is because the primary way of challenging the discursive, cultural and political framings of the memory of the air war is by bringing it into direct contact with the material traces of the destruction on the ground. As an Anglo-American visitor, I bring these framings with me to my visit; my visit is in a way a collision and entanglement of the two. Golanksa's (2020) collision approach therefore guides the approach, which engages and captures both the material and sensory elements of the site and also the discursive contexts in which it is situated. The method and primary sources of photographs and auto-ethnographic observations explored in the following chapter are a way of accounting for myself as a researcher interacting with both the sites' materialities and their cultural meanings, in the hope of complicating the latter with the former.

3

Methods – Gleaning cultural memory from sites in Berlin

Introduction

The four analysis chapters of this book are structured around material-discursive, culturally situated ethnographic observations of Teufelsberg. Whilst Teufelsberg forms the central pillar of analysis, both as the main site of analysis and as a methodological framework, I also draw on visits and analyses of eight other sites in Berlin. This chapter details the conceptual framework that structures both the methodology and the practicalities of data collection and analysis, including the twenty-seven sites visited, the sites identified for analysis, how and why Teufelsberg was developed as a central site, the forms and methods of collecting data and the ways collected notes and images were developed into analyses and findings.

The hill of Teufelsberg forms the conceptual and methical framework through which I examine the potential of encounters with Berlin's urban environment to complicate Anglo-American cultural memories of wartime violence. The hill is literally and figuratively layered, a palimpsest of not only traces of Berlin's violent past but various commemorative and representational frames for understanding violence and the past: ruination, haunting, stratigraphical and geological layers, archaeology, piles of rubble and remnants, and burial grounds. In addition to Teufelsberg I identified five further sites for analysis (from the twenty-seven I visited): the Topography of Terror (the site of a Gestapo prison), Anhalter Bahnhof (a ruined train station), the Schwerbelastungskörper (heavy load-bearing structure, built by 'Hitler's architect', Albert Speer), a Jewish memorial cemetery in Mitte, and Gleis 17 (a memorial at Grunewald S-Bahn station to the thousands deported from there during the Holocaust). These are sites (but not the only sites) in Berlin where an Anglo-American visitor might encounter the traces of area bombing from the Second World War, either as textual artefacts or material marks left on the city, and most often as both. In addition to Teufelsberg, I also draw on encounters with the seven other *Trümmerberge* in Berlin. These sites' material and commemorative elements speak to and inform the detailed analysis of Teufelsberg and Berlin's landscape more broadly, each drawing out varying commemorative frames of understanding and encountering traces of urban violence for English-language visitors. Because they are likely to be encountered by Anglo-American tourists, the grounded, material perspectives engendered by visiting these sites can therefore become layered with perspectives that habitually structure the discourses that Anglo-American visitors 'bring' to the sites. This makes them ideal sites through which we might complicate the assurances about wartime guilt and responsibility that continue to structure Anglo-American cultural discourses about the war (outlined in Chapter 1).

My methodology specifically engages the situatedness of the researcher to explore how a cultural memory can be formulated and reformulated through the act of reading these sites as texts. The sites are read through material and sensory encounters with them – sunburn, mosquitoes, wild boars, rain, cold wind – as well as cultural texts – film, television, literature, speeches, Tweets. To engage these elements, this method draws on the emerging new materialist perspectives of memory studies discussed in the previous chapter.

As well as my material and sensorial encounters with the sites in May 2017, I also situate these encounters within wider cultural and political contexts of remembering urban violence in Berlin, particularly from an Anglo-American perspective. The findings and analyses are therefore also situated specifically within the ongoing political and cultural debates that I outlined in Chapter 1: resurgent neo-fascism and Euro-scepticism, the re-negotiation of national history and memory associated with the Trump presidency and the Black Lives Matter movement, elements of the German victimhood debate (as it unfolded in the Anglo-American sphere) and the continuing mythification of the war in Anglo-American cultures. The method therefore foregrounds, rather than elides, the cultural and political specificity of my encounters with the sites as much as the material-sensory elements. Drawing again on Foucault's (1977) history of the present, which he also calls 'effective history' (p. 153), this methodology delineates the potency of the researcher in data and analysis, understanding 'knowledge as perspective' (p. 156). This approach sees any knowledge generated by research as inherently bound with the perspective of the researcher. Potential 'biases' of the researcher – her history, perspective, politics, identities – are considered productive of this knowledge, rather than elements that obscure an 'objective' truth.

This entanglement of the sensory with the cultural-discursive is what I argue can bring about a more nuanced cultural memory of area bombing, in which the assumed absolute innocence of the Allies might be complicated – not replaced – by the material and subjective reality of their bombing campaigns 'on the ground'. My method entangles the sensory encounter with the sties' materiality with the normative cultural memory the Second World War, not unlike Golanska's (2020) 'collision' approach (p. 74).

Finally, this chapter details how I employed a model of documentation to engage my own physical and material perspective as productive of knowledge and to account for the layered experiences of Teufelsberg and the other sites. At the sites I took photographs, made extensive ethnographic notes, observations and reflections, and collected tourism materials, that is, brochures, fact sheets, maps. This forms the data of my analyses of Chapters 4–7, including more speculative writing that develops my findings as the reader and researcher move from one chapter to the next. In an attempt to avoid the tendency to anthropocentrism that often characterizes more ethnographic and autoethnographic methods, photographs and observations of the sites are layered with analysis, drawing on a range of sources. This layered method and form of documentation reflect the multiple temporalities at and of the sites and further enact the idea of 'knowledge as perspective' (Foucault 1977, p. 156).

Site identification

The method of this research consisted of a fieldwork trip to London and Berlin in May and June 2017. I visited these cities to understand the influence encounters with 'bombed sites' could have on my understanding of the war, which are usually structured around narratives that omit, downplay or frame memories of Allied area bombing (see Chapter 1). I visited sites in London that had been marked by falling ordnance, many of which have been memorialized in accordance with the more dominant ways of understanding aerial bombing, particularly through the lens and language of the London Blitz. The after images of these experiences came with me to Berlin, as did other dominant discourses surrounding the war that had been formed long before touching down in Heathrow. In the German capital I again visited sites at which I could encounter marks of the bombings. These encounters became entangled with the ways

I have habitually imagined the war through nascent cultural narratives, the sites in London perhaps being the most recent instance of this.

In London, I visited two churches that had both been severely damaged during the Blitz: Christchurch Greyfriars and St Giles Cripplegate. The remains of Christchurch Greyfriars have been turned into a public garden space as a memorial to the victims and survivors of the Blitz, whilst St Giles Cripplegate has been reconstructed, but contains information boards commemorating its history before and after the Blitz. I also visited the memorial for Arthur 'Bomber' Harris, the head of British Bomber Command during the area bombing campaigns. The statue stands in front of St Clements, a church that was also damaged during the Blitz and is now associated with the British air force. Finally, I visited a memorial to Bomber Command in Hyde Park, memorializing the efforts of the British air crews who flew bombing missions during the war.

In Berlin, I visited eight *Trümmerberge*, or 'rubble mountains'. These are hills that were formed from the rubble of Berlin's buildings after the war, and are now mostly urban green spaces in and on the outskirts of Berlin: Teufelsberg, Prenzlauerberg Volkspark, Volkspark Hasenheide, Volkspark Friedrichshain (Grossbunker and Kleinbunker), Dorferblick, Insulaner, Marienhöhe and Humbolt Flaktower/hill. I also visited other sites that have been memorialized for their destruction during the war, such as Anhalter Bahnhof, the Kaiser Wilhelm Memorial Church and the Berliner Schloss. I also visited a range of other sites in Berlin through which tourists tend to formulate cultural memory of the war. This included Cold War era memorials such as the Neue Wache, the Jewish memorial cemetery in Grosse Hamburger Strasse, a memorial to the thousands of women who cleaned up Berlin after the war and the Soviet War Memorial in Treptow Park. I also visited more contemporary memorials and monuments: the Memorial to the Murdered Jews of Europe, the Memorial to the Sinti and Roma Victims of National Socialism, the Memorial to Homosexuals Persecuted Under Nazism, Gleis 17 at Grunewald Bahnhof, the Topography of Terror and the Bebelplatz memorial. My visits also included surviving Nazi architecture such as the remains of the Tempelhof airport and the Schwerbelastungskörper.

From these twenty-seven sites, Teufelsberg emerged as a site that spoke the most comprehensively to the tangled web of remembering and comprehending the violence on Berlin in a way that might complicate some of the assurances of dominant Anglo-American memory structures. I describe the site below, as well as how I developed the site into both a site of analysis and a framework through which I could draw out the overlapping and intersecting ways of remembering the air war in Berlin. I also selected five other sites that prominently engage the intersecting and overlapping commemorative and narrative frames present at Teufelsberg: the Schwerbelastungskörper, the Jewish memorial cemetery, Gleis 17, the Topography of Terror and Anhalter Bahnhof. These sites are introduced below.

There were many other sites I might have visited in Berlin but did not, and there are also sites I did visit that I might have included in my analysis and did not – the Neue Wache, a memorial that was heavily damaged during the war by artillery and aerial bombing and which courted controversy when it was reopened in 1957 as a memorial 'to the Victims and Fascism and Militarism' by the East German authorities; and the Kaiser Wilhelm Memorial Church, carefully maintained in its partially ruined state since an Allied bombing raid destroyed most of the chapel and heavily damaged the spire in 1943. The practical and necessary restrictions of fieldwork capacity, funding and scheduling partially explain the exclusion of these sites from the analysis, but a desire to focus on sites at the intersection of the material marks of bombing, the cultural memory of the Holocaust and Anglo-American visitors and their dominant cultural memory structures of the air war necessarily lead to these sites being excluded from analysis. That said, I do provide a detailed investigation of the cultural memory of area bombing at the Kaiser Wilhelm Memorial Church elsewhere (Florence 2019) and briefly discuss it in Chapter 8. What's more, Berlin is a living, ever-evolving city, and in the time between my visits and publication the fabric of the city has shifted in its memory landscape.[1] I look forward to future works incorporating these changes into studies of the cultural memory of area bombing for Anglo-American visitors.

Teufelsberg

Teufelsberg (the name translates to 'devil's mountain') is a *Trümmerberg* (rubble mountain), an artificial hill made up of the rubble that remained after the destruction of Berlin during the war. Teufelsberg is located on the north-western edge of the city and is part of the Grunewald forest, the largest green space in Berlin's city limits. The hill rises about 80 metres above the otherwise flat Teltow Plateau on which Berlin is situated and was made using approximately 25 million cubic metres of rubble, all that remained of about 15,000 destroyed buildings. Beneath the pile remains one of the only examples of Nazi Master of Armaments and War Production Albert Speer's neo-classical architecture in Berlin to survive the war, a military training facility. The occupying Allied forces in the immediate

Figure 3.1 Teufelsberg, Berlin. Photograph by Eloise Florence, 2017.

post-war era were unable to destroy it completely (Stöver 2013). It was therefore buried beneath a pile of rubble and the resultant hill was re-integrated into the Grunewald. Teufelsberg is today used as a green space for hiking, cycling and swimming in the nearby lake, Teufelssee (or 'devil's lake').

During the Cold War, the American National Security Agency (NSA) established a 'listening station' at the top of Teufelsberg. The station was designed to listen to and spy on USSR activities in East Berlin. After the fall of the Soviet Union, the site fell into disrepair and was used by local art and music communities for events and as an alternative art space through the post-reunification decade. In 2007, the site was bought by American director David Lynch, who announced he would be using the site to build a 'university devoted to Transcendental Meditation' (*Der Spiegel* 2007). This university was never built. In November 2018 the entire hill was listed as a protected monument. The Berlin Cultural Senator Claus Lederer called the old spy station 'a unique and multilayered historical monument of the twentieth century' (*The Local* 2018).

Through my analysis, Teufelsberg emerged as a series of fragmentary layers. The various politics, ideologies, destruction, construction, decay, chemicals, bodies and designs that have shifted across Berlin's modern history intersect and coalesce at Teufelsberg, creating a kind of palimpsest. Looking to Teufelsberg allows us to draw out these intersecting and overlapping layers as a possible way of complicating some of the more straightforward and discrete elements of the dominant cultural narratives about the war explored Chapter 1.

The following four analysis chapters will therefore draw out these overlapping and intersecting layers as potential frames of references through which the violence of aerial bombings might be remembered, and how these are often couched in related frames of remembrance about the war. These frameworks include ruination, such as the ruins of the Cold War spy station atop the hill and a Nazi training facility buried beneath the hill. Ruins might also be haunted, and Teufelsberg thus also allows us to draw out the narrative and sensorial effects of haunting on the cultural memory of the bombings, which has particular impact when the complicated temporality of haunting is applied to some of the more assured notions of cause-and-effect that relate the bombings to the Holocaust (see Chapter 4). Teufelsberg is also distinctly unruly, a churning, changing mass of rock, rubble, earth, forest, sunshine, mosquitoes and wildlife. This allows the possibility of considering memorial sites such as Teufelsberg as *actants*, active participants in the production of cultural memory. Approaching the materials of Teufelsberg in this way, as is done through Jane Bennett's (2010) networked model of accountability and agency, allows for a more networked view of the responsibility for violence of the bombings (Chapter 5). Furthermore, the physicality of Teufelsberg, as well as the physical labour that is required to access and experience it, introduces the possibility of more bodily and sensorial encounters with the traces of the violence of the bombings, which has been traditionally held at arm's length through aerial photography and military history's objectivity. Walking urban sites of violence like Teufelsberg offers the possibility of evoking the bodily and subjective nature of this violence, thereby reintroducing violence as a lived experience into its cultural memory (Chapter 6). Finally, the pieces of stone, metal, ceramics, brick, glass and wood that make up Teufelsberg can also be read as forensic records of the historical violence committed against Berlin, which also introduces the disturbing possibility of human remains entangled with the dirt, rubble, rocks and tree roots. I therefore explore Teufelsberg as a site of the Anthropocene, embodying the blurred lines between humans' and nature's effects on the planet, and the implications this has for the kinds of entangled cultural memory that can be formed there (Chapter 7).

Teufelsberg is thus both a site of analysis and a conceptual frame, drawing out the intersecting and overlapping ways of remembering the bombings and ways of complicating the established frames of historical responsibility and guilt that continue to pervade this cultural memory. Several other sites in Berlin that are introduced below – including seven other *Trümmerberge* – assist in drawing out and exploring these themes and frames of reference, contributing to the potential of encounters with Berlin's urban environment to complicate normative historical narratives of wartime violence. The material and commemorative elements of these other sites speak to and inform the detailed analysis of Teufelsberg and Berlin's landscape more broadly.

Trümmerberge

In addition to Teufelsberg, I also visited seven other *Trümmerberge* in Berlin's city limits. These hills are constructed out of the approximate 55 million cubic metres of rubble that littered Berlin after the war (Diefendorf 1993).

The destruction of significant parts of German cities during the war entailed a massive clean-up effort. Diefendorf (1993) calls the scale of the damage on cities 'incalculable – quite literally so, since compiling accurate statistical data often proved impossible, and since words were seldom adequate to describe the experience of living in the midst of falling bombings, explosions, fires, the collapse of homes, and the end to the comfort and security of normal life' (p. 10). In Berlin, estimates of the damage vary from source to source. Diefendorf estimates that in the large cities 'with 100,000 inhabitants in 1939, on average about 50% of their built-up areas were destroyed' (1993, p. 11). Berlin's central suburbs lost almost half their housing stock to wartime destruction.

This damage created immense amounts of rubble, which had to be dealt with in order for Berlin to function as a city. 'Removal or salvage – those were the two options for handling the rubble' (Diefendorf 1993 p. 26). Salvage was attractive, not the least as a way to offset the huge debt German cities found themselves in at the end of the war. Berlin's city administrators offered 380 contracts for the clearance of 549 designated rubble sites, and the contractors attempted to recover their costs by selling building materials salvaged from the rubble (Diefendorf 1993). A national association of experts on rubble processing (*Deutsche Studiengesellschaft fur Trümmerverwertung*) was founded. The mayor of Stuttgart held an exhibition in the middle of town to demonstrate the kinds of building materials that could be salvaged from the wreckage.

But relocation and reuse of the rubble remained the most attractive option in lieu of a comprehensive salvage program. Hamburg filled in some of its unused canals and strengthened the banks of the Elbe with its rubble. Munich used its rubble to construct the grounds for the 1972 Olympic Games. Essen used rubble to 'fill in sinkholes and other depressions left from earlier mining, to strengthen dikes, build new road and rail beds, and to enlarge the airport' (Diefendorf 1993, pp. 26–7). In Berlin, the rubble was ground into the runways at Tegel, Gatow and Tempelhof airstrips, the latter being particularly of use during the Berlin Airlift in 1948–9.

Much of the rubble of Berlin, however, was used to fill in, enlarge or landscape city parks. Berlin's flat, marshy topography became hilly and raised over the postwar years as *Trümmerberge* rose across the city. The forest around Teufelssee was first home to one of Albert Speer's megalomaniacal constructions and embodiments of his 'theory of ruination' (see Chapter 4). After the war it became home to millions of cubic meters of a destroyed Berlin, piled high over the institute, resulting in Teufelsberg.

The other seven *Trümmerberge* I visited on my fieldwork were built in much the same way. Prenzlauerberg Volkspark, Volkspark Hasenheide, Volkspark Friedrichshain (Grossbunker and Kleinbunker), Dorferblick, Insulaner, Marienhöhe and Humbolt Flaktower/hill are all located in a kind of public park; some large, some small. They make up some of the urban green spaces for which Berlin has become somewhat famous; sites of community recreation, with the accompanying memorials, skateparks, playgrounds, hiking trails, even a planetarium.

In the inner city neighbourhood of Neukölln, Volkspark Hasendheide hosts the small rise of rubble called Rixdorfer Höhe. There is also a small monument to the *Trümmerfrauen* (rubble women), the women who helped clean up the city after the war by moving masses of rubble, and who became somewhat of a folkloric hero, especially in East Germany.[2]

A large urban park in the former East, Volkspark Friedrichshain hosts two hills made of rubble – the Grosser Bunkerberg and the Kleiner Bunkerberg. The park is an exemplar of Berlin's urban parkland, populated by *Grillplatz*, ponds, fountains, concession stands, runners, skateboarders, picnickers in the summer, sledders in the winter. Volkspark Prenzlauerberg, just to the east of the city, and Insulaner and Marienhöhe in the city's south west, are all similarly urban green spaces, with varying degrees of memorialisation of the war, the *Trümmerfrauen*, and the rubble.

More suburban than urban, Dorferblick lies deep in the southern edge of Berlin's limits, right on the border between Berlin and the surrounding Brandenburg region. Like Teufelsberg, Dorkerblick can be accessed by a walking track that winds around and over the hill. From the peak you can see back over the city of Berlin to the north, and the Schönefeld airport[3] to the south.

Some of these sites – like the statue in Volkspark Hasenheide – actively commemorate their post-war rubble make-up. At some – but perhaps none so much as Teufelsberg – one can make out the larger pieces of rubble on the ground, amongst leaf litter, shrubbery and tree roots. But it would be easy, likely in fact, that many people could walk these hills and not know their roles as the burial grounds of pre-war Berlin's buildings. They are largely sites of play, relaxation and recreation, rather than memory.

Nonetheless, the *Trümmerberge* are included in my analysis because they persist as material traces of the violence inflicted upon Berlin. In the very least, these small hills stand out against Berlin's notoriously flat and marshy topography (Anderson 2015). The *Trümmerberge* could be considered a topographical result of the material task of post-war recovery; what is estimated as 50 million cubic meters of destroyed Berlin had to be dealt with in a physical as well as a political or memorial sense. The construction of the *Trümmerberge* was also deeply entwined with Berlin's political and cultural response to post-war destruction and reconstruction. 'Dealing with' the destruction of the bombs and the resultant rubble ran parallel to the famous 'dealing with' the past or *Vergangenheitsbewältigung,* and often followed similar vagaries of leadership, urban planning and political and ideological stances on history and the past in the countries emerging either side of the Wall. The fate of Berlin's rubble speaks to the continued intersection of the pragmatics of urban post-war reconstruction with cultural and political processes of post-war remembering and forgetting, particularly that of post-war German memory cultures. In a more immediate and material sense, however, and as I will explore in the analysis chapters that follow, the presence of the *Trümmerberge* as hills, as things to be climbed or looked at or used as a vantage point from which to see the city are presences in former Allied visitors' comprehension of the city. Thus the violence that caused the rubble and the post-war memory and reconstruction processes that followed take up space in the comprehension of Berlin as a city, even if it is only in the form of sore leg muscles after climbing a steep slope.

The other sites

The Topography of Terror

The Topography of Terror is the name of a permanent on-site exhibition and documentation centre about the creation, methods, victims and organizational structures of the central institutions of Nazi persecution and terror: the Secret State Police Office (Gestapo), the leadership of the *Schutzstaffel* (SS) and the Reich Security Main Office. The site is situated on the city block that housed these institutions, now mostly empty thanks to the bombing raids of the 1940s, the Battle of Berlin, post-war processes of denazification and Cold War memory politics over the following decades. A self-guided tour path winds around the site, describing the buildings that once stood there and their varying uses across the twentieth century with photographs and text in English and German. A small documentation centre houses a permanent exhibition about the SS and Gestapo and a library on state terror. Behind the documentation centre is the result of an archaeological dig from 1985, when two West German civic groups worked to uncover the traces of Berlin's Nazi past that remained at the site. The groups unearthed the remains of the Gestapo prison and mess hall. The foundations remain uncovered and visible today as part of the tour around the site. The site also became a loci of the German Historian's Debate (see Chapter 2), a vigorous and often vitriolic debate about the possibility of a history of German victimhood and suffering (Habermas 2018). The whole government district in which the Topography of Terror is situated was effectively cut in two by the Berlin Wall, and various lines, pavements, art works and street signs mark out where the Wall ran. One can follow one set of pavers in the road about 500 metres up Zimmerstraße and find the bustling and overtly touristy Checkpoint Charlie. The Topography of Terror is home to the second largest surviving piece of the Wall, which ran along Niederkirchnerstraße and into Zimmerstraße. Visitors can approach, photograph and touch the Wall fragment, which has been left largely in the condition it was in at reunification.

Anhalter Bahnhof

Anhalter Bahnhof was a major train station in central Berlin, constructed and opened in 1880 (Presner 2001). The station was one of three in Berlin that was used for the Nazis' mass deportations of Berlin's Jewish populations and other so-called 'enemies' of Nazism to concentration camps (Brett 2015). During the war the main terminus was bombed heavily, leaving the station barely usable, but it continued to be a hub of both exportation and evacuation – Goebbels ordered a mass evacuation from the Allied air raids on trains departing from Anhalter in 1943 (Brett 2015). The shell of the station sat in dereliction throughout the Cold War, occupying the fringe area of West Berlin adjacent to the Wall (Elkins 2005).

Today the ruin of the facade remains, just in front of a sports field and an aquatics centre. Anhalter S-Bahn station, established just next to the main terminus, is still functioning today. Behind the aquatic centre, amongst trees and the tents, bedding, clothes and rubbish belonging to the people who appear to live there temporarily, one can still see the remnants of the original train tracks and platforms. There is a small sign near the facade explaining, in German and English, the station's role in the forced expulsions and deportations of the Holocaust. The area surrounding the site is often used for public and community events.

The Schwerbelastungskörper

The Schwerbelastungskörper is an experimental column built by the Nazis, designed to test the load-bearing capacities of Berlin's sandy foundations – it literally translates to 'heavy load-bearing structure'. The pillar was built to test the possibility of a large archway, echoing but outstripping the Arc de Triomphe in Paris. The archway would be a key piece in Albert Speer's 'Germania' – what he and Hitler envisioned as the renewed capital of the Third Reich that would be built after a German victory. 'Germania' carried echoes of the Roman Empire, the ruins of which Hitler and Speer aspired to echo with what they imagined would be the ruins of the 'Thousand Year Reich'. A nearby sign calls the structure 'witness to the most megalomaniacal construction project Berlin has ever seen', noting that 'the Second World War put an end to the National Socialists' inhuman urban planning'.

Today the structure stands in an obscure spot near a railway in the residential suburb of Tempelhof. There is a small visitor centre attached with information on the structure and the proposed megacity of Germania. A large metal fence topped with spikes regulates the site's opening times. There is a stair case, separate from the structure, that allows visitors to view the structure from several viewing platforms at varying heights, all the way to the top of the pillar. Visitors can also enter the pillar at ground level, and find several concrete rooms with remnants of machines and metal structures.

Gleis 17

Gleis 17 (Platform 17) is a memorial on what used to be Platform 17 of the Grunewald S-Bahn station in north west Berlin, from where more than 17,000 of Berlin's Jewish citizens were sent to Theresienstadt and Auschwitz or the ghettos of Łódź and Riga. It can be accessed in much the same ways as the other platforms at the station, and consists of a series of large steel plates that line the platform. On the plates, the numbers of people exported from the station each day are recorded, covering the period between 1941 and 1945. The website for Deutsche Bahn, who created the memorial in 1998, states: 'The vegetation that has developed at Platform 17 over the years has been left to grow between the rails and now forms and integral part of the memorial as a symbol that no more trains will ever depart from this platform' (Deutsche Bahn AG 2019). Grunewald S-Bahn station remains one of the best ways to access Teufelsberg on foot or on a bike.

Jewish memorial cemetery

The Jewish memorial cemetery is the remains of the oldest Jewish cemetery in Berlin, on Grosse Hamburger Strasse in the central suburb of Mitte. The site was the chosen burial ground for much of Berlin's Jewish community from as early as 1671, when the site was still outside the city walls but at the heart of a newly arrived Jewish community. Smaller, but also far older than Berlin's largest Jewish cemetery in Weissensee, the site had around 2000 graves, including that of the philosopher Moses Mendelssohn, before it closed in 1827. An aged care facility was built nearby, and the site of the cemetery became a public park for the home (Jacobs 2008).

The site was hugely desecrated by the Nazis. The aged care facility was used as a Gestapo prison until it was destroyed by Allied bombs in the final days of the war. The Nazis tore up the cemetery to build an air raid shelter, using the ancient headstones of generations of Berlin's Jews to reinforce the walls. The grounds were later used as a mass grave for victims of both the prison and aerial bombing – some 3000 people were buried there by the close of the war.

The cemetery is now a memorial garden with a few of the original surviving headstones scattered throughout. The site fell on the eastern side of the Wall, and the GDR uncovered and memorialized the centuries old stones and placed them in a symbolic sarcophagus. A few of the headstones have been replaced, including a new stone for Mendelssohn. At the front gate, a memorial sculpture by Will Lammert commemorates the fate of Berlin's Jews, alongside a commemorative plaque and information on the history of the site.

These sites figure in my analysis as places through which Anglo-American visitors might encounter traces of the violence of the bombs. These sites were selected as instances of the material traces of the bombings that are accessible to English-speaking visitors to Berlin in 2017. All the sites are public, free,[4] and more or less democratically accessible.[5] They are places in Berlin one can physically visit to encounter the destruction caused by Allied bombs dropped on the city from 1940 to 1945. What is more, the consistent presence of English-language texts at the sites, as well as their location within established historical tourism networks in Berlin, marks them as tailored to a specific visitor population. This makes them highly amenable to examining the meanings of the war on the ground in Berlin as they can be interwoven with Allied-American discourses that privilege more detached perspectives of area bombing 'from above'.

These sites also were selected for analysis because they draw out the varying frames of reference through which Allied tourists might comprehend the violence of the bombings. At each, the traces of the air war are present through ruins, rubble piles, forests, archaeological digs, remnants, burial grounds, dark tourism sites and memorials. Teufelsberg is an assemblage of the various ways one can both approach and disrupt the cultural and material memory of destruction, and these other sites' material and commemorative elements speak to and inform the detailed analysis of Teufelsberg and Berlin's violent landscape more broadly.

Self-reflexive method

Encountering Teufelsberg is a decidedly bodily experience. Visiting it entails walking paths, paying entry fees, catching trains, walking or riding a bike to, from, and around it. But it is also an experience distinctly embedded within the cultural, political and discursive contexts of remembering the war, couched in the wider cultural currents that accompany the English-speaking visitor. My method of data gathering as an English-speaking tourist from a former-Allied country therefore reflects 'collision' of both the material and discursive.

I employed a method to account for the ways both the visitor's body as well as the wider discursive negotiations of cultural memory become implicated in meaning-making about the past at these sites. Morris (2004) argues to consider the relationship between people and their environments as a 'feedback loop' (p. 677), less a dialectical model of bodies and cities interacting, more 'contingent and contextual assemblages' (p. 692). Drawing on the interdisciplinary approaches outlined in Chapter 2, my method considers the relationship between humans and urban environments as co-constitutive.

I visited Teufelsberg and the other sites multiple times, over multiple days, at different times of day. I walked in and around them, interacting with them as a tourist but also following a particular interest in the traces left by the air war. I paid attention to information boards written in English and collected other tourist materials such as brochures and guides. I took photographs and videos and recorded my observations and thoughts in notebooks which evolved into a site not only of record but of exploration, discussion and thinking-through. I then reviewed these materials and continued to think through the ways that these sites could be part of productions of cultural memory of the bombings as both material encounters with destruction and communicative texts.

Such an approach echoes the new materialist attention to both the material and cognitive situatedness of the researcher (Alaimo 2010; Barad 2007; 2014; Bennett 2010; Haraway 1988). Knowledge, Barad (2007) argues, emerges from 'a complex network of human and nonhuman agents, including historically specific sets of material conditions that exceed the traditional notion of the individual' (p. 23). Barad's (2014) 'material-discursive' (187) and Haraway's 'semiotic-discursive' (1988, p. 585) and 'naturecultures' (2016, p. 24) in particular blur the boundary between material encounters and cultural or discursive meanings. In her 'collision approach' (2020, p. 74), Golanska argues for the integration of experience into analysis of memory sites, to include 'how these sites absorb us, also at the affective, bodily level, which sometimes happens regardless, or even in spite of, our critical or resistant attitude towards meanings they convey' (2015, p. 774). The focus of my approach is therefore on the moment of interaction, but not only bodily interactions; taking the discursive in the material-discursive encounter seriously means a continued inclusion of the political-cultural subjectivities included in the encounter. Furthermore and as I shall explain below, the cultural memory that can be formed at and through these sites has potential to disrupt and complicate normative cultural memory narratives about area bombing *because* of their continued discursive and cultural presence at these site encounters.

A collision approach

Rigney (2017) argues that a posthuman approach to memory looks specifically to the 'continuous interactions between humans and non-humans, between mediations and materialities, within particular social and physical environments' (p. 465). An approach to memory and place that draws in part on new materialist thought sees cultural memory as constituted by both the bodily (material) context of the sites as well as the cultural and narrative (discursive) context of dominant memory cultures of the war. Golanksa's (2020) 'collision approach' (p. 76) is instructional in that it seeks to layer the material and sensory encounters with sites with their discursive and cultural contexts. Experiences produced at memory sites, Golanska argues, are not purely affective or aesthetic, and nor are they purely representational. 'Quite the contrary, they are intertwined in complex ways and often harnessed for political purposes' (2015, p. 786). Cultural memory emerges through the dynamics between discourse and materiality that circulate at the site. The collision approach does away with dualism such as representable/unrepresentable, material/discursive, affective/intellectual. Rather, Golanska's collision 'offers its productive reformulation, focusing on the complex, entangled nature of mnemonic processes' (2020, p. 76). Rather than positing the material and sensory effects of memory sites are countering, disrupting or counter-acting the representational aspects of memory, Golanska approaches them as inherently inseparable and co-constitutive.

Like Golanksa, my approach to cultural memory at these sites in Berlin brings the normative, typically representational, readings of Anglo-American cultural memory of the Second World War (explored in Chapter 1) into collision with the material encounters with the sites in Berlin. This method therefore does not pay attention to the sensory and bodily encounters of a memory site alone. The two become entangled, and it is this entanglement of what (as I show in Chapter 1) has traditionally kept separate – the dominant discursive narrative of absolute Allied righteousness with the material impacts of the bombings 'on the ground' – that can create new, more inclusive and comprehensive forms of cultural memory of area bombing.

The researcher, as a site of this interaction between discourse and materiality, is central to such a collision approach. Kennedy and Radstone (2013) argue that 'place' 'refers not only to the actual geographical site but also to the embodied location of the investigator – the location, physical or geographical, felt through the senses, imagined or remembered – from which the critic writes' (240). Foucault's (1977) history of the present similarly engages the researcher as a critical location. Foucault argues for the interrogation of the specificity of the researcher in any historical project:

> Historians take unusual pains to erase the elements of their work which reveal their grounding in a particular time and place, their preferences in a controversy – the unavoidable obstacles of their passion.
>
> (pp. 156–7)

Foucault argues to engage, rather than elide, these elements that reveal the grounding of the historian's work in a particular time and place. The knowledge and cultural memory generated at Teufelsberg and the other sites are therefore inextricable from the experience and knowledge – perspective – of the Anglo-American visitor-researcher.

This also echoes Walter Benjamin's 'poetic thinking', which Jackson (2007) describes as:

> ... neither focused on one's own subjectivity nor on the objectivity of the world, but on what emerges in the space between. It thus refuses to create an illusion of impartiality and authority by excluding from its picture of the world the author's relationship with others, and the particular circumstances in which his or her understanding was reached.
>
> (pp. xii–xiii)

This space in between subjectivity and objectivity engages the researcher as not only materially but culturally embedded, a specific cultural and political subject engaging the 'objectivity of the world'. Whilst my own biographical subjectivity is not interrogated in the below analyses, the fact the researcher belongs to a particular transnational population that in many ways has been defined by particular frames of remembering the war (see Introduction) remains balanced with my subjective experiential encounters with these sites. This means that the data remain restricted to the time and place of visiting Teufelsberg and the other sites, but is also concerned with wider, socio-cultural meanings and significances that emerge through my interactions with them.

It is through such an entangled or 'collision' method that documenting these sites as an Anglo-American visitor-researcher can disrupt the oppositional either/or matrix of cultural memory I identified in Chapter 2. This either/or dichotomy tends to specifically characterize different perspectives in the memory of area bombing, and a collision method brings them into direct contact and collision with one another. As an example, many of the hegemonic Anglo-American narratives about the war are told through aerial perspectives. Visual technologies of surveillance, aerial navigation and policing embody these aerial perspectives and are also technologies of (or *actants* in) the scientific objectivity through which aerial bombing is habitually documented and conveyed. Kaplan (2017) identifies an inherent opposition at the heart of how we think about aerial viewpoints and aerial bombing, between 'powerful panopticism and subterranean resistance' (p. 2). Aerial viewpoints often 'play a villainous role'

(p. 2) in representations of warfare, argues Kaplan, tying visual documentation to systems of military control and surveillance:

> Until the coincidence of the ramp-up of visual technologies that became associated with the war on terror after 9/11 ... the 'God's-eye view' of violent scenes was either classified as 'secret' by the military or released on an extremely selective basis ... For most of the twentieth century, aerial photography of traumatic or violent events was usually associated with official surveying, documenting, and conducting of surveillance and reconnaissance rather than the capturing of images at the 'human' level of individualized suffering that is usually associated affirmatively with photojournalism.
>
> (p. 5)

In short, the separation between the objective view from above and the embodied, sensory encounter with these sites 'from below' exemplifies ongoing power relations and discursive frames that continue to structure dominant cultural memory about the war. Entangling these perspectives, through a collision method, holds potential to bridge this separation and thus disrupt these dominant frameworks.

However, whilst I may appear to play the role of photojournalist Kaplan describes, my method of visiting Teufelsberg and the other sites – walking, climbing, photographing, smelling, feeling and writing – is not *subversive* per se, nor a specific attempt to refocus on the 'human level of individualised suffering' (Kaplan 2017, p. 5). The terrestrial nature of my method does not claim to present the reality on the ground as *counteracting* more objective perspectives in dominant depictions of the war that represent aerial bombing from above. Examining the sites as a researcher-visitor actually includes these perspectives from above that are so entrenched in dominant ways of understanding the war and layers them with the material encounters with the sites on the ground. It is the act of bringing them into contact with one another that can disrupt a framework that has determinedly kept them separate.

My physical perspective as I visit Teufelsberg and the other sites implicates specific power relations between aerial and grounded views inherent in aerial bombing and aerial viewpoints. On the ground, visiting and documenting the sites was not in the slightest distinct and separate from those abstracted and conceptual representations that dominate English-speaking war mythologies. In Chapter 2 I discussed cultural memory as the outcome of particular communicative practices. My cultural communicative practice of visiting these sites, camera and notebook in hand, also continues to produce the very cultural memory under study. My notes show how I positioned what I encountered on the ground in Berlin within specific frameworks, navigating the sites through the cultural and literal viewpoints through which I habitually understand the bombings. This navigation occurred even on the most pragmatic level: I mostly navigated my way around Berlin and the sites themselves using Google Maps, orienting my position on the ground within an aerial viewpoint and thus rendering these often confusing and unintelligible places more legible through the mastery of a birds-eye view. Simultaneously, the legible viewpoint from above was often rendered illegible by what I found on the ground, in a road that should be there but wasn't, or an 'estimated arrival time' that flagrantly ignored the additional time required to climb a steep hill in 32°C. My method is therefore not an attempt to counter these abstracted aerial views, or to use the human effects of the bombings to somehow undermine the military, scientific objectivity of traditional histories of the bombings. My method instead investigates how these perspectives might be entangled and the effects of this entanglement on the cultural memory of area bombing.

This entanglement can trigger a critical engagement with the normative cultural memory of the war. Golańska (2020) argues that 'the physicality of the encounter with the memorial space as well as its jointly generated material-semiotic qualities engraves invisible (sometimes unrepresentable) micro-traces on the bodies involved in the process. This encounter is what might trigger production of critical thought' (p. 85). Bringing the normative memory discourses into collision with the material traces of the bombings might trigger critical thought in relation to those cultural memory structures.

Data collection

Accordingly, the 'data' from this research were both experiential and cultural, sensory and discursive, material and semiotic. It revolved largely around field visits but, as explained above, drew on wider negotiations of memory and history that expand beyond several sites in London and Berlin in the spring and summer of 2017. It is therefore perhaps somewhat misleading to outline the 'data' of this research, or the 'data collection', but this section attempts to at least outline the system of documentation, collection and analysis through which I encountered Teufelsberg and the other sites to explore the relationship between cultural memory and urban places marked by violence. To collect data I gathered photographs, ethnographic observations and other textual materials from the sites.

Photographs

At Teufelsberg and the other sites, I took photographs. These were initially conceived as a way to 'capture' as much as I could of the sites, to act as mnemonic aids for later analysis. I took photographs of the features of the sites, the signage, the surrounds, the layout of the sites, the points of entry and exit, the beautiful parts, the ugly parts, the parts that seemed to speak directly to the bombings and the history of the war, and the parts that seemed to speak to the mundanity of these sites as they existed as tourist spots, commuting hubs or public parks. I was trying to capture as much of the sites as I could before I had to leave, trying to have as much material with which I could think through the ways of negotiating the cultural memory of the bombings.

As I worked, I became aware of the ways that photography's history is bound up with the rampant destruction and change of the environment, destruction like that of the bombings. As I 'captured' these sites of destruction in photographs, I showed what Sontag identified as a desire to capture something on the brink of disappearing:

> Cameras began duplicating the world at that moment when the human landscape started to undergo a vertiginous rate of change: while an untold number of forms of biological and social life are being destroyed in a brief span of time, a device is available to record what is disappearing.
>
> (Sontag 1979, pp. 15–6)

As I clicked my camera at chunks of rubble in the grass, spray paint on walls and signs, I was working to freeze time for later analysis, to fix these objects to an image, holding them still and preserving them against the flow of time. I also inadvertently established a large archive of these sites, a 'snapshot' of their condition on several Spring days in 2017, which continued the tradition of photographs preserving against time and decay.

The photographs, like my collision method, worked to capture both the semiotic and material encounters with the sites. By photographing the sites as I encountered them – and also by the note taking I explore below – I worked to capture their interactions with me, or mine with the sites.

But the function of photographs expands beyond the documentary. 'Photographers document something "out there,"' Sontag (1979) argues, which purports photographs are some kind of 'more innocent, and therefore more accurate, relation to visible reality than … other mimetic objects' (p. 6). This has resulted in what Sturken and Cartwright (2018) call 'the myth of photographic truth' (p. 24), the idea that photographs capture reality in earnest. Against this myth, Sontag (1979) argues that 'the camera's rendering of reality must always hide more than it discloses ... only that which narrates can make us understand' (p. 23). Whilst I initially took photographs for their documentary value, they soon became key tools in constituting notions of verisimilitude that characterize the Anglo-American perspectives of the bombings I brought with me to the analysis. I found that I began to frame these photographs (so to speak) as documenting not only the sites and objects they depicted, but the perspective they simultaneously conveyed. Photography always entails a point of view, an implication of the perspective and agency of the photographer. These images therefore disclose the sense-making and noticing of myself as the researcher, and by association the cultural frameworks I and other Anglo-American tourists are likely to rely on to make sense of these sites. The photographs show the preoccupations of the photographer as much as they do the material and visual elements of the sites.

Notebooks

The extensive observation notes I took at these sites further help to identify and explore what ethnographer Lewis (2015) calls 'the complexity and ambiguity of the role of the researcher in undertaking embodied, participatory research' (p. 349). These observations were both attempts to document the sensory aspects of the site that could not be captured by a camera – smells, sounds, atmosphere, temperature – as well as my own cultural political perspectives and thought processes that emerged through the site visits. My notes speak quite directly to the inner sense-making processes that I brought with me to the sites, and therefore to the ongoing cultural and political embeddedness of myself as a visitor-researcher. This method is grounded in what DeSilvey (2007) calls 'a different kind of materialism ... a materialism that accepts the presence of the researcher as a creative and catalysing element in the construction of knowledge' (p. 420). Many observations in my notes, some of which appear in the below analyses, reflect how the common narrative tropes discussed in Chapter 1 continue to frame and reframe my encounters with the sites.

The sense-making processes of this kind of experiential method are inherently entangled with the material reality of the sites under study, the researcher's and the sites' bodies each claiming influence. These notes occasionally take the form of a record of thoughts: 'Cognitive mapping is failing, I am less a walker and more a cartographer'. At other times my notes are an attempt to make sense of the site's materiality interacting with my own body: 'Difficult to move, to navigate the area. Noisy'. 'Birds, sun breeze, green. Idyllic, ordered (can hear strauss [sic] playing)'. Still in others, the historical and conceptual meaning of the sites intersect: 'Is the forest healing or forgetting? What's the difference?' 'I don't think any tourist would come here [Rain just started] I wonder what this spot is called on the map'. Including these notes in my analyses brings my own sense-making processes to the fore, in an attempt to remain faithful to the fact that making sense of these sites consistently draws on a myriad of historical, conceptual and practical readings, but also physical idiosyncrasies, accidents, and contingencies like rust, rain, decay, wifi, traffic.

Palimpsests

The photographs and notes have emerged as a way to foreground my layered experience of attending these sites as an Anglo-American visitor, producing and reproducing the cultural memory of the bombings. The notes and impressions I collected at the sites in the following chapters are therefore somewhat of an attempt to reflect W. G. Sebald's (2000; 2002; 2004; 2001) well-known palimpsestic writing and publishing style. Sebald intertwines his writing with images, descriptions, histories, anecdotes, personal narratives, archival documents and poetry. 'At times', argues Wilson (2013), Sebald's images 'occupy an indexical relation to the text, by pointing back to the language that surrounds them or by becoming a kind of silent indicator or unspoken word within it' (p. 50). Sebald, the self-titled 'collector', presents a fragmentary, collage-like encounter with the past through a bricolage of 'memoirs, diaries, gravestones, oral histories, annotated maps, artworks, newspaper articles, literature, postcards, and dictionaries ... in the forms of quotations, translations, photographic reproductions, or curious combinations thereof' (Elcott 2004, p. 203).

My own palimpsest collection of images and impressions are also an attempt to render the multiple temporalities of the sites and of cultural memory that might be formed at them. It is an attempt at simultaneity, flexing and realigning horizontal, linear time to consider many moments at once. Sebald's layout resembles superimposition, 'disparate historical or chronological moments [appearing] somehow contemporaneous' (Wilson 2013, p. 51). Photographs, analysis and impressions of the sites are therefore presented below interwoven in a palimpsest, bringing together disparate times, people, places and stories – much like visiting a place. My form of presenting my analyses is also informed by Ingold's (2010) description of images drawing the reader/viewer into an act of walking, wandering and exploring through a collection of images, that in a way mirrors visiting a place: 'we have to find our ways through and among them, inhabiting them as we do the world itself' (p. 16). The images and texts of the following four chapters attempt to replicate this, to draw the reader into the act of visiting these sites through the grounded perspective of my camera and notes, walking through the pages in a way that might evoke the act of walking through the sites. Representing my findings like this spatializes my readings of the sites across the page, allowing my knowledge-as-perspective generated at and through the sites to come through as prose and photographs.

The resultant four chapters are therefore studies of the sites that interweave their historical contexts and theoretical and conceptual scholarship (of the sites themselves and of other concepts related the past and place, such as archaeology, burial, memorial, nature, geology and so on) with my corporeal and practical encounters with the places themselves. Each chapter begins with a brief summary of the chapter and its findings, followed by an analysis of the sites told through a more contemplative style of writing than the first three chapters, in collage-like collections of quotes, narratives and fragments from a range of texts, from novels to news reports. The photographs and notes I collected, as well as the more heuristic writing style, form fragments in a palimpsest, overlapping and interacting with one another. Discourses about the Second World War area bombing similarly overlap and interact with the sensory encounters available at the sites. From this palimpsest I tease out the ways the bombings can be remembered in Berlin today by English-speaking audiences visiting these sites.

Conclusion

This chapter has outlined the practical and theoretical elements of a method developed to account for the layered and variegated readings of area bombing that can be enacted at Teufelsberg and the other sites chosen for study. I have constructed a model of documentation that accounts for the encounters with the past at Teufelsberg, utilizing an interdisciplinary mix of techniques. Through its layering and intermingling of mnemonic frames and material evidence of area bombing, Teufelsberg emerged as both a site of analysis and as a methodological framework through which we might approach the ways cultural memory of the air war can be framed and reframed.

Photographs, initially used to capture the visual elements of the site, further developed in the analysis stage into reflections of the perspective of the researcher. Extensive observations of the sites were recorded in notebooks, as well my own interaction with the sites, and how these interactions came to intersect with the particular cultural narrations of the Second World War that I 'bring' to encounters with these sites.

The second half of this book walks through Teufelsberg and the other *Trümmerberge*, discovering ruins, archaeology, memorialization, museum practices, reconstruction, aerial photography, nature, geology and rubble, and draws these out into conversation with five other sites across Berlin. The method has been designed to confront, rather than avoid, the pre-existing narratives of area bombing and the Second World War that an Anglo-American visitor-researcher uses to frame her encounter with Teufelsberg, bringing them into direct conversation with the sensory and material traces of destruction and violence. The following four chapters disrupt and tease apart common communicative and material practices of remembering as we walk across Teufelsberg's slopes, to interrogate some of the underlying assurances and belief systems that continue to frame how we remember the war. By entangling different subject positions and perspectives, these site studies of Teufelsberg can complicate the normative Anglo-American discourses that continue to reaffirm the historical innocence and righteousness of the Allies.

4

Layers of history

Introduction: Strata

It is a steep climb to the top of Teufelsberg, along small pathways, through dense forest, and at the time of my visit, intense summer heat and mosquitos. At the top of the hill, I found the former NSA listening station, surrounded by a wire fence with a gate and adorned with graffiti and thousands of objects repurposed into chairs, sculpture, art. After paying my eight Euros, the men lounging at the gate directed me to follow the yellow cats painted on the ground. The felines led me through hallways of the spy station facility, through doorways, up flights of stairs. Eventually I found myself at the top of the tallest building, amongst the now quite iconic large white antenna radomes. There is a definite sense of accumulation at Teufelsberg, the accretion of layers of earth, metal, rust, graffiti, stickers, photographs, history. Standing atop the building, there seems to be much beneath my feet; decades of art and performance, spray paint and beer cans, concrete, iron and electronics of the listening station; meters and meters and masses of rubble, dirt and roots, stretching deep down beneath me; and beneath it all, a Nazi facility, lurking still in the dark.

***

At first glance, it is fruitful to consider Teufelsberg as a series of geological strata. As both a field site and a methodological frame of analysis, one might first imagine walking Teufelsberg as walking over one episode of Berlin's past layered over the last. If one were to slice downward, from the top of the listening station to the sands of the Teltow Plateau, then a history of Berlin would reveal itself vertically, like strata of the earth.

To begin with the first 'layer': The spy station is a popular tourism destination, and in 2018 was listed as a protected historical monument. On my visit in 2017, visitors were charged eight Euros for entry and an extra four Euros for a guided

Figure 4.1 Artwork at the spy station at Teufelsberg, Berlin. Photograph by Eloise Florence, 2017.

tour. Through a stratigraphical view of Teufelsberg the layer of the spy station would signal Berlin as a global city of tourism, art and (often counter-) culture.

The ruins of the spy station emerged as a hub of the post-reunification era trend of alternative cultures occupying and re-purposing Cold War buildings. The site was (and to some extent still is) used as an alternative art and music space. Underneath the signs for tour groups, promotional pamphlets and fences with signs written in English, lie reclaimed and repurposed furniture, improvised stages and performance spaces, and layers of graffiti that has been applied since the fall of the Wall.

Beneath those layers of graffiti, the politics of hyper-surveillance that epitomized the Cold War then materialize in the buildings of the listening station. During the Cold War this station was part of the American international Echelon spy network (Smith & Shand 2016). The American National Security Agency (NSA) utilized Teufelsberg as the highest point in West Berlin to track communications from the other side of the Wall.

This culture of hyper-surveillance was literally built on top of the remains of a destroyed city. Roughly 55 million cubic metres of rubble was generated by the destroyed buildings of Berlin (Anderson 2015). After the war, this rubble was swept into piles, ground into gravel for roads and runways, or heaped over any surviving Nazi architecture. Teufelsberg is literally composed of wartime Berlin, constructed using rubble blasted apart by Allied bombs, Russian artillery and post-war demolition crews.

Beneath those layers of rubble at and of Teufelsberg lie the remains of a Nazi military training facility (Anderson 2015). The building was one of the only examples of Albert Speer's infamous neo-classical architecture in Berlin to survive the war, the embodiment of his famous 'theory of ruination' (explored below). It was buried beneath the rubble of Berlin and the Grunewald was allowed to grow over the hill that now hid the institute from view, reclaiming the area and integrating it back into the forest. Teufelsberg now stands over the history of Berlin as the capital of the Nazi Reich.

Finally, the Nazi Reich and the military training facility both built on a legacy of Romantic notions of home and homeland that had followed Germany since unification in 1871 and found voice in forests like the Grunewald. Speer and Hitler deliberately chose the Grunewald as the site for the institute. The trees under which Hitler stood on the day he laid the foundation stone for the facility and the forest through which one must walk to climb Teufelsberg 'has itself swayed synonymous with darkness and magic far predating its wartime vocations and the rhetoric of blood and soil' (Smith & Shand 2016, p. 185). Speer's neo-classical and neo-Romantic architecture, embodied in buildings like the military institute (and Anhalter Bahnhof, explored below), is often thought of as 'built upon' modern Germany's imperial and Romantic nationalism origins. This Romanticism, in turn, drew largely on this 'darkness' and 'magic' inherent in German forests like the Grunewald.

Thinking through Teufelsberg in this layered, linear, stratigraphical way, one can see the hill as a rather straightforward metaphor for Berlin's past: one event or idea layered upon the last in a steady, vertical progression, from German unification in 1871 through to contemporary tourism and cultural practices.

But a closer look at Teufelsberg reveals nothing so straightforward nor even linear. The more recent past doesn't lie neatly piled atop more distant history, and one cannot simply 'read' Berlin's history through the strata of Teufelsberg. In this chapter, I will outline the limitations of such an approach in forming cultural memory for Anglo-American visitors, not only as an incorrect description of Teufelsberg as a place, but also as a problematically linear understanding of cultural memory of and in Berlin. I offer the potential of the ruins, rubble and forests of Teufelsberg to complicate this stratified sense of Berlin's history.

As both a site and a conceptual and methodological framework, Teufelsberg offers insight into possible nuanced, complicated forms of Anglo-American cultural memory of the air war in several ways. Firstly, I explore both the physical act and rhetorical device of burial, digging and archaeology as a means of both reaffirming and complicating some of the more established frames of reference for remembering the air war that remain in English-language cultural texts. Burial and archaeology are also found at the well-known tourist site the Topography of Terror, where the burial and digging up of Nazi buildings speaks directly to wider English-language (not to mention German) debates about the cultural memory in and of Berlin in the post-war period, with specific implications for the cultural memory of the air war. Drawing on analyses of other sites of ruination, namely that of Anhalter Bahnhof, I then explore the cultural histories of ruins, including Albert Speer's 'theory of ruination' and the Romantic ruins so hijacked by the Nazis (Zill 2011) and popular visual ruin motifs of the Second World War that continue to influence contemporary Anglo-American notions of guilt, responsibility and victimhood. I also focus specifically on ruins' tendency to be experienced as 'haunted' (Edensor 2005b; Gordon 2008). Looking to the ruins of the Cold War spy station as haunted offers new ways of considering wartime area bombing as entangled with other episodes of Berlin's past. Such an entanglement offers potential to complicate the linear causality that underlines normative cultural memory of area bombing, that is, the Allies bombed Berlin *because of* – ergo in response to – Nazi war crimes and genocide. Encountering Teufelsberg as a haunted, unruly, messy mass of rubble opens the possibility of remembering the bombings occurring alongside Nazi atrocities. What follows is the possibility of a contemporary cultural legacy of the war in which the Allies can be remembering fight a just war against the Nazi machine of genocide *and also* responsible for mass destruction and civilian deaths.

Views of history: The problem of forests and Nazis

As a set of strata, Teufelsberg initially appears to cement a linear reading of Berlin's history. Such a reading of the past echoes the very linear progress of time that Foucault is trying to counter with his genealogy and history of the present, the assumption of an 'unbroken continuity' stretching out behind us into history (see Chapter 1). Similar too is the 'chain of events' that we see while Benjamin's Angel of History sees a single catastrophe (in Sebald 2004). As I will argue below, reading Teufelsberg in a particularly linear way continues, rather than complicates, normative Anglo-American cultural memory structures of the war. But it also speaks to particular Anglo-American understandings of Germany's past, particularly its relationship with its Nazis past. Before moving to a more complicated view of the histories that can be found at Teufelsberg, I will briefly outline some of the dangers of this view of the past.

Uncomfortably, this fundamentally linear understanding of history is exemplified by Hitler's and the Nazi Minister for Armaments and War Production Albert Speer – often called 'Hitler's architect'. Speer and Hitler famously articulated the 'Thousand Year Reich' as a continuation of the ancient mythic Germany imagined through nineteenth-century Romantic nationalism and embodied this in architecture and design. Speer in particular was known for his tendency to create physical structures and environments that provided aesthetic and narrative links to particular aspects of Germany's past. This took expression in his so-called 'theory of ruination' which I explore below, but which in no small part drew on Germany's relationship with nature and forests.

The forest that spreads out over and away from Teufelsberg today once stood as an example of this kind of thinking. Speer replanted the Grunewald with deciduous trees in the late 1930s; one must pass through what are ostensibly the descendants of these trees to reach Teufelsberg. Speer (1970) claimed he replaced the trees to 'restore the old mixed forest which Frederick the Great had cut for lumber to finance the Silesian War' (p. 78). Speer was naming what he saw as a 'bridge of tradition' embodied in the forest that the Nazis claimed linked them with Germany's ancient Teutonic origins.

Figure 4.2 The forest at Teufelsberg, Berlin. Photograph by Eloise Florence, 2017.

The mythic, timeless Germany that Speer and the Nazis utilized, and which fed Speer's 'theory of ruination', is analogous with forests. The Nazi obsession with landscape is often linked back to the importance of the landscape in late nineteenth-century expressions of European national mythologies and imaginaries, on which Speer is drawing when he refers to Friedrich the Great. The forest was used as a nationalist source of unity in the period following German unification in 1871, in no small part because it was a common motif of Romanticism and Romantic nationalism (Lekan 2009; Smith & Shand 2016). Six decades later, the Nazis incorporated Romantic themes of sublime naturalism into their ideology to imagine a Germany built on ancient origins and racial purity. Historians have particularly focused on the concepts of *Heimat* and *Lebensraum* (roughly 'homeland' and 'living space'), which the Nazis used to imagine the longevity and permanence of Germany's origins in the geography of Europe, and which created a biological and sublime connection to the land and justified their racist ideology, policies and genocide.

The links between the Romantic love of forest and nature and Nazism emerged as a crucial post-war question in English-language circles, particularly those regarding the future of German identity. Lekan (2009) describes British novelist Stephen Spender touring the war-ravaged German countryside in 1946 and asking:

> How did the same culture that had inspired Heine and Friedrich also generate Adolf Hitler? Had the Nazi appeal to 'Blood and Soil' perverted the Romantics' appreciation of nature, or had Romantic mysticism itself endowed the landscape with volatile moods and menacing intentions?
> (Spender in Lekan 2009, p. 2)

We can see here the view of history challenged by Foucault and Benjamin and a framework of historical memory I hope to explore and push beyond below. Spender draws direct causal lines between the Romantic nationalist period and the Nazis' obsession with mythic pasts. Spender feared the Romantic nationalist obsession with the landscape had fed directly into the racialized nationalism of the Nazis. From this perspective of history, when Speer planted his deciduous trees he imbued the Grunewald with the racial purity and timeless mysticism with which Nazism had endowed 'the Fatherland'. To be sure, the forest covering Teufelsberg does often feel like a fairy tale forest, dark, foreboding, mysterious, magical and ancient. Even when the full summer sun is blazing overhead, the thick trees create dim shadows. Sound moves strangely through the trees, often exaggerated, louder or bigger than their source. Small sounds make me jump, and large sounds are muffled and distant. Sometimes noises sound a lot closer than they are. Other times, a person or creature comes right up close before I hear or see it.

So are the dark and mysterious shadows in Teufelsberg's forest teeming with the dark origins of Nazism? Are the 'volatile moods and menacing intentions' (Spender in Lekan 2009, p. 2) that Spender was searching for lurking beneath the trees of the Grunewald?

As much as continuity between contemporary Germany and its Nazi past is strictly policed, many claim that linkages between the Romantic obsession with land and geography continue to haunt contemporary expressions of German national identity. A vertical, episodic view of history, where past horrors can seep into the present and threaten the future, structures many of the debates surrounding remembering and forgetting the Holocaust.

The uproar at a much more recent event concerning Teufelsberg is predicated by this view. In 2007, the spy station was bought by American director David Lynch, who announced he would be using the site to build a 'university devoted to Transcendental Meditation' (*Der Spiegel* 2007). Announcing the project, Lynch caused controversy when his 'guru' opened the press conference dressed in a gold robe and wearing a crown, chanting 'Invincible Germany!' 'That's what Hitler wanted!' an attendee in the crowd is reported to have yelled in reply (*Der Spiegel* 2007). The world remains wary of evocations of Germany's recent past unless it is explicitly – and completely necessarily, as I demonstrated in Chapter 1 – framed as continuing Germany's collective guilt and responsibility for the war. The wariness of Lynch's heckler was built on a view of history wherein time and events build upon one another vertically, like the layers of and beneath Teufelsberg.

As I noted in the opening chapter, we should remain vigilant against parties who downplay Germany's fascist past, not the least because of the tendencies of resurgent neo-fascism and nationalistic groups to do so to further their racist agendas. The wariness of Lynch's heckler is built on very real threats of resurgent waves of neo-fascism, neo-Nazism and Islamophobia across the world, including in Germany. But, as I also noted in the opening chapter, it also remains important to be wary of cultural criticism that posits a *direct* causal relationship between the past and present through a linear model. Huyssen (2003b) identifies the danger of creating an 'ever-expanding present' (p. 171), where similar events and ideas across different time periods and geographies can become conflated. Huyssen specifically criticized the German anti-Iraq War movements in the early 2000s using the imagery of the 1943 firebombing of Dresden and Hamburg to draw parallels with the 2002 bombing of Baghdad. Huyssen identified that Jörg Friedrich's *The Fire* (2006 (released in German in 2002)), which provided a vivid account of the bombings, had political impact on the protests. Huyssen said the book helped 'close the gap between past and present by collapsing fundamental political differences: America and England bomb and civilians suffer – a facile and fallacious historical analogy between the German past and the Iraqi present' (2003b, p. 171). Considering Teufelsberg as layers of German history not only risks similarly conflating essential political and historical differences between Germany's twentieth- and nineteenth-century attachments to landscape, but also fails to interrogate the ways the memory of these periods interact, overlap and entangle. Furthermore, it risks obscuring the particulars of contemporary incarnations of fascism and racism.

When exploring the cultural memory of the air war that can be formed at Teufelsberg, it is therefore important to be sceptical of the assumption that any contemporary German expressions of cultural and political connection to the landscape flow directly from Imperial Germany's Romantic forests through to the racially charged mythology of the Nazis hijacking of *Heimat*, much less to the dark and mysterious forest of present-day Teufelsberg. Lekan and Zeller (2005) argue for regarding attachment to landscape as a politically volatile tool, rather than an inherent cultural or biological trait of the German people stretching back in history. This is a somewhat problematic way of challenging Anglo-American narratives that continue to link contemporary Germany with its racialized past, but, as I explore below, can also serve to complicate some of the assumptions in normative Anglo-American cultural memory discourses of the war, which tend to reinforce this link.

At Teufelsberg, the layers of the hill, like the strata of dirt in an archaeological dig trench, do not 'build upon' or cause one another, nor do they remain clearly defined and separate. The rubble of pre-war Berlin is not 'covered by' or 'built upon' the forest, but literally integrated into it – it blends almost seamlessly into the surrounding Grunewald, complicating the notion that the destruction of Berlin (which the rubble represents) is simply 'built upon' Germany's Romantic attention to forests cultivated by the Nazis. The spy station was built upon the rubble of the Second World War, but it does not cover the rubble completely, nor does it remain separate from it, complicating the notion that the hyper-surveillance culture of the Cold War was simply 'built upon' the destruction of the Second World War. The spy station is partly built out of, as well as on top of, the rubble. Using the hill of Teufelsberg as a metaphor for the cultural legacy of Berlin's twentieth-century history is fruitful, but at the hill itself I find these histories interacting with and influencing one another, and not in a strictly vertical, linear fashion.

In what follows, I will explore ways of comprehending Teufelsberg that allow for a more complex, nuanced and entangled form of cultural memory to emerge. Frames of burial, digging, ruination and haunting all emerge as ways of comprehending the past at Teufelsberg, and how this might contribute to a more complex understanding of guilt, responsibility, victimhood and accountability with regard to the air war.

Burial and digging

As well as a metaphor for the layered episodes of Berlin's history, Teufelsberg has been described as a burial ground for a destroyed city (Anderson 2015). Through a similarly participatory method of walking, photographing and imagining, Anderson investigated the forest planted over Teufelsberg as an act of forgetting. Walking over Teufelsberg, Anderson argues, is an act of 'self-induced amnesia' (Anderson 2015, p. 81), akin to walking over an unmarked grave. As a means of interrogating the potential of Teufelsberg to complicate normative culture memory structures of the air war, I would like to build on this notion to consider whether Berlin and its destruction are actually 'buried' at Teufelsberg at all. Instead, as I shall demonstrate below, it might be more fruitful to consider the remnants of the city in a more active, unruly sense.

Anderson (2015) draws on a common narrative that burial equals suppression, that the destruction of Berlin is absent from possible remembering at Teufelsberg because it is absent from the visible surface of the city. Anderson identifies the hill as the mark of 'a society consumed by guilt for the murder of millions at the very moment when it was faced with the immense task of reconstructing its cities' (p. 79). 'To walk on and over Teufelsberg', Anderson continues, 'is to be complicit with the ruination of Berlin without ever experiencing its effects' (p. 79). When considered as a burial ground, the reality of Berlin's ruination remains hidden beneath Teufelsberg's surface. Anderson calls for an archaeological dig to remedy this, engaging a revelatory rhetoric often associated with archaeological digging. Gonzalex-Rubial (2008) identifies the revelatory potential of archaeology, calling each dig 'a revelation that allows the return of the repressed, the unsayable ... It is from this point of view above all that archaeology can perform a therapeutic – as well as political – function .... performing the political act of unveiling what the supermodern power machine does not want to be shown' (p. 262). Anderson argues the 'unheard story' of Berlin's destruction can and should be seen by bringing these stories to the surface. By digging down, opening up the surface of Teufelsberg to the public gaze, the fog of 'self-induced amnesia' about the destruction of the city at the hands of the Allies would lift.

Rhetorical uses of digging

Anderson's study speaks to the rhetorical power of digging and uncovering in cultural memory spaces (Florence 2016). The presence of rubble, buried remnants, and ruins at Teufelsberg echoes that of another site at which these have been used as a rhetorical device, the Topography of Terror. The site is the remnants of the foundations of the institutions that designed and administrated the Holocaust and other Nazi atrocities in Berlin: the Secret State Police (Gestapo) Office, the leadership of the SS and SA, and the Reich Security Main Office. Today it is a major tourism destination, but its modern history is that of an archaeological dig.

Thanks in part to aerial bombing (as well as the Battle of Berlin and Cold war and reunification memory politics; see Czaplicka 1995; Elkins 2005; Fulbrook 2009; Ladd 1997; Till 2005), much of the physical traces of Berlin's Nazi past were buried at the Topography of Terror at the close of the war, and then unearthed as the end of the Cold War approached. In the decade leading up to the fall of the Wall, the area near Niederkirchnerstraße was marked for the construction of a highway. In response to this, in May 1985 two civic groups from West Berlin staged a symbolic dig at the site, uncovering the site of Nazi state-terror and demanding its preservation. Under community pressure and in deep awareness of related cultural memory cultures on the other side of the Wall, the West Berlin senate cancelled the plans for the highway and established a temporary exhibition over the site in 1987. The exhibition displayed the information that is today housed in the documentation centre.

The dig at the Topography of Terror occurred at a time when calls for more open and responsible acknowledgement of Nazi crimes on the part of Berlin's two governments were growing.[1] The motto of the West German 'activist archaeologists' in 1985 was 'act, dig where you stand' (Till 2004, p. 76), embodying a narrative of probing the foundations of one's home to 'uncover' the truth. The Topography of Terror is thus often spoken of in language of exposition. 'The rubble of the Gestapo [was] now present in the urban imaginary' argues Till (2012, p. 6), speaking of what occurred when the remnants of Nazi state terror were uncovered by the activist archaeologists in the late 1980s. The dig was seen to reveal a truth long buried in West Berlin's consciousness, and National Socialism was revealed to be embedded in the foundations of the soon-to-be-reunified city, buried by layers of 'forgetful' dirt and sand.

One can see here how archaeological digs in particular contexts speak not only to the uncovering of the truth but the *burial* of its truth. On an international stage, the archaeological digs at Niederkirchnerstraße seemed to physically embody the exposure of a hidden history, exemplifying not only the history that had been buried but the act of burial within the context of post-war remembering and forgetting in both East and West Germany. The dig exemplified the ability of archaeology 'to bring these debates [about Berlin's Nazi past] into the public sphere, potentially undermining the hegemony of the officially sanctioned memory' (Moshenka 2006, p. 59). In a city plagued by a history of atrocities, the exposed remnants of the Topography of Terror seemed to reveal physically not only Berlin's violent Nazi's past, but also 'the refusal of the state to come to terms with its violent past in the attempt to become a "good" democracy through economic recovery' (Till 2012, p. 6). The fragments and remnants at the Topography of Terror came to embody a narrative familiar in Anglo-American post-war cultural spheres: a nation's shameful history could be exposed through a determined act of unearthing lost fragments and remains, but so too could state acts of suppression. The dig of 1985 uncovered Berlin's past, but also evidenced the fact that this past had been buried.

This narrative of 'hidden family secrets' or 'the buried truth' at the Topography of Terror was perhaps so quick to take because it had become a well-established trope in Anglo-American perceptions of post-war Germany and its struggle with remembering Nazism. International audiences have been privy to many movements in which (particularly West) Germany wrestled with its post-war identity, often on an international geo-political and cultural stage. For example, in the 1970s a new generation of West Germans began to ask questions of their parents' generation about their participation in the war and the Holocaust, a process epitomized in 'the *Nasty Girl* controversy' (see Geisen 2004). Geisen goes on to note this took place on an international stage, and in a context in which asking these sorts of questions were often considered the trait of 'outsiders' (p. 127).

The truth that was 'uncovered' by the digs at the Topography of Terror, and to be later found by Anglo-American tourists, is therefore not only the committal of these atrocities, but the efforts of German governments to cover them up. This form of remembering purports that beneath the surface of Berlin lay a dark past that had been actively suppressed and then uncovered. The activist-archaeologists 'dug up the "forgetful" layers of grass and denial that covered up a shameful national past' (Till 2012, p. 6). The digs of 1985 appeared to reveal both Berlin's dark past and the city's efforts to hide that past from the light of day.

These revelatory themes at both Teufelsberg and the Topography of Terror have specific connotations in the context of well-known official attempts to control the narrative of the past in Germany. The dig at the Topography of Terror exposed the layers of what Sebald (2004) called 'the well-kept secret of the corpses built into the foundations of our state', and what Steinbach (qtd. and trans. in Czaplicka 1995) calls 'perpetrator history' (p. 181):

> [The Topography of Terror] is in my opinion especially impressive because it opens up not only the historical site, but also its meaning for 'remembering' in the post-war period. Sand mountains and plateaus become symbols of the active suppression, the excavation symbols of a new recollection.
> (qtd. and trans. in Czaplicka 1995, p. 181)

Steinbach identifies the potential of the Topography of Terror to undermine German state-sponsored narratives of the past, which Sebald argues is a characteristic of post-war Germany (see also Young 1993; Kettenacker 2010).

One can hear the echoes of Anderson's depiction of Teufelsberg here. Like it does at the Topography of Terror, Anderson argues that an archaeological dig would bring the remains of the city, and thus the memory of its destruction, 'to the surface'. But it is worth noting how describing rubble as 'hidden beneath' the surface of Teufelsberg relates explicitly to the German victimhood debate and the debates over the cultural memory of area bombing. If thought of as an unmarked grave, Teufelsberg would represent Berlin 'burying' its own destruction at the hands of Allied air forces under layers of forgetful dirt and sand. Anderson (2017) wants to use archaeology to reveal both the stones and 'the forces of silence and forgetting that helped to create an environment that could allow a people to bury their city' (p. 161). Like those at the Topography of Terror, the *acts* of possible excavation of the rubble at Teufelsberg would perform the cultural and political task of reckoning with the past, by bringing the rubble into the realm of what is visible. Furthermore, the power of material objects to reveal the truth is often explicitly linked to the cultural memory of Second World War aerial bombing. This relates directly to a common argument in the German victimhood debate explored in the opening chapter: the cultural memory of area bombing has been taboo, if not actively suppressed, in mainstream expressions of Second World War cultural memory. It has been buried. Framing Teufelsberg in this way is somewhat dangerous, given that the rhetorics of 'taboo' and 'state repression' are the realm of the far-right and neo-fascism that often aim to use the memory of the bombings to further their revisionist and often racist and anti-Semitic agendas (see Chapter 1). We must be careful, therefore, when approaching Teufelsberg as a site of 'buried' or 'suppressed' history, such as the history buried at the Topography of Terror; care must be taken not to frame the buried history of aerial violence in anything close the buried history of Nazi atrocities. What's more, as Moeller (2006) argues, the 'taboo' was 'not one on speaking; rather, it was on listening' (p. 116). Perhaps what is signified by the burial of rubble of Teufelsberg is not Germany trying to 'tell their story' of area bombing, but of the former Allies refusing to hear it.

Whilst Anderson's proposed dig is a way of showing these interacting layers of history, it still implies that the surface of the hill represents the covering or hiding of this history. But given that the ground of Teufelsberg does not so much cover the layers of Berlin's history as it does entangle them together, digging is in fact likely insufficient to properly grasp the cultural memory available through walking the hill. Digging, as I discussed in regard to the Topography of Terror, implies the uncovering of some hidden truth, the 'point of origin' (Foucault 1977, p. 10), an idea that Foucault's genealogy refutes. As Till (2004) explains:

> As people search for this underlying essence, a seemingly unchanging reality, as they dig toward a mythical bedrock or truth, they encounter instead transgenerational phantoms. How does one dig when time and space intersect, fold upon each other, and are mutually co – created? What does it mean to dig for ghostly presences?
>
> (p. 77)

Non-linear histories

When one looks at Teufelsberg more carefully, this supposedly buried, hidden and then exposed history does not materialize in quite the same way as at the Topography of Terror. The destruction of Berlin is not buried at Teufelsberg and the other *Trümmerberge*, nor is archaeology required to appreciate the massive destructive forces of the bombing raids. For one, there is no digging required to see the material traces of Berlin's destruction or remnants of wartime Berlin at these sites. Teufelsberg and the other *Trümmerberge* that scatter the city are *constructed out of* the resultant rubble. The ruined city does not 'hide beneath the surface' of the hills – it composes the hills, makes up their surfaces and makes up their substance. Shattered pieces of rock, brick, marble, terracotta, porcelain tiles, twisted metal and concrete slabs are literally everywhere on the hills (see Chapter 7 for more on this). Furthermore, rather than being hidden beneath the ground, the rubble rises up out of the Teltow Plateau, transforming the formerly flat city into 'a city with an undulating geography of hills and elevated views' (Anderson 2015, p. 75). If the destruction is hiding, it is in plain sight. Nor is the rubble covered by forgetting forests. The rubble is sometimes huge, particularly at Teufelsberg, with hard edges juxtaposed against the soft curve of trees and soil. One tree at Teufelsberg had fallen over and exposed roots that were entangled with rubble to the sky. Another piece of rubble was huge, half the size of a car. And finally, the hills do not remain dormant; they are not the solid, impenetrable foundations of a city. Wind, rain, tree roots, roads, campers and hikers constantly reshape them. Particularly out at Teuflesberg, there is a sense the soil is constantly churning, shifting and throwing up new pieces of rubble. Geologists Wessolek and Toland (2014) documented how 'artefacts such as tile fragments, bricks, and glass shards are readily brought to the surface by burrowing animals and isolated points of erosion due to recreational activities and natural weathering processes' (p. 2) (see Chapter 6 for detail on the geology of Teufelsberg). The rubble, as material remnants of the bombings, is constantly shifting and changing, and constantly demanding attention.

Figure 4.3 Rubble entwined in the roots of a tree in the forest at Teufelsberg, Berlin. Photograph by Eloise Florence, 2017.

Figure 4.4 Rubble in the forest at Teufelsberg, Berlin. Photograph by Eloise Florence, 2017.

Berlin therefore does not remain 'buried' at Teufelsberg and the other *Trümmerberge* in the same way that the remains of the Gestapo prison were buried at the Topography of Terror. The unruly and unstable nature of the hill, as well as the fact it is walked over, not just gazed at, allows the possibility of considering the hill as a continuous opening and reopening of the evidence of pre-war Berlin and its destruction. Pushing beyond simple metaphors of 'burial equals forgetting' and 'digging equals remembering' opens up a more complex engagement with the material substance of Teufelsberg as a way to figure the city of Berlin that existed before the war and its destruction at the hands of Allied bombers.

In short, Teufelsberg is an apt physical metaphor to describe new, disruptive kinds of cultural memory that can be produced through it by Anglo-American visitors. Berlin's past as a bombed city is not the least bit dormant and buried at Teufelsberg, in safely separated layers beneath the earth. Whilst Nazi architecture is far from in view, Berlin's past is much like the hill itself – insistent, never still and settled, built over itself but never strictly following the vertical progression of time; it is folded back and upon itself, its various layers showing through one another.

As we shall see below and as I have already alluded to in the opening chapters, this model of Berlin's past sits somewhat uncomfortably with the dominant Anglo-American structures of the memory of the war. Because they are often viewed through the lens of justification and even retribution for Nazi atrocities, these memory structures must keep the bombings quite separate from the violence of Nazi atrocities. As I documented in the opening chapters this separation is also a well-founded precaution: conflating or even comparing the two is a well-used tactic of historical revisionism, the far right and neo-Nazism. At the same time, holding Nazi atrocities as separate from the bombings is central to narratives which posit the bombings as a response to these atrocities, that is, justified by them, and therefore is central to the continued regulation of historical accountability for violence and suffering in Anglo-American spheres. If the bombings are to be culturally framed as justified by Nazi atrocities, they must be held clearly and temporally separate. Approaching these historical events as entwined, if not contemporaneous, as is allowed by the entanglement that can emerge through a closer look at Teufelsberg, Anhalter Bahnhof, and the Jewish memorial cemetery, offers the notion the Allies bombed before *and* after the Nazis committed atrocities, and thus the two are more entwined than the hegemonic cultural memory narratives purport.

Ruins

Viewing the history of Berlin along the messy, entangled lines of the *Trümmerberge* allows a less linear, more variegated reading of Berlin's past to emerge. But this may also emerge through the usage of ruins and ruination, which both play a significant role in the mnemonic impact of these sites. Teufelsberg is perhaps best known as a site of ruins, the remnants of the Cold War spy station infamous as a site of alternative art and counter culture. Ruination, as a conceptual tool, speaks more to the entangled, complicated readings of the past that emerge at other ruinous sites as well, such as the Jewish memorial cemetery and Anhalter Bahnhof. Rather than carefully held separate, the layers of Berlin's past show through and interact with one another at these ruins and burial sites, like Till's (2004) 'transgenerational phantoms' that are freed from the earth when one 'dig[s] for ghostly presences' (p. 77). By encountering the ruins of pre-war Berlin at the same time I encounter the ruins of the Cold War, the straight line of history becomes instead a tangled mess, and I can then consider the cultural memory of Nazi atrocities alongside and entangled with that of the bombing of Berlin. Approaching Teufelsberg through the framework of ruins, as at other sites of ruination, we might continue to draw out these overlapping and interacting episodes of Berlin's past, and explore the potential of a more complex, nuanced form of Anglo-American cultural memory of area bombing.

Iconography of ruins

Approached as a ruin, the spy station echoes scores of other post-war and Cold War ruins across Berlin, perhaps the most notable being the Kaiser Wilhelm Memorial Church[2] and Anhalter Bahnhof. Anhalter emerged as a site of study in this research because of its striking romantic ruins that were layered with a more sinister history as a site of deportation during the Holocaust. As a site of analysis, Anhalter allows us to further draw out ruination as one of the mnemonic elements present at Teufelsberg, and demonstrates how the presence of ruins might allow for a more complex cultural memory of the air war to emerge.

Anhalter's ruins are almost monumental, the portico making clear that the former train station would have once dwarfed its surrounding buildings. With its columns, arches, statues and accompanying greenery, the facade recalls magnificent and picturesque ruins of the classics. Anhalter therefore draws on certain narrative tropes of ruination, engaging familiar themes of time, nature and destruction, particularly common in Anglo-American cultural memory patterns. Ruins have their own rhetorical currency, and, like archaeology, they can be thought of as 'representational device[s]' (DeSilvey & Edensor 2012, p. 465), or 'mnemonic trope[s]' (Clark 2015, p. 84) with a history of meaning. When she remembers the air war at and through Anhalter, an Anglo-American visitor draws on these archives of imagery, narratives and framings that are associated with ruins.

In particular, ruination plays an important role in wider memory cultures that emerged in post-war Europe in relation to the air war. The ruins of Teufelsberg's spy station or Anhalter's facade are read amongst an established lexicon of ruin images in the post-war Anglo-American imagination. This, argues Dillon (2005), is part of ruins' appeal, 'totter[ing] on the edge of *kitsch*' and 'endlessly repeatable' (para 16). The 'endlessly repeatable' image of ruins is similar to Benjamin's 'optical unconscious', an archive of memories of images on which we draw when interpreting a place (Dobraszczyk 2017, p. 34). As a ruin, both Teufelsberg and Anhalter are loaded with cultural and historical meanings of ruin-imagery that can be replicated to achieve cultural-political outcomes that are caught up in the continual production and reproduction of cultural memory of the war.

Figure 4.5 The ruins of Anhalter Bahnhof, Berlin. Photograph by Eloise Florence, 2017.

But what do these images communicate?[3] Common utilizations of ruins are difficult to pin down and predict. One more sinister expression also draws in the buried ruins of Nazi architecture beneath Teufelsberg, with which Hitler and Speer aimed to harness the aesthetic power of ruins and attach them to the 'future ruins' of Nazi architecture, which they believed would last hundreds of years. 'What had remained of the emperors of Rome?', Speer argued. 'What would still bear witness to them today, if their buildings had not survived?' (1970, pp. 55–6). Speer was drawing on what Clark (2015) argues is the function of ruined monuments to communicate memory across time. Clark points out how ruins can be a substitute for religion: ensuring temporal continuity, permanence, timelessness. 'To statesmen, ruins predict the fall of Empires', argues Woodward (2001), 'the futility of mortal man's aspiration' against time (p. 2). Woodward (2001) assures us 'regular people' view ruins as signs of transience, not permanence: 'To Hitler the Colosseum was not a ruin but a monument' (p. 30), but to the rest of us, Anhalter is a sign of the inevitability of time and nature over all human endeavour, the reassurance that even the most despicable of human endeavours like Hitler's Germany will fall to time, decay or Allied bombing raids.[4] This poses an ethical question: in Speer and Hitler's eyes, would the ruins of Anhalter evoke both the past and the future, the destruction of wars past, and the possibility of a future in which they were remembered as a glorious ancient empire (Zill 2011)?

The transience of Anhalter, its crumbling masonry and jagged edges, is therefore as much a warning as it is a comfort for those on the other side of their downfall.

There are also much more familiar utilizations of ruin imagery in the Anglo-American post-war lexicon than those of Hitler or Speer. Scenes of London torn apart by bombs, foundations exposed, civilians camped out in shelters, became emblematic of the Allied (particularly British) war experience, and were deliberately cultivated in the immediate post-war history-making projects of the British establishment as part of the 'good war' narrative. This narrative transformed London's houses, churches, museums, train stations, hotels, monuments, universities and libraries into sublime, almost magical ruins, that came to epitomize the national unity, solidarity and stoicism of the British Blitz Myth during the war. When London was transformed into ruins by aerial warfare, it became a 'powerful ideological symbol of civilian endurance' (Bell 2012, p. 157). In the intervening years, these images have continued to circulate through the historical consciousness of Western populations. Today, there are still several memorial sites in London in the ruins of bombed-out churches: St Giles Cripplegate and Christchurch Greyfriars are the two most well-known. In these instances, ruins of city buildings represent patriotism, persistence, stoic endurance, as well as sadness, pain and sacrifice.

This only adds to the nebulousness of Anhalter and Teufelsberg's ruins. At Anhalter, the familiar image of the ruined house, church or train station that has previously symbolized endurance, sadness and sacrifice in places like London accompanies Anglo-American visitors to this ruin in a very different context. One might encounter this familiar imagery in the capital of the nation that *caused* the destruction in London, destruction that came to epitomize civilian stoicism and endurance. As a tourist, it is possible to visit St Giles Cripplegate in London one day and Anhalter the next, even one in the morning and one in the evening. Anhalter therefore echoes an image familiar to visitors well versed in the normative Anglo-American cultural memory structures, not in the least the familiar tone of sadness and pain associated with urban wartime ruins. Somewhat radically, by echoing the imagery of the London Blitz but occurring in the context of a bombed Berlin, Anhalter has the potential to evoke this sadness and pain and direct it towards the citizens of Berlin. Arnold-de-Simine (2015) concludes visitors mourning through ruins 'are affected by the past in a way that would enable them to experience their own position and role in the complex micro – and macrostructures of fear, which cannot safely be positioned as the "other" in terms of time, geography, and ideology' (p. 102). There is potential for Anglo-American audiences to bring with them and apply the well-practised rhetoric and imagery of the London Blitz to Anhalter, and thus to the reality of Berlin's wartime destruction, without allowing the destruction to be safely othered in terms of time and geography.

Considering the familiar imagery of ruined London buildings in an unfamiliar setting – that of 'the enemy' and 'the bomber' – has the potential to 'make strange' Anglo-American narratives of the war that have remained largely unquestioned. This highlights the function of ruins that Edensor says is 'partly captured by the notion of the uncanny or *unheimlich*, wherein the familiar and homely suddenly become strange' (Edensor 2005b, p. 835). When the familiar and homely suddenly become strange, the system of representation through which one sees ruined buildings as emblematic in normative structures of cultural memory might be complicated, if not outright questioned. At the very least, the mythology of the London Blitz emerges as only one of many narratives, as but one way of framing the meaning of the destruction of a city from the air. In doing so, the veracity and totality of these narratives might be drawn into question, complicating these cultural memory structures.

Haunted ruins

Ruins also have a long history of being haunted:

> [Ruins] seethe with memories, but these wispy forms can rarely be confined. They haunt the visitor with vague intimations of the past, refusing fixity, and they also haunt the desire to pin memory down in place.
>
> (Edensor 2005b, p. 829)

Haunting is deeply disruptive. Walter Benjamin famously looked to ruins as a means of challenging the otherwise smooth and untroubled experience of modern cities: 'the visible presence of historical ruins … may awaken the viewer to history's forgotten or rejected voices and jolt him or her into seeing new political possibilities that may help "redeem" society' (in Dempsey 2007, p. 271). These forgotten and rejected voices are often conceptualized, as Edensor does, as ghosts. Till (2005) calls Berlin a city crowded with ghosts, 'unnamed, but powerfully felt absences' (p. 9), full of what Kolk (2020) calls unresolved, forgotten or suppressed history. Ladd (1997) argues that the city's 'buildings, ruins and voids groan under the burden of painful memories' (p. 3), the memories of the war 'cleave[d] onto the physical setting' (p. 1). Approaching Teufelsberg has a ruinous site is therefore a way to engage it as haunted, as a site that might seethe with these unnamed but powerfully present absences.

I wander through an open door in one of the abandoned buildings of Teufelsberg's spy station, picked at random. I turn right, walk through several dark graffitied hallways, turn left, push through another door, and another one after that. The interior of the building is dark, lit only by windows. It is cold after the blaze of the May sun, and smells heavily of dust. In a room with some old machinery, I find information boards and photographs lining the walls in a haphazard manner. On a small table at either end of the row of photographs is a brief explanation of the project. The exhibition is about the women who cleaned up Berlin after the war, cleaning and sorting rubble, and transporting loads of rubble to collection points that became the *Trümmerberge*. Their eyes, granite and black and white, stare at me quite intently.

It is not hard to feel the ruins of Teufelsberg are haunted. Even with the layers of graffiti, art installations, damage, deconstruction and reconstruction that accumulated once the listening station closed, the place seems to hold memories or presences of long-gone people, machinery, equipment, radar signals, dust, politics, mutually assured destruction. Inside the spy station, the multiple layers of time that have accrued on the hill become evident. The spy station's use as a listening post during the Cold War, a counter-culture centre in the post-reunification era, and as an art and events site today, coalesce and overlap in the dark, metal-lined rooms. Somewhat of a maze, there are many dark corners

Figure 4.6 The interior of the abandoned spy station at Teufelsberg, Berlin. Photograph by Eloise Florence, 2017.

and long corridors in which ghosts might lurk. From these corridors, American and British intelligence listened to their Stasi counterparts over the Wall. An American veteran who served at 'the hill' has described the loud music that was often played over the loudspeakers of the facility, 'to thwart any attempts to listen to conversations' (Cocroft & Schofield 2019, p. 49). In an archaeology of the listening station, Cocroft and Schofield (2019) describe the range and quantity of equipment that would have filled the rooms, providing a link to a YouTube video[5] of the sound of a teletype machine to suggest how one room might have sounded. The sound is loud, harsh, but quite satisfactory; one is keenly aware that a room full of such machines would create a distinctive cacophony of clicks and whirrs as intelligence streamed in from over the Wall. But the echoes of the past are also material; rusted machinery, exit signs, warning signs, desks, office chairs, graffiti on graffiti on graffiti. These traces of a time long past quite easily offer the possibility of ghosts, of powerfully present absences lurking in the corners of these old and otherwise abandoned buildings.

Bennett (2020) highlights the dangers of aestheticizing ruins, particularly those from the Cold War era. Aestheticization, they argue, risks erasing the people who inhabited, and more significantly, laboured, in these spaces. The traces of this labour might form a kind of haunting, lingering traces of the past not only as ephemeral, ghostly bodies, but as the material traces of the system of workers, spies, diplomats, base analysts, researchers and linguists (Cocroft & Schofield 2019; Smith & Shand 2016) who once wandered the halls. The spy station is host to tours by American veterans who served at the listening post, endowing the buildings with this labour of the past through storytelling and tourism. Whether this negates the risks of aestheticization isn't clear, but it does work to maintain the presence of people, labour and politics in these rooms, if only as ghostly presences.

In all, the spy station at Teufelsberg emerges as a site layered and laden with the past, even to the point of excess. Cocroft and Schofield (2019), who conducted an in-depth archaeology of the listening station and its history at the centre of Cold War intelligence gathering, nonetheless stated that as of 2019, 'the point has now been reached where the Teufelsberg has spent more time as derelict structures than as operational units, and all now have complex post-abandonment biographies' (p. 144). There are so many layers of history and graffiti it can be difficult to comprehend. What is key, however, is the disruptive potential of these layers, the unsettling nature of the site as haunted by nebulous and often shadowy ghosts of past people, events, machines and politics that refuse to remain assigned to neatly ordered episodes of history. Through this palimpsest of layers, Teufelsberg offers potential for complicated and nuanced forms of cultural memory.

Anhahlter Bahnhof's history as a site of the Holocaust means the ghosts that circle the site also have the potential to be disruptive of normative memory cultures about the Second World War. Behind the crumbling remains of its facade and the sports field that stands behind it, a visitor can find the original platforms of the overland station. Cracked and crumbling, these platforms remain in a heavily overgrown, somewhat derelict area, covered in rubbish and the bedding belonging to people sleeping rough. A walking track encircles the site and connects to a wider network across the city. There are birds in the trees in the summer, occasionally a runner or walker, and the hiss of trains coming in and out of the nearby S-Bahn station. Some red and white tapes encircle the area in 2017, come loose in some places.

From these platforms departed thousands of Berlin's (overwhelmingly Jewish) citizens, exported by the Nazis to Theresienstadt in Nazi-occupied Czechoslovakia, and from there to concentration camps. A small sign next to the ruined facade informs visitors of the operation, detailing the amount and date of departures. Rather than the ghosts of NSA operatives or post-reunification artists and musicians, the ghosts that haunt Anhalter are those of Holocaust victims. It's not difficult to imagine them standing on the platforms in their little

Figure 4.7 The remains of the original platforms at Anhalter Bahnhof, Berlin. Photograph by Eloise Florence, 2017.

groups, clutching suitcases, talking quietly. At Anhalter, the deportees are those ghosts and memories that 'have not been consigned to dark corners, attics, and drawers, or been swept away, reinterpreted and recontextualised' (Edensor, 2005b, p. 836). Anhalter, like Teufelsberg, can be thought of as one of these dark corners in which the ghosts of Berlin lurk, but because it is simultaneously a ruin of area bombing, Anhalter evokes and overlaps multiple, intersecting temporalities (Florence 2021).

A similarly haunted site, the Jewish memorial cemetery on Grosse Hamburger Strasse in Mitte, allows a similar temporal entanglement as Anhalter. As I explained in Chapter 3, the site was the resting place of many members of Berlin's Jewish community until it was closed in 1827. During the war it was not only desecrated by the Nazis, who used the centuries-old headstones to fortify the walls of an air raid shelter, but the neighbouring home for the elderly was used as a so-called 'collection point', a site where thousands of the city's Jews were told to gather before being sent to the death camps. Up to 2000 victims of air raids were also buried here during the war in a mass grave, and there is very good evidence that some top-ranking Nazis were even buried here in the closing days of the war, including Gestapo Director and Holocaust planner Heinrich Müller (Brown 2013). Today, the site has been marked by a memorial to Holocaust

Figure 4.8 The only photograph taken on my research visit to the Jewish memorial cemetery on Grosse Hamburger Strasse in Mitte, Berlin. Photograph by Eloise Florence, 2017.

victims (originally intended for the Ravensbrück concentration camp), and is a peaceful and overgrown space through which visitors can walk and sit.

I found the memorial cemetery to be teeming with ghosts. The site evoked the most noticeable affective response of all the sites I visited in my fieldwork. This is evidenced, if nothing else, by the noticeable lack of photographs I took during my site visit. At the other twenty-six sites I visited as part of my fieldwork, I took hundreds of photos, and thousands at Teufelsberg. At the memorial cemetery, I took just one, and one video. Whilst the Memorial for Murdered Jews of Europe closer to the city centre holds anger and horror, the cemetery was, for me, marked by only an incredible sadness. The sadness felt related to the *absence* of millions of people that was markedly noticeable at the site, Till's 'unnamed, but powerfully felt absences' (2005, p. 9). The memorial at the front gate of the cemetery, the remaining few gravestones lining the northern wall and the few gaps in the greenery where some gravestones had been returned and restored spoke a gentle but unblinking evocation of what was once here and what is no longer, traces of the centuries old culture, people and history the Nazis worked so hard to erase. The one video I took captures the birdsong I found so common and striking at these sites during a Berlin spring, as well as the almost mundane noises of the city – cars, bikes, tourists chatting, cheers from a nearby football match, children playing at the school nearby. On that beautiful spring day, the millions of murdered people sent into oblivion by the Nazis felt incredibly close. I am reminded of what W. G. Sebald writes of the blurred lines between life and death, both in his essays on Corsico (2006) and his novel *Austerlitz* (2001). In the latter, the titular figure speaks of his time as a child learning about ghosts from the neighbourhood cobbler, Evan:

> If you had an eye for them they were to be seen quite often, said Evan. At first glance they seemed to be normal people, but when you looked more closely their faces would blur or flicker slightly at the edges. And they were usually a little shorter than they had been in life, for the experience of death, said Evan, diminishes us, just as a piece of linen shrinks when you first wash it.
>
> (Sebald 2001, p. 75)

Sebald writes of the dead as among us, thinly separated from us by a substance no thicker than a veil, or a piece of cloth. And the dead seem close at both Anhalter and the memorial cemetery; perhaps because of the prevalent mundanity of the sites as compared to more 'sacred' sites such as the Memorial to the Murdered Jews of Europe or the remnants of the death camps. But more likely it is the physical presence of the dead one accepts when one visits a cemetery.

At the memorial cemetery, the awareness of 'what is missing' is accentuated by the memorial and the plaque at the front gate, but is also felt quite keenly in a more affective, haptic sense. 'While standing in this former cemetery, observers are clearly aware that they are looking at worlds that are forever gone,' argues Dempsey (2007, p. 270). Dempsey demonstrates how material traces allow the past to become available to the present and resist erasure, but the traces of the past at this cemetery are also distinctly immaterial. Haunting, Edensor (2005a) argues, occurs not in the form of 'empiricist, didactic or intellectual knowledge, but an empathetic sensual apprehension, understood at an intuitive level' (p. 847). It falls to a visitor, walking through a haunted site, encountering the sites in a material, sensuous way, to bring these ghosts out of the dark shadows under the trees. The deportees are huddled on Anhalter's platforms again, the masses of Berlin's Jews and the mass grave of victims of Allied bombs hover around the edges of the cemetery, but they are, in a way, imagined into being by this Anglo-American visitor, and the cultural imagery of the war and wartime Berlin that accompany her.

Importantly, and unfortably, the dead that I imagine are of *both* the Holocaust and area bombing. In the final days of the war, the cemetery on Grosse Hamburger Strasse was used as a mass grave for victims of aerial bombing (Black 2010).[6] I find this fact deeply disruptive, the knowledge that centuries of Berlin's Jews are buried alongside the dead from Allied air raids, and even possibly the remains of Nazi commanders. It is unsettling to consider the dead of the Holocaust at the same time I consider the mass grave of victims of air raids, or to consider the bombs falling on the Nazi air raid shelter at the same time Berlin's Jews were being assembled not 50 meters away for deportation and annihilation.

Haunting and time

With all these ghosts at Anhalter, Teufelsberg and the memorial cemetery, time feels 'out of joint' (Derrida 1994, p. 31), no longer following the rules of one-thing-after-another. Arnold-de-Simine (2015) points out that ruins 'suspend time altogether, allowing us to step out of history and question the neat linear temporality of historical progress' (p. 95). This recalls Gordon's (2011) assertion that haunting has effects on the linearity of time:

> Haunting raises specters, and it alters the experience of being in linear time, alters the way we normally separate and sequence the past, the present and the

future. These specters or ghosts appear when the trouble they represent and symptomize is no longer being contained or repressed or blocked from view.

(p. 2)

What is disruptive about the haunted platforms of Anhalter is that they are encountered in the context of the bombed and damaged portico of the station. Ghosts possess a certain kind of liveliness, and at Anhalter, like in the layered depths of Teufelsberg's rubble, the ghosts of the Holocaust intermingle with ghosts of the air war. The haunted cemetery also creates a sort of temporal entanglement. In a way akin to Teufelsberg's 'strata' of history, the memorial cemetery is also made up of several layers of Berlin's past. Like at Teufelsberg, where the episodes of Berlin's past become embroiled and interact in the soil, Berlin's history is a swirling mess of gravestones, air raid shelters and 'collection points' at the cemetery. This entanglement is violent; the graves of Berlin's Jews were viciously desecrated by the Nazis to build air raid shelters, the sacred headstones used to fortify walls. And again like Teufelsberg, these episodes of history are not held separate or in clearly defined layers, either literally or in material-discursive encounters. Similarly at Anhalter, the memory of the bombings reaches out and through the memory of the Holocaust to the present, seeping into the tangled mess of trees, platforms and rubbish.

At the Jewish memorial cemetery, this entanglement is uncomfortable and quite literal. Black (2010) calls the burial of a group of 'probably SS' men at the cemetery evidence that 'even as the Nazi state imploded, attempts were continually being made to claim as German those spaces that had been specifically Jewish' (p. 142). As far as researchers can tell from shreds of records and oral history, the ground contains traces of Berlin's deep rich Jewish history entangled with traces of men who set out to destroy that history, and further entangled with victims of the war that tried to stop those men. This is uncomfortable, borderline intolerable – desecrated Jewish graves mixed with Nazi remains. But it is again disruptive not only in the moral, sacrilegious sense described above by Black. The mixture of what lies beneath the cemetery is another kind of temporal entanglement, which disrupts the dominant Anglo-American structures of cultural memory of area bombing that position the bombings as a response to the Holocaust. These structures, outlined in Chapter 1, often rely on a conceptualization of time as the 'neat linear temporality of historical progress' (Arnold-de-Simine 2015, p. 95) that can be so disrupted by haunting (Florence 2021). Both narratively and temporally, the foundational assumption of these dominant frameworks for remembering the bombings involves viewing the bombings as occurring because of, ergo *following*, Nazi atrocities. This is despite, as I outline in Chapter 1, the fact that the full extent and horror of the Holocaust was not fully understood by British and American commanders until after 1945, nor was it ever cited as a reason for beginning and escalating the bombing campaigns (Hansen 2008).

A look to histories of bombing (many of which engage the objectivist military historical perspective on time discussed above) suggests that Berliners could have sheltered at the air raid shelter on Grosse Hamburger Strasse as bombs fell just hours before or after the last of Berlin's Jewish community was 'collected' for deportation nearby, or as they fell on Anhalter as the deportations took place. Deportations occurred from Anhalter during every month that saw Allied bombing raids on Berlin, with the exception of March 1943 and April 1945 (Grayling 2007).[7] The collections point near the memorial cemetery was established in 1942 and continued to operate through to February 1945 (Bella 2012; US Holocaust Museum, n.d.; Yad Vasham, n.d.), which overlaps with RAF bombing raids over Berlin in 1943, 1944, and 1945 (Grayling 2007). Therefore, one could reasonably assume that the machinations of the Holocaust and the violence of area bombing could have occurred contemporaneously, if not simultaneously.

However, these official histories, dates, statistics and chronologies aren't necessarily readily available for the Anglo-American visitor to Anhalter or the memorial cemetery. The actual chronology of the bombs literally falling upon machinations of the Holocaust as they operated is therefore almost irrelevant to the study of the cultural memory that might be formed at these locations. The chronology remains important to discussions of the morality, justifiability, effects and necessity of the bombings, as mentioned in Chapter 1 and explored in detail by many (Friedrich 2006; Grayling 2007; Maier 1988; Overy 2014; Schaffer 1988; Werell 1986). It is the *narrative* of simultaneity, and the affective entanglement of these past events that are available to Anglo-American visitors at the memorial cemetery, as they form and reform cultural memory and through this site, that it is of importance here. These events become both physically and affectively embroiled at Anhalter, the memorial cemetery and Teufelsberg. These episodes of history become less episodic or sequential, and therefore the narrative structures that rely on them being held separate begin to crumble. The liveliness of ghosts and the material entanglement at these sites allow the memory of area bombing and Nazi atrocities to intersect and interact, allowing a nuanced and complicated cultural memory of the war to emerge, one in which the violence of the bombings cannot be framed as a response to, and therefore justified by and even excused by, Nazi atrocities.

Conclusion

This first of four analysis chapters has begun the process of examining Teufelsberg as a way of opening up some of the more rigid and restrictive cultural memory frameworks around area bombing in Berlin. Beginning with the framework of strata, I first showed the limitations of approaching Teufelsberg as neat layers of Berlin's history laid upon one another, opting instead for considering Berlin's past, and thus the memory of its area bombing past, as a complex palimpsest of intersecting and interacting layers. Such a comprehension of the past is in keeping with Foucault's 'history of the present' laid out in Chapters 1, 2 and 3. A stratified conceptualization of history is central to more normative structures of the cultural memory of the war I explain in Chapter 1 and which this book seeks to disrupt. Burial and digging, common motifs associated with memory in Berlin, were also shown to be valuable as conceptual frameworks through which we might appreciate the memory of the bombings in the city, like at the Topography of Terror. But as motifs and metaphors, burial, digging and archaeology only get us so far with Teufelsberg; instead of being 'hidden beneath the surface', waiting to be revealed and understood like the Nazi remnants at the Topography of Terror, the memory of the bombings is more accurately heaped on top of and indeed made out of the surface of Teufelsberg. So too does ruin and ruination emerge as a potentially problematic epitomization of Albert Speer's 'theory of ruination' and the Romantic ruins so hijacked by the Nazis (Zill 2011), and popular visual ruin motifs of the Second World War that continue to influence contemporary Anglo-American notions of guilt, responsibility and victimhood.

Teufelsberg therefore offers new ways of remembering the air war that might complicate the normative structures of cultural memory outlined in Chapter 1. By examining Teufelsberg beyond the limiting motifs of burial and archaeology, encounters with the hill emerge as a technology of remembering the bombings that brings the underlying truths of some of the more established cultural narratives regarding the war into interaction with other episodes of Berlin's history. Furthermore, the motifs of ruination give rise to unexpected linkages of events, such as those of the London Blitz and Berlin's area bombing, complicating more traditional ways of understanding the war through ruins and ruination. Ruins are also well-known to be haunted, and taking the effects of haunting at Teufelsberg seriously opens up possibilities of understanding the bombings' relationship with the Holocaust, complicating the cultural memory of the war that relies on the two being held separate. Encountering the destruction of the falling bombings at the same time I encounter displays evidencing the Holocaust and Nazi atrocities at sites like Anhalter and the Jewish memorial cemetery opens up some of the more traditional ways of thinking about the responsibility and accountability of the Allies for mass civilian casualties, which are generally cast as justified by these atrocities. This chapter has therefore also reaffirmed the finding in Chapter 1 that the memory of Nazi atrocities plays a central role supporting Anglo-American cultural memory of area bombing. Entangling the results of a bombing campaign with the results of Nazi atrocities, like at these sites, allows the righteousness of the Allied cause (ending the Nazi regime) to exist alongside a more comprehensive accountability for the bodily and material damage caused by the Allies' air forces.

We move now to other ways of understanding the memory of the bombings at Teufelsberg and how these necessitate a more dispersed model of accountability in relation to deaths and destruction caused by the bombs. Another way of remembering the air war through and at Teufelsberg is through the networked systems that caused and accounted for the violence of the bombings. In the following chapter we will again see how this is inherently entangled with that of Nazi atrocities, and can thus complicate the hegemonic narrative structures of post-war cultural memory, leading to more nuanced, entangled forms of remembering.

5

Vibrant, unruly rubble

Introduction

I am struck by the insistence and persistence of the rubble. It is stubborn, intrusive, agentic. It trips me up, often grazes or cuts my skin, gets in my way as I try to navigate the forest. I can pick up the rubble pieces, throw them down the hill, but they (and gravity, fatigue, the hot sun) can similarly send me tumbling down the hill if I don't watch my step.

And yet overlaid with this is a continuing awareness of what the rubble is. The persistence and intrusiveness – the liveliness – of the rubble makes it all the more apparent, not only how these stones can act, but also how they have acted in the past. At times, the stones seem to hold the violence of the destruction of Berlin within them. Their activeness or disruption of my walk, combined with their status as records of violence, makes me suddenly very aware of their past as a participant in this violence. At other times, they're simply rocks.

A page of my notebook on which I muse on the origins of a particular rubble chunk I found bears a small brown mark. Blood, from a small graze on my hand, after the rubble pushed back, acted back and tripped me over.

***

This chapter explores the possibility of a dispersed model of accountability that might be engendered by considering the materials of Teufelsberg as *agentic*. It takes Jane Bennett's (2010) theory of vibrant materialism to radically expand what we can consider as 'agents' of change to include non-human materials and objects. Affording the rubble of Teufelsberg agency encourages us to remember the bombings as an assemblage of Latour's (2004) *actants* – objects with the capacity to act and create change, some of which are human, most of which are not (see also discussion in Chapter 3).

In her 2005 essay 'The Agency of Assemblages and the North American Blackout', and further expanded in her 2010 book *Vibrant Matter*, Bennett offers the example of a widespread blackout to understand an electrical power grid as an assemblage of *actants*:

> [a power grid] is a material cluster of charged parts that have indeed affiliated, remaining in sufficient proximity and coordination to function as a (flowing) system ... the elements of this assemblage, while they include humans and their constructions, also include some very active and powerful nonhumans: electrons, trees, wind, electromagnetic fields.
>
> (2005, p. 446)

The bombings, as a cultural, political, and technological phenomenon, can be remembered as a similar assemblage of many actants, some of which are human, but many of which are not: electricity, earth, paper, plastic, wind, metal, roof tiles, radio waves, propellers, cameras, uniforms, thermite, magnesium, phosphorous, air pressure, gravity. If we consider these materials, as Bennett does, as possessing a kind of agency, this spreads accountability and responsibility for death and destruction across this assemblage in cultural memory structures. The rubble over which I walk, which I pick up and trip over, with which I interact, is thus more active than a record of violence – it is a participant in this violence. This prompts interesting questions: can a metal casing of explosives, as well as – that is, not instead of – the humans who designed and manufactured it, be held 'accountable' for deaths? Can a toppled statue be 'responsible' for a changed memory culture?

In the context of both Teufelsberg and the other sites of memory considered in this chapter – Anhalter Bahnhof, the Topography of Terror, and the Gleis 17 memorial – blurring distinctions between human and non-human actants also reveals the humans and machines involved in the mechanized systems of violence of both the air war and the Nazis' genocide, particularly that of train stations (Anhalter and Gleis 17), which in turn feed into dominant cultural memory structures of area bombing. This chapter explores how long chains of cause and effect, technology, bureaucracy, intelligence networks and policy lengthen the emotional, psychological, moral, causal and conceptual distance between air war deaths and the individuals responsible for their violence. Specifically, I explore how this plays out in the Anglo-American cultural memory of area bombing where it overlaps and interacts with that of the Holocaust. The definition of a 'legitimate' target and the formulation of these definitions in relation to the operations of the Holocaust are at the heart of ongoing discussions about the legitimacy and morality of the Allies' bombing campaigns, and thus remain at the heart of the dominant memory structures surrounding the bombings explored in Chapter 1. As integral parts of the machinations of the Holocaust, the bombing of train stations (Anhalter and Gleis 17) and the political and administrative centre of Nazi terror (the buildings that once stood at the Topography of Terror) can be remembered as 'legitimate targets' in the Allies' war against the Nazis. However, each of these sites remains deeply embedded in the everyday function of Berlin as a city, thus making evident the dispersal of both the Nazis' and the Allies' violence across wide and complex systems of infrastructure, bureaucracy, policy, urban social and cultural functions, and more. Such a view of violence across a system allows for the drawing out of yet more actors and *actants* that can be imbricated in systematized violence like the bombings. However, this is not without ethical concerns. This chapter explores the contribution that a more dispersed network of accountability can make to the more restrictive Anglo-American memory cultures that continue to regulate who – and what – can and cannot be held accountable for mass deaths during the war.

Materials active in destruction

Area bombing of the Second World War transformed the buildings of Berlin into part of what Wigley (2002) calls an 'economy of violence' (p. 84). The stones of Teufelsberg were participants in their own destruction in the most literal sense. The damage of area bombing occurs not in the air but on the ground, argues Friedrich (2006). Most civilians were not really killed by the bombs but by their effects – falling masonry, firestorms, bomb shelters that became death traps. The bombs themselves did not cause the most damage to stone, but the fires they spread and propagated, and the avalanches of debris they created. In fact, the air raids were designed to turn German cities into a giant weapon against themselves and their inhabitants:

> [an air raid's] violence unfurled only … in burying people and property in rubble, in creating fire bridges and draft conditions in the buildings … The dwellings of generations did not merely split in two, they became masses of stone that struck people dead, glowing ovens that asphyxiated, dungeons that gassed to death …[1]
> [stone] was the main tool of the enemy, its most pernicious aggregate.
> (Friedrich 2006, p. 461)

Area bombing specifically targets built-up areas because of the self-perpetuating nature of incendiary and block-buster bombs on urban environments. The very nature of most German medieval Old Town districts was what made them such attractive targets to the Allies. Area bombing simply will not cause the same amount of damage in rural or sparsely populated areas. Closely packed buildings, attics full of flammable material – books, documents, artwork, photographs, clothing – and narrow, inescapable streets, made the Old Town centres of German cities the materials for their own destruction.

The Allies systematically planned their attacks based on how incendiary they determined different districts of German cities and towns to be. Using reports by geographer R. E. Dickinson, the Research and Experiment Department of the British Air Ministry designed maps that split German cities into zones that corresponded to population and building densities. The zones were assigned based on which densities would provide the best conditions for creating firestorms. This guide to the flammability of German cities was nicknamed 'The Bomber's Baedeker', and contained descriptions of cities such as this one of Kassel:

> The Old Town area of zone 1 in Kassel is considered to be of a higher degree of vulnerability of IB [incendiary bomb] attack than the 18th century Town or the

Figure 5.1 Rubble in the forest at Teufelsberg, Berlin. Photograph by Eloise Florence, 2017.

closely built up areas extended northward. This is due to the mixed character of the buildings, the absence of normal compartmentalisation by visible parapeted fire walls and the presence of narrow winding streets.

(qtd. in Hohn 1994, p. 228)

The rubble at Teufelsberg, as well as being records of this violence, is therefore also a participant. The seemingly inert matter of bricks and ceramics at Teufelsberg can emerge as active players in a system of physical, bodily violence. The rubble is an *actant* in the assemblage of 'the bombings', as well as in practices of cultural memory (as discussed in Chapter 2). The possibility of material substances being active participants in destruction relates to some of the fundamental ways we conceive our relationship with our built environment, but also to the ways we assign agency beyond the human.

Many scholars, both preceding and drawing on Bennett (2010), have begun taking the agency of non-human actors in violence seriously. Some have looked beyond the human and built environments to animals. When defined by its agents – rather than its 'perpetrators' – Driscoll (2019) argues political violence has always been 'a multispecies affair' (p. 199). Tim Cole (2014) has examined of the 'role' of trees and forests in Holocaust victims and survivors' experiences of hiding and escaping Nazi persecution as a way of exploring the place of environmental history in Holocaust studies (and the Holocaust in environmental history). Cole argues 'nature functioned both materially and imaginatively during the Holocaust and its postwar retelling' (p. 667), identifying forests and trees as simultaneously disorienting, havens, benevolent and insufficient. Pointing specifically the violence of European colonization, Driscoll (2019) points out how the projects were carried out not only by humans against animals but also involved the use of animals against humans. Driscoll details how the very ontological distinction between human and non-human (which the discipline of animal studies pushes against) is at the heart of projects of colonization and genocide, but colonization was also carried out *by* non-humans, an 'array of animals, from domestic animals and livestock to vermin and microbes, which played a crucial role in the colonial project' (p. 199). Gregory (2016) similarly examines the militarization of the non-human as a form of weaponization, exploring the function of gravity, stone and air pressure as agents in the destruction of bodies and houses in the major wars of the twentieth century. Gregory looks to the potential for vibrant matter to be violent matter, matter with capacity to inflict damage, violence, suffering. Gregory examines the mud and trenches of the Western Front as a non-human actor with capacity for violence, 'bio-physical formations that became entangled with armed conflict' (p. 4). Gregory goes on:

> In much the same way that "space" is not only a terrain over which wars are waged ... but also a medium through which military and paramilitary violence is conducted, so "nature" is more than a resource bank whose riches can trigger armed conflict and finance its depredations: the problematic of resource wars and conflict commodities ... nature too is a medium through which military and paramilitary violence is conducted.
>
> (p. 4)

Considering the shock of the 2001 9/11 terrorist attacks to the American psyche, Wigley (2002) documented a shift in the way Americans think about danger and safety in relation to architecture. Wigley argues that in their destruction, the two towers of the World Trade Centre became more than inert matter that was attacked by terrorists. As falling steel beams crushed office workers, collapsed and burning staircases trapped hundreds of people 500 meters above the ground, as the immense forces of a falling building pulverized concrete, melted steel, and turned bodies into dust, the buildings around us suddenly seemed not only active, but volatile:

> Things that we have been living with for some time were disturbingly revealed. The everyday idea that architecture keeps the danger out was exposed as a fantasy. Violence is never a distant thing. Security is never more than a fragile illusion. Buildings are much stranger than we are willing to admit. They are tied to an economy of violence rather than simply a protection from it.
>
> (Wigley 2002, pp. 83–4)

A history of the violence of area bombing must therefore take account of this capacity of the non-human, the seemingly inert matter of buildings, mud, water and the more obviously 'lively' matter of animals, microbes and gravity, to create and perpetuate violence.

Whilst these scholars argue for taking these non-human presences more seriously in histories of violence, including those of the Holocaust, many do not go so far as to attribute the trees and steel beams and mud their own *agency*. This is, I will explore below, largely because the concept of agency remains tied up with that of intent, a rational quality traditionally reserved for humans. However, in later writing Cole (2020) draws out how environmental histories can 'expand the range and nature of actors studied as we seek to understand genocide and its aftermath ... the range and nature of sources and methods drawn upon in genocide research ... [and] the chronological boundaries of study when conceptualizing histories of genocide' (p. 273). It is this sense of expansion, of incorporating more actors, sources and boundaries of 'what counts' when assigning accountability that I incorporate in my analyses of assemblages of violence like the bombings. Bennett's (2010) Latourian approach to agency takes this expansion most seriously, and specifically attributes agency to an expanded range of actors. This is done, as we shall see, by a decoupling of agency from the human, and a posthuman view of affect and effect.

Distributed accountability

To rise to the question of 'who' or 'what' might be remembered as 'responsible' for the large-scale destruction of the bombings, I now introduce the formulation of actor network theory (Latour 2004) so effectively explored by political theorist Jane Bennett in relation to a massive blackout (2005; 2010) and explored earlier in Chapter 2. When the boundary between human and non-human forces dissolves, as it does in the posthuman view, questions of responsibility for destruction are drawn outward, and encapsulate many different players, both human and non-human. The agency Bennett (2010) affords matter, against which I brush while walking Teufelsberg and tripping on its stones, disperses agency and therefore accountability, horizontally across a networked assemblage of all these elements. This, as I will outline below, has radical implications for questions of moral responsibility, the chief of which is the potential uncoupling of accountability from intentionality.

Bennett's (2010) theory of distributive agency draws on Spinoza's (1992) 'affective bodies' and Deleuze and Guattari's (1988) 'assemblages'. Bennett looks to assemblages as 'living, throbbing grouping, webs with uneven topographies' (p. 23). Across this topography is power, which, while not evenly distributed (see Chapter 2), nonetheless crosses the human/non-human divide. Bennett posits that agency, in the sense that something has the capacity to effect change, is distributed across this assemblage, that is, the assemblage, as a confederacy of actors, has its own capacity to act and make change:

> On close-enough inspection, the productive power that has engendered an effect will turn out to be a confederacy, and the human actants within it will themselves turn out to be confederations of tools, microbes, minerals, sounds, and other 'foreign' materialities. Human intentionality can emerge as agentic only by way of such a distribution.
>
> (Bennett 2010, p. 37)

Viewing political violence such as the bombings as assemblages allows a way of 'capturing the interelationality of discourses, institutions, materiality, and power relations' that contribute to that violence (Grayson 2016, p. 2). Intentionality is identified as a human-centric notion, which Bennett's 'emergent causality' theory pushes against. Bennett and those preceding her draw agency away from intentionality and free will, or 'the realm of the rational human(ist) subject' (Driscoll 2020, p. 201). 'An intention becomes like a pebble thrown into a pond', argues Bennett (2005), 'or an electrical current sent through a wire, or a neural network: it vibrates' (p. 475). 'Rather than being the property of this or that individual, agency by this definition is instead an emergent effect of the interaction between various agents' (Driscoll 2020, p. 200). Distributed agency shifts the focus to a linked series of effects, 'the cascade of becomings' (Bennett 2005, p. 457), decentring both the individual and rational intention from discussions of accountability and responsibility.

Expanding what (and who) we consider agentic in the assemblage of a bombing raid requires an expanded definition of accountability, cause and effect, even moral responsibility. Despite drawing on Bennett heavily to explore the emergent causality of the bombings, this chapter does not offer an in-depth exploration of the effects of such emergent causality on *moral* ethics or responsibility of the air war – to do so would grossly overstep my qualifications and the scope of this book. What this chapter does explore is the effects that such a model of accountability, when engendered as a way of remembering at and through Teufelsberg's agentic and active rubble, may be a key way in which the established cause-and-effect narrative at the centre of dominant cultural memory discourses about area bombing can be disturbed.

Billy Pilgrim encounters a host of actors involved in the bombings when he becomes 'unstuck in time'[2] (Vonnegut 2000, p. 19). Billy is the protagonist in Kurt Vonnegut's *Slaughterhouse Five* (2000). Billy (like Vonnegut) survives the infamous February 13 firestorm created by the American air force in Dresden in 1945. But unlike their countrymen dropping incendiaries, both Billy and Vonnegut experienced the raid on the ground as American prisoners of war. In the novel, Billy watches a movie about the American crews who dropped the bombs 'backwards, then forwards again' (p. 60). As Billy watches, the bombings play out in reverse:

> Seen backwards by Billy, the story went like this:
> … The formation flew backwards over a German city that was in flames. The bombers opened their bomb bay doors, exerted a miraculous magnetism which

shrunk the fires, gathered them into cylindrical steel containers, and lifted the containers into the bellies of the planes. The containers were stored neatly in racks ... When the bombers got back to their base, the steel cylinders were taken from the racks and shipped back to the United States of America, where factories were operating night and day, dismantling the cylinders, separating the dangerous contents into minerals. Touchingly, it was mainly women who did this work. The minerals were then shipped to specialists in remote areas. It was their business to put them into the ground, to hide them cleverly, so they would never hurt anybody ever again.

(Vonnegut 2000, pp. 60–1)

Vonnegut's depiction of the bombings 'unstuck from time' unfurls outward to implicate some of the many additional actors that were and are a part of the bombings. Introducing Bennett's (2010) idea of human and non-human matter to the bombings similarly widens what we can consider the scope of *actants* involved in the bombings, opening up questions of who and what we might consider 'responsible' for the destruction.

Below I explore the effects of such an expansion on narratives of historical responsibility, but for now it is worth examining what becomes encapsulated if we widen the net(work) to capture more actors that are involved in the bombings.

An expanded network

The assemblage of the bombings, if approached as Bennett does the North American blackout, threatens to stretch ever outwards without limits (and this is precisely the point). 'Area bombing of German cities in the Second World War' is an assemblage with similar characteristics to that of the North American blackout, with material elements, both human and non-human, that work together and affect one another but also take on their own agency, the agency *of* the assemblage. In order to comprehend the implications of viewing the bombings in this way, we must first survey who and what nodes, agents or *actants* might be caught in this network. This entails both widening the field of vision and pushing through the divide between the human and non-human.

To look first to some of the non-human elements that might be included in this networked assemblage. The metal casings, high explosives, incendiary materials and chemicals of the bombs are included, as are the raw materials of these chemicals, phosphorus, magnesium, ammonium nitrate and those of the planes that dropped them. When considering the runs of the bombers over

Germany, we turn then to gravity, air resistance, wind, light, propulsion, navigation. Elements here are not only non-human but often not earthly: RAF navigators used the stars to find their way over Germany and therefore in the selection and plight of victims on the ground. The moon played its part, strictly limiting the times and amounts of Bomber Command's missions. The dark of moonless nights provided cover for RAF pilots, but the blackouts of German towns often confused navigators and resulted in the turning back of planes or the dropping of bombs indiscriminately (Overy 2013). Blackouts – themselves an assemblage of the human and non-human actors so aptly described by Bennett – had agency over the outcomes of missions, over the results of the bombs loaded into planes. Weather proved vital in the shockingly inaccurate hit-rates of early Bomber Command raids (Overy 2013), which often resulted in more civilian deaths than destruction of key strategic targets like railroads or oil refineries. The British Research and Experiments Department of the Ministry of Home Security employed scientists who specialized in anatomy, physics and explosives to study the effects of blasts and fire on the human body and residential architecture to inform a strategy of mass bombing urban areas. The chemistry of incendiary bombs that wreaked such havoc on the ground can be seen as the result of alternatively fruitful and frustrating interactions between the human (scientists) and the non-human (magnesium).

Unshackled from temporal frames of the raids themselves, as Billy Pilgrim is, this network also reaches outward to implicate factory supply lines, kilometres of railways, endless paper trails and chains of command that form production lines that supplied the bombing runs, the factories and mines that made bombs and munitions, the trains that transported them. The network not only stretches across the boundaries of human and non-human but also across geography: the bombs fell on Germany but left the ground in Britain, on planes flown by pilots from France, the Netherlands, Norway, Czechoslovakia and Poland, trained in Canada, Australia and New Zealand. They were made with parts made all over Britain from raw materials sourced from all over the British Empire and American import networks. The American Airforce set up a truck transport system that moved 1.5 million ton-miles each month (Overy 2013, p. 317). Their storage facilities covered more than 9 million square feet.

Attached to this supply network are the humans who have not yet been implicated into mainstream cultural cause-and-effect models of responsibility for the bombings: RAF and USAAF pilots and their commanders and department heads, obviously, but also British and American factory workers, weapons experts, clerks and secretaries at manufacturing companies, public servants, radar technicians, the workers Billy sees working day and night 'dismantling the cylinders, separating the dangerous contents into minerals' (Vonnegut 2000, p. 19). This includes aircraft fitters, training and operational training units personnel, labourers, builders, technical specialists. Aircrew and their support staff also spent time in the civilian communities in which their bases were located, drawing in countless civilians: bartenders, cooks, bus drivers, billet hosts. 'The nature of air battle required numerous well-equipped permanent bases, and extensive maintenance organisation, a large stock of spares and, in the case of the Eighth Air Force, a long trans-oceanic logistics tail' (Overy 2013, p. 312–3). By the end of the war British Bomber Command was made up of a combat strength of 49,000 air crew with a supporting force of 174,000 men and women, 'a ratio of 1:3.5' (Overy 2013, p. 313). The factories, air bases and training facilities were manned by cleaners, bakers, drivers, waste management, builders, medics, nurses, drawing this 'long logistics trail' into the ever-expanding assemblage of the bombings.

Then there is the ever-expanding network caught up in the *effects* of the bombings: air raid shelters, mud, concrete, nets strung over the Unter den Linden to hide the street from view, flak towers, battery guns, evacuation trains, radar systems, anti-radar systems, searchlights. If uncoupled from time we can draw in the rubble itself that was heaped into Teufelsberg, the carts, wheelbarrows, trowels and shovels of the famous *Trümmerfrauen* cleaning up the streets, the chalk of the messages scribbled on the ruins of houses by people searching for survivors. The assemblage moves ever outwards, drawing in more and more *actants*.

This somewhat indulgent listing of just some of the possible *actants* in the assemblage of the bombings is not an attempt to fully and thoroughly account for *all* the actants in this assemblage in any kind of comprehensive or systematic way. Nor is it to say that all the actors, human and non-human, in this assemblage are responsible for the mass deaths and destruction of the bombing raids.[3] Rather, it is to show the radical potential of expanding this frame of reference – if one 'extends the time frame or widens the angle of vision on the action' as Bennett (2005, p. 458) says – to have implications for disrupting dominant structures of understanding the air war and historical responsibility. Much of these structures rely on somewhat restrictive, rationalist, unilateral flows of cause-and-effect: the Nazis committing atrocities and *therefore* the Allies bombing their cities, which I explore in Chapter 1, is just one example. Bennett calls this 'billiard-ball causality' (2005, p. 458). Haunting and the possibility of spectral and material entanglement explored in Chapter 4 offers one way of disrupting this directional flow of time and cause-and-effect. Properly engaging the vitality of sites like Teufelsberg offers another, in that it forces us to expand our scope of who or what is capable of affecting change and enacting violence. In turn, this holds potential to draw in new and unexpected actors into the question: who can be remembered as responsible for the deaths and destruction of the bombings? It is these effects of a distributed model of agency on historical responsibility that I argue can have implications for the dominant models of cultural memory surrounding the air war, and to which I now turn.

Dispersed accountability and narratives of historical responsibility

What might it mean to assign accountability across the assemblage of the bombings when remembering? Can a man be held accountable for writing the memo that results in an air raid over a small town and kills civilians? Can the pen he used be held accountable? Or the paper? And, perhaps most importantly, if the pen and paper are ensnared in this networked accountability, is the man *less* accountable?

Bennett (2005; 2010) argues the purpose of a dispersed model of agency is not to absolve responsibility from any one *actant* or even to dilute responsibility across many individual actors. Dispersed agency widens the scope of who and what can be held accountable. Individual *actants* are never absolutely removed from this network of accountability but neither are they ever made solely responsible. A dispersed model of accountability broadens, rather than dilutes, the loci at which responsibility rests. Bennett (2005) is careful to assert that she is not ignoring the notion of 'efficient causality', where a force is identified as the most responsible for an identified effect:

> To understand agency as distributive is not to deny this kind of causality. George W. Bush and his advisers, for example, can be said to be the efficient cause of the post-9/11 invasion of Iraq. But if one extends the time frame or widens the angle of vision on the action, such billiard-ball causality falters and appears as only one of the operative modes of causality. Alongside singular and integral agents, one finds a more diffuse or distributed series of actants, with partial, overlapping, and conflicting degrees of power.
>
> (2005, p. 458)

In a vertical concept of agency – which underpins most structures of cultural memory in English-language populations – Hitler and the Nazis fulfil this role of the 'efficient cause' for the bombings. Efficient causality identifies only *the most* responsible party, and the bombing raids on German cities are therefore traced back to head of RAF Bomber Command Arthur 'Bomber' Harris and Commander of US Strategic Air Forces Carl Spaatz, but ultimately to Hitler's declaration of war, disdain for international peace and morality, and the determination to exterminate the Jews of Europe.

In place of this, Bennett (2005) offers 'emergent causality' (p. 459). Emergent causality opens up this 'billiard-ball' relationship of cause-and-effect to be profoundly non-linear:

> Emergent causality is another way of conceiving a nonlinear, indirect causality, where instead of an effect obedient to a determinant, one finds circuits where effect and cause alternate position and redound back upon each other.
>
> (p. 459)

The vibrant materiality of Teufelsberg allows for the responsibility for mass violence to be seen more in terms of this emergent causality. Teufelsberg brings the agentic and unruly matter of the stones to the foreground, blurs notions of natural and human efficacy, brings bodily violence into contact with normative visual perspectives and thus brings a wide-spread network of *actants* involved in the bombings into view. Remembering through Teufelsberg allows us to encounter the governments and military of the Allies positioned somewhere *within* this network of causality. This network includes Hitler and the Nazis *as well as* the metal hulls of Lancasters made by British labourers, the pilots that flew them and the bodies that were struck by the bombs they dropped. Dispersing responsibility in this way, rather than alleviating German historical guilt, instead simply broadens the 'angle of vision' (Bennett 2010, p. 458) to encompass Allied as well as Germans *actants,* along with the phosphorous and rivets and hulls of planes, when remembering destruction.

Through such an expansive model of accountability I hope to widen the scope of who can and cannot be considered 'responsible' for mass deaths and violence in dominant cultural memory structures of the Second World War. But, as Cole points out, 'expanding the range of actors (and factors) beyond the human raises questions that are not simply historiographical and methodological, but also ... ethical' (2020, p. 274). There is a danger, as Cole and others point out, that the dispersion of accountability can lead to a *dilution* of responsibility. There is therefore a need to draw 'a line between making the claim that nature mattered and matters, without this being mis-read as either excusing human behaviour on the part of the perpetrators, or downplaying human experience on the part of the victims' (Cole 2020, p. 274). Might taking

Figure 5.2 Rubble pieces entwined with vines and leaf litter at Volkspark Prenzlauerberg, a *Trümmerberg* in Berlin. Photograph by Eloise Florence, 2017.

the agency of the stones I slip on at Teufelsberg *more* seriously in the violence of the bombing cause me to take the agency of the men who dropped the bombs *less* seriously?

Howard Zinn (1997), himself a bombardier during the war, identifies the so-called 'kill-chain' that selected and destroyed targets an 'infinite chain of causes, that infinite dispersion of responsibility' (in Gregory 2011, p. 279) across the many actors involved in wartime destruction. Such a problem has been raised in relation to contemporary aerial bombing, in which selecting and destroying a target is carried out by a range of actors, some of which are human – although often geographically distant from the target – and many of which are not, such as software programs and remote sensing technology:

> With the stretched and de-centralized network of kill-chains, UAVs and precision weapons, concentrating the focus and strike of the target into ever decreasing circles of intensity, the so-called 'reach-back' of the drone's targeting process, from the Area of Operations to air force bases thousands of miles away, makes deliberation over who is a combatant increasingly imprecise.
>
> (Adey et al. 2011, p. 178)

Gregory (2011) argues that in the context of the Second World War this chain of cause and effect diffuses accountability and responsibility for the destruction

Figure 5.3 Remnants of a metal pipe at Teufelsberg, Berlin. Photograph by Eloise Florence, 2017.

and deaths caused by the falling bombs. In fact, it is its purpose. It is therefore possible that opening this network to non-human actors only offers more potential for dilution. If the metal casing of a bomb or a falling wall of masonry is active in the death of a German civilian, does it render the pilot who dropped the bomb 'less' responsible? What can it mean to take seriously non-human actors as 'perpetrators'?

This question, I argue, is also indicative of the continually restrictive and binary understandings of 'victim' and 'perpetrator' that I discuss in Chapter 1 and which continue to regulate dominant memory cultures of the Second World War. Driscoll (2020) specifically explores the possibility of the non-human perpetrator through the lens of animal studies. He looks to the use of guard dogs in patrolling the Berlin Wall during the Cold War and the fences of concentration camps during the Second World War, or European settlers using vermin and microbes in their projects of colonization:

> No doubt whatever guilt or responsibility these animals bear for these processes is only 'by association', yet those processes could not have taken place in this way without their involvement. Clearly, it is inadequate, therefore, to conceive of them as purely passive objects or 'tools' in the hands of human actors.
>
> (p. 199)

Figure 5.4 Berliners enjoy the summer in Volkspark Hasenheide, a park built on a *Trümmerberg*. Photograph by Eloise Florence, 2017.

Driscoll, a perpetrator studies scholar, looks to the agency of animals in these violences as close to a 'scope for action' (p. 200), perpetrator studies term used to describe the actions available to individuals within a system of violence. In perpetrator studies, assigning responsibility must take into account this scope for action, rather than just an individual's intention, and how this scope is bounded in a geopolitical system of violence: 'Even in humans, agency is always contingent and only ever expressed in relation to a given set of circumstances, many of which will be beyond the individual's control' (p. 200). The set of circumstances, events, effects and other actors in which we are imbricated becomes more important than pure, rational(ist) intentionality, when considering things like guilt and responsibility.

In ways that have clear implications for the dominant Anglo-American memory cultures of the air war, such a lens on accountability allows for a more flexible understanding of the 'categories' of 'perpetrator' and 'victim', providing 'a recalibrated understanding of humanist history and subjectivity that displaces (without entirely eliminating) the positions of victim and perpetrator' (Rothberg 2013, p. xvi). In memory and trauma studies, Rothberg[4] has drawn on the term 'implicated subjects', to speak of individuals – humans, specifically – who are 'more than bystanders and something other than direct perpetrators' (2013, p. xv) in systems of violence. Pointing particularly to the structures of globalization that underpin this dispersal of cause and effect across broad and complex supply chains, Rothberg points to the simple fact that most of us are 'beneficiaries of a system that generates dispersed and uneven experiences of trauma and wellbeing simultaneously' (p. xv), and therefore implicates us in this trauma. Because of this dispersal of agency across the assemblages in which we are caught, we are, Rothberg argues, 'neither simply perpetrator nor victim, though potentially either or both at other moments' (p. xv). This echoes Alaimo's (2016) reflection on 'the networks of harm and responsibility that entangle even the most modest of actions' (p. 2). It is this nuanced, 'both/and also' approach to the categories of guilt and innocence that has the most potential complicate dominant articulations of the cultural memory of the air war.

Implications: Networked accountability for area bombing

A networked model of accountability is disruptive to the cultural memory of area bombing in that it does not allow actors – be they human or not – to fall only into the established categories surrounding responsibility that have come to be applied to the cultural memory of the war: victim, perpetrator, witness, complicit, bystander, guilty, innocent. As I discuss in the opening chapter, these categorizations restrict accountability being taken for mass deaths during the war by groups other than the Nazis, largely because under this model one cannot simultaneously be a victim *and* a perpetrator. But viewing accountability as distributed, as Bennett does, allows for these constrictive categorizations to dissolve somewhat, and allow the possibility of an actor being both a perpetrator and victim. Their historical responsibility, guilt, innocence or position as a witness is determined not by absolute, linear models of cause and effect, but rather by their position in intersecting networks of agency – an assemblage.

The effects of such a model of accountability on the traditional memory constructs surrounding the Second World War are profound. These memory constructs are built and continually rebuilt around binaries of good and evil, guilty and innocent, perpetrator and victim. An assemblage view of the bombings as allowed by the vibrant materiality of Teufelsberg might trigger a more nuanced remembering of the air war wherein these categories dissolve. In the least, it reveals the restrictive binaries underpinning the narratives that continue to regulate who can and cannot be held responsible for mass deaths during the war. At best, it can hold Allied actors accountable for these mass deaths without detracting from their role in defeating a genocidal regime, or detracting from the immense historical guilt and responsibility of Germany and Nazi perpetrators and collaborators for other and indisputably more significant mass deaths.

Conceptual distances

Such a view of assemblages 'emphasises the relationality of component parts, the incorporation of disparate elements (including the non-human), their power dynamics, and the plasticity of assemblages' (Grayson 2016, p. 15). Assemblage thinking calls for a radical expansion of who and what is included, but it also appreciates the inter-related nature of these components. In fact, it is in this interrelatedness that an *actant* finds its 'thing power' (Bennett 2010, p. xvi), its capacity to effect change:

> While the smallest or simplest body or bit may indeed express a vital impetus, conatus or *clinamen*, an actant never really acts alone. Its efficacy or agency always depends on the collaboration, cooperation, or interactive interference of many bodies and forces.
>
> (Bennett 2010, p. 21)

The assemblage of the bombings therefore also emerges as a bureaucratic one. The network includes analysts, commanders, strategists, clerical staff, operations support, radar technicians. And within this incredibly complex system are yet more non-human actants: interdepartmental committees, communiques, doctrines, technical guides, memos, paper, wire, ink, typewrites, chairs, seals, envelopes, paper clips. Engaging the bureaucracy of the assemblage of the bombings also demonstrates Bennett's assertion that assemblages have their own agency derived from the interaction of its components.

Through the lens of the bureaucracy of the bombings we can see quite clearly the agency of an assemblage acting almost outside a single human's or group of humans' 'intentionality'. Many have described the impetus of the area bombing campaign as it was operationalized through bureaucracy and chains of command as taking on 'a life of its own', that once it had begun there was no stopping it.[5] Military historian Richard G. Davis (1991) said that by July 1944 'the notion of massive missions directed against German civilians morale had, like many bureaucratic notions, began to gain its own momentum' (p. 94). Sebald (2004) writes that from the organizers' point of view, 'so much intelligence, capital, and labour went into the planning of destruction that, under the pressure of all the accumulated potential, it *had* to happen in the end' (p. 65, original emphasis). The inherent bureaucracy of the area bombing campaigns not only disperses responsibility but also disperses cause-and-effect, creating agency from the very fact it is an assemblage. Despite being driven by very human decision-making, it was not through one single decision, nor through one non-human act that the Allies destroyed Berlin and created Teufelsberg and the other *Trümmerberge*. The assemblage of the bombings held agency because of the inherent relationality of its composite *actants* – '[an assemblage's] efficacy or agency always depends on the collaboration, cooperation, or interactive interference of many bodies and forces' (Bennett 2010, p. 21). Bennett continues: 'Each member and protomember of the assemblage has a certain vital force, but there is also an effectivity proper to the grouping as such: an agency *of* the assemblage' (p. 24). Gregory (2011) calls the 'kill chain' – the process of identifying and destroying targets in aerial bombing – 'a matrix of measurements, a lethal calculus that abstracted, ensnared, and transformed living cities into dead ones' (p. 267). Gregory explores this conceptual yet deeply material process of abstraction (which I will explore in more detail in Chapter 6) and identifies that many of the cities destroyed by Allied raids were destroyed 'from the moment the intelligence photographs land[ed] safely at Bomber Command' (p. 270).[6]

In practice, the ever-expanding network of actors worked to lengthen the conceptual distance between intent, decisions and their effects. The American air force and the RAF formulated 'targets' out of German cities through a system that thoroughly detached the destruction from its human perpetrators and, by extension, its human victims. This detachment lingers in popular imaginings of the bombings today, not in the least in recollections of the aircrew, a chief medium through which populations remembered and continue to remember the war, not in the least because of the disproportionately high death rates in Bomber Command as compared to the rest of the British military during the war. For example, after flying as a navigator for the RAF, Australian bombardier Harold Nash recalled trying to comprehend the people on the ground during his missions: '[T]hey weren't people to me, just the target. It's the distance and the blindness which enabled you to do these things' (in Taylor & Davidson 2012, p. 447). This detachment has thoroughly characterized Anglosphere representations of aerial bombing, which are explored in the more representational and optic sense in Chapter 6.

Gregory argues the Allies deliberately conceptually transformed the cities into abstract 'targets' in order to carry out the bombings within the confines of morality:

> [each air force] rationalized its own kill-chain by subdividing its production and regulating its practices through standard operating procedures. This rationalization entailed not only an abstraction of the target *but also an abstraction of the process through which the target was produced*, which was made to appear inevitable – target as telos – and its destruction the terminus of a more or less 'natural' history.
>
> (p. 270, original emphasis)

Adey, Whitehead, and Williams (2011) identify this system and its lengthening of the conceptual distance between perpetrator and target as the system that enables aerial warfare, particularly modern drone warfare:

> aerial targeting seems to work precisely because it subjects its users to a distanced and rational bureaucratic orientation, so that the effects of their actions can never be fully realized.
>
> (p. 180)

I will explore the implications of verticality and aerial imagery on conceptualizations of violence further in Chapter 6. But it is important to note here how extending the 'frame of action', as Bennett (2010, p. 34) writes, allows the very networks that were used to separate the destruction on the ground from human agency to be brought into view, circumventing 'the existential difficulty of recognizing the ruined landscape as the product of human action' (Gregory 2011, p. 265). These lengthened conceptual distances allowed by the complexity of the assemblage of the bombings mean their devastation is often considered outside the realm of human capabilities,[7] and therefore almost foregoes completely the need to assign an identity to the perpetrator. Again I have discussed the ethics of this expansion of agency above, but it is worthwhile pointing out that this dispersal or dilution of responsibility is already existing in these dominant frames of understanding the bombings.

I turn now briefly to three other sites at which an expansive and disruptive sense of accountability emerges as a system of language, bureaucracy and infrastructure, drawing one's attention to the wider networked assemblages involved in violence. One I've mentioned above – the Topography of Terror, or what are today the remains of the administrative and political centre of the Nazis and SS in Berlin, bombed, demolished, buried and dug up across the second half of the century. Another two are train stations from which thousands of Berlin's

Jews were deported – Anhalter Bahnhof and Gleis 17 at Grunewald Bahnhof. As well as sites of aerial destruction from bombing, these sites are well-known and marked as cogs in the machine of the Holocaust through texts and signs. These three sites therefore also emerge as what we might call 'legitimate targets' of area bombing. This marks them as sites around which the more dominant frames of cultural memory regarding the air war can coalesce, particularly those of justification and retribution.

A quick aside on comparisons of systematized violence: the consideration of the Holocaust as an assemblage, and the implications of this on historical moral and/or legal responsibility, is not the purpose of this section nor of the book. A networked model of accountability, Bennett identifies, poses problems for the dispersal of responsibility, which become ethical problems when applied to systems of violence, and these are no more pronounced than when they are explored in relation to the Holocaust. A conceptual, rational and emotional distance enabled by long lines and networks of bureaucracy has been argued by many as central to the carrying out of the Holocaust, the implications of which have been so well documented and identified by Hannah Arendt and Zygmut Bauman, among others.[8] Explicitly refusing to compare the two incommensurable assemblages of violence, Gregory nonetheless points out that:

> Both the Holocaust and the air war were a systematic, concerted campaign of the mass killing of noncombatants that combined a thoroughly modern, scientific-technological apparatus with an atavistic dehumanization and, at the limit, a nullification of the enemy other.
>
> (p. 261)

How the Nazis' wholescale murder of millions came to be a bureaucratic function, an act whose responsibility was so thoroughly dispersed across orders, memos, directives, subordinates, chains of command, desks, stamps and balance sheets that it often posed a real danger of eventually *dissolving*, is the realm for moral philosophers and Holocaust scholars. The dispersal of guilt across that particular network is not a matter for this book; it has been and continues to be interrogated and explored by more qualified and insightful perspectives than I can bring. I raise it here only to acknowledge that any discussion about guilt and responsibility for the bombings must be had in direct context of cultural *narratives* about guilt and responsibility for the Holocaust, not in the least because of the (im)moral equivalence (Lipstadt 1993) and potential for revisionism and denialism identified in Chapter 1.

Blurring distinctions between human and non-human actants reveals the vastness of the network of actors involved in the mechanized system of violence of the air war, and how this network is often remembered in specific relation to the well-known systems of violence that made up the Holocaust. Explored below, Anhalter Bahnhof, Gleis 17, and the Topography of Terror emerge as a means of interrogating the overlap of these memory cultures in terms of how their violence is remembered as dispersed (and possibly diluted) across complex systems of humans, non-humans, technologies and conceptual systems (bureaucracy, organizations, command chains and so on). The three sites played significant parts in the complex systems of violence and the remembering of the violence of both the Holocaust and the area bombing campaigns, and thus form fertile sites at which to explore where these memory cultures might overlap in encounters in Berlin. Anhalter, for example, emerged in the previous chapter as a site of the entanglement of the cultural memory of the Holocaust with the cultural memory of the bombings, in such a way that it disrupted dominant cultural memory structures that often insist on keeping them separate. Gleis 17's proximity to Teufelsberg entangles the memory of the deportations with that of the massive clean-up effort resulting from the bombings, so bringing the scale of Berlin's destruction embodied in Teufelsberg into contact with the immeasurable scale of the violence of the Holocaust. Finally, as the 'nerve centre' of the SS, as well as a central target for the Allies and a well-known site of wartime destruction in modern day Berlin, the Topography of Terror draws these two overlapping systems of violence together as well (as well as overlapping German memory cultures during the Cold War, discussed in Chapter 4). I turn now to examine these sites as ways of remembering the complex systems of infrastructure, bureaucracy, technology and policy of mass destruction of the bombings.

Gleis 17 (Platform 17) is a memorial on what used to be Platform 17 of the Grunewald train station in north west Berlin, from where more than 17,000 of Berlin's Jewish citizens were sent to Theresienstadt and Auschwitz or the ghettos of Łódź and Riga. It is accessible in much the same ways as the other platforms at the station, and consists of a series of large steel plates that line the platform. On the plates, the numbers of people deported from the station each day between 1941 and 1945 are recorded. The website for Deutsche Bahn, who created the memorial in 1998, states: 'The vegetation that has developed at Platform 17 over the years has been left to grow between the rails and now forms and integral part of the memorial as a symbol that no more trains will ever depart from this platform' (Deutsche Bahn AG, 2019).

The memorial is highly liminal, similar to Anhalter in its half-way point between the everyday and the profound. The platform is at the same level as the rest of the platforms of the still functioning S-Bahn station, and yet is blocked by trees from view. There is a normal city hiking and cycling path that runs through here. On my visit, a runner jogs past me, stops at the end of the platform, turns around and runs back towards the city. Shops and cafes are nearby, and the breeze, scent of flowers and laughter of hikers are all very ordinary for a Berlin summer day.

And yet the path along the platform, following the list of names, is uneven, throwing one somewhat off-kilter. The list of dates and numbers seems to continue on a long way backwards and forwards through time, listing off the dead that departed. Despite, or perhaps because of, being thoroughly embedded in a thoroughly 'everyday' site such as a train station, the memorial at Gleis 17 is extremely moving. I found an overwhelming sense of obscenity at trying to approach a site like this through the lens of 'academic rigour' or using it as a 'research data point', much in the same way I felt at the Jewish memorial cemetery on Grosse Hamburger Strasse (see Chapter 4). The large steel sheets on which the number and date of victims transported from the platform are printed turn archival, fragmentary records into something much more concrete, weightier and permanent. The memorial laid out alongside the tracks seems to lead the eye and self back towards Berlin, to where these people came from, not where they were going. The focus of the memorial is on the platforms, rather than the tracks, the spot on which people stood and from which they left their home. The visitor can stand there too, much like at Anhalter, and briefly occupy a space from which thousands perished. The visitor, unmoored from time, can therefore briefly occupy a space in the immense complex machinations of the Nazis' murderous plans.

Notably, the memory of the bombings is largely absent at Gleis 17. There is no ruinous portico like at Anhalter, no empty space or aerial photographs of the Topography of Terror pointing to a great force of destruction that once rained down on the site. The bombs are present only through their role in 'creating' Teufelsberg, which is nearby but barely close enough to register in my or likely anyone's experience of the site. Grunewald station remains the easiest way to access Teufelsberg and the surrounding forest, but Gleis 17 registers only as a cog in the machine of the Holocaust in the cultural memory that can be formed there. It matters, in other words, only as part of a more conceptual, but also deeply material, assemblage.

As already examined in detail in Chapter 4, Anhalter Bahnhof was another site from which the Nazis deported their victims. The war turned Anhalter into a symbol of the 'destruction and dislocation that had become commonplace in Hitler's capital' (Beilenberg 1984, p. 202). In her memoirs of life under the Nazis in Berlin, Bielenberg described the station as 'a symbol of disintegration' (p. 242), part of a machine that fragmented lives, families and histories. Anhalter is explicitly positioned within the dominant framework of cultural memory surrounding the war. This is mostly enacted by a sign that designates it as a site of deportation. Like in the quote from Bielenberg above, Anhalter is thus explicitly identified as part of the regime and system that the Allied bombs were ostensibly aimed against. Layered with the markers of the bombings and time – the crumbling masonry, the support beams, the headless statues – encounters with the station therefore have the entangling effect described in Chapter 4, complicating some of the assuredness of dominant frames of cultural memory that often try to keep the bombings temporally separate from the Holocaust, or at least in a strict cause-and-effect relationship. Nevertheless, the bombings can still fit quite easily into a category of preventative or punitive violence against the Nazi regime at Anhalter, because they are positioned here as a move against the genocide machine of which Anhalter was a cog.

There is similarly very little ambiguity about the effects Allied bombing had on the Nazi regime at the Topography of Terror. The site is the remnants of the foundations of the institutions that designed and administrated the Holocaust and other Nazi atrocities in Berlin: the Secret State Police (Gestapo) Office, the leadership of the SS and SA, and the Reich Security Main Office. The site is situated on the city block that housed these institutions, now mostly empty thanks to the bombing raids of the 1940s and the political processes of denazification and memory work over the following decades (described in Chapter 4). A self-guided tour path winds around the site, describing the buildings that once stood there and their varying uses as apparatuses of Nazi state terror. A small documentation centre houses a permanent exhibition about the SS and Gestapo and a library. The signs also display images of the destruction of the buildings from the air, occasionally showing 'before and after' shots of the city block's damage by aerial bombardment and divided Cold War memory politics and urban regeneration. The Topography of Terror is like Anhalter, clearly positioned as a clear instance of what the bombings were against.

Retribution and justice

In the context of the damage caused by the bombings, the sign at Anhalter and the site tour and documentation centre at the Topography of Terror specifically

Figure 5.5 Signage at the Topography of Terror, showing the use of the site as Gestapo headquarters and the damage they suffered under Allied bombs. Photograph by Eloise Florence, 2017.

identify the buildings that once populated the sites as apparatuses of state-sponsored terror. The bombings can therefore easily be positioned as an act against these apparatuses within Anglo-American cultural memory structures. The historical function of the buildings at these sites means the buildings can be framed not just as symbolizing the Allies' reasons to bomb cities in wartime Germany, but also as active sites of the administration and implementation of crimes against humanity: they were 'the target'. The documentation centre and the exhibition trench at the Topography of Terror, and the small sign accompanying the portico at Anhalter, serve as reminders of this, and the destruction of these buildings is therefore quite defensible, even welcome. This reproduces the dominant Anglo-American cultural memory of the war that is centred around victims of Nazi war atrocities, which I discussed in Chapter 1. The theme of retribution and justice (identified in Chapter 1) is a prominent theme in this cultural memory structure. Sebald (2004), for example, quotes Winston Churchill responding to the bombing of Germany 'those who have loosed these horrors upon mankind will now in their homes and persons feel the shattering strokes of just retribution' (p. 19). Dominant discourses continue to frame area bombings as a response to Nazi atrocities – recall, for example, the comments beneath British news articles commemorating the bombing of Dresden: 'they started a war'.

Again, it is a legitimate claim; regardless of their intent and despite the fact they were not designed or intended to (Hanson 2008), there is some evidence the air raids halted or hindered the Nazis' effort at the Holocaust. This evidence is often anecdotal but nonetheless powerful. Henni Brenner, a young Jewish girl in Dresden during the war, described how she and her family avoided deportation because of an American air raid in February 1945:

> In the morning my father received the order to report for the transport. He became very depressed and said: 'Henni, only a miracle, a bolt from the blue can save us now.' We survived the air raid and then walked down towards the city centre.
>
> [Journalist]: 'What did you feel?'
>
> It was terrible, the bodies, the city burning. But my father wanted at all costs to see what had happened to the Gestapo building. We couldn't get that far, because everything was burning, but from a distance we saw that it was ablaze. Well, then we felt some satisfaction.
>
> (qtd. by Chalmers in Klemperer 2013[1945], p. xi)

The absence of the buildings at the Topography of Terror is therefore not only explained by the details of Nazi atrocities in the documentation centre, but welcomed because the destroyed buildings enacted a brutal dictatorship. This was also seen in attacks on the 'normal' function of Nazi cities. Moeller (2006) interrogates this notion through the diaries of the Jewish scholar Victor Klemperer, who was also spared deportation by the bombing of Dresden. The night before he and his family were due to be taken away, 'the Allies' destructive bombing of the city in February 1945 [meant] Nazi officials had to turn their attention away from deportations to more pressing problems, allowing Klemperer to move freely about the city' (Moeller 2006, p. 120). The bombings here are a saviour, a 'miracle, a bolt from the blue', but only inasmuch as they disturbed the complex but mundane function of the Nazis' genocide machine.[9]

Legitimate targets

The evidence of the bureaucracy of the Holocaust and the capture, torture and murder of dissidents that is presented in the documentation centre engenders us to feel some of Henni Brenner's satisfaction at their destruction. Both the existence and the absence of these buildings therefore reinforce the righteousness of the Allies' bombing campaigns. Subsequently, in the era of 'total war' and within the mechanized system of destruction described above, that system – any part of it – becomes a 'legitimate' target of the air war. Implied in the cultural memory structures that justify the violence of the bombings with the incommensurable violence of the Holocaust is the idea of that any part of wartime Germany was a 'legitimate target' because any part of wartime Germany was a part of their genocidal war effort. Gleis 17, the Topography of Terror and Anhalter are unquestionably part of this machine. So too is another site of interest: the memorial cemetery at Grosse Hamburger Strasse. Jordan (2006) writes that because of its role as a collection site, the cemetery should be considered not on its own but as part of a network that sent millions to their deaths:

> The site must also be seen as connected to the thousands of places from which entire familiarise were taken to Grosse Hamburger Strasse, where they were held until being sent to a train station like the Bahnhof Grunewald or Anhalter Bahnhof and transported to distant death camps. These small stones in oases of urban greenery trace parts of the interconnected geography of Nazi violence – not systematically, and non-comprehensively, but as pieces of a much larger picture and nodes in a much larger system, in ways that are not always immediately apparent in the urban landscape.
>
> (Jordan 2006, p. 71)

Figure 5.6 Anhalter S-Bahn station, showing photos of the overland station that now stands in ruins, Berlin. Photograph by Eloise Florence, 2017.

At Anhalter and the Topography of Terror, an argument is made that the sites were bombed *because* of their participation in Germany's war and genocide machine. In his memoir *No Moon Tonight* (1987), Charlwood describes an attack on a Germany city: 'In that listening darkness, there was one vast animal-machine, its tentacles these frenzied beams' (p. 45). To pilots and navigators, whose recollections have flowed down to cultural perceptions of the air war (see Chapter 1), a German city is an 'animal-machine', a non-human, complex system of violence. But more often than not, rather than bombing a target that already exists, systems of aerial bombing actually will a target into being. Anderson (2010) identifies that 'targets only appear or materialize in relation to a specific tactical or strategic problem' (p. 225). Area bombing *created* a target out of morale, establishing the 'will to war' as a thing to be attacked and destroyed. At the centre of doctrines of both strategic and morale bombing was the notion that modern societies operate as a complex network of interdependent parts, and disrupting this network is key to defeating a society. Davis Biddle (1995) argues that underpinning both the moral and strategic bombing arguments was the notion that:

> modern industrial states are made of what Liddell Hart described as a 'complex and interdependent fabric'. [The Allies] believed that the delicate sinews – whether material or moral – holding together such intricate creations ought to be easily subject to the overwhelming offensive power of aircraft.
>
> (p. 127)

The very interconnectivity of modern industrial societies – and the war and mass extermination project that emerged out of the Nazi German one – itself was put forward as a target of aerial bombing. This could mean, theoretically, that a site may not necessarily need to be explicitly marked as a cog in the machine of the Holocaust or Nazi terror to still be considered a 'legitimate' target in dominant cultural memory frames. As Adey and colleagues (2011) point out:

> the consequence of aerial violence is the destruction of parts of the environment 'not for what they individually represent (military target, cultural heritage, conceptual metaphor)' [as Coward (2006, p. 430) writes] but for the conditions such environments provide for the performance of ways of life and life itself. The targeting of these nodes or integral points on a relational network or 'battlespace' has become a primary method in the doctrine of contemporary air power.
>
> (p. 177)

The doctrines of both morale and strategic bombing transformed the capacity of German society to function *into* a target. This capacity therefore could take the form of a train station or a butchers shop, because both would in some way incapacitate the 'machine' and prevent it from functioning smoothly.

Such an understanding of the sites' position within this machine as it feeds into cultural memory for the Anglosphere is engendered by the fact Anhalter and Gleis 17 are still positioned within this system today. When visiting both sites, a visitor is likely to use the Anhalter and Grunewald S-Bahn stations, becoming implicated in a city that continued to function as a vital mechanism of the Holocaust, and today still functions immersed in the memory of the Holocaust. Today trains arrive at Grunewald station from Berlin on Platform 1 on the S7 line. The crowds of swimmers, hikers and artists stream onto the platform and stroll down the ramps to the underground concourse. Turn right, and you can wander across the road and into the woods of the Grunewald, and eventually up the hill of Teufelsberg or along to Teufelssee. Turn left, and you can see a small sign for the memorial, where another ramp takes you up into the sunshine and to Gleis 17. The unveiling of the Gleis 17 memorial was notable because it was seen by many as the first time Deutsche Bahn engaged with its history of involvement in the deportation of Berlin's Jews (Merrill 2015), bringing attention to the continued presence of an apparatus of Nazi terror in the everyday lives of Berliners. The sign explaining Anhalter's use in the deportations is situated right next to the ruined facade, and immediately redirects the viewer's attention and narrative to the fact that the Holocaust was carried out through an urban transit system not unlike the one that functions mere meters away, and which still bears Anhalter's name. The sign stresses the mundane and (literally) 'every day' occurrence of these deportations, taking care to indicate that it was 'clear for all to see' and making explicit mention of 'the normal station traffic'. At both Anhalter and Gleis 17, the embedded nature of the Holocaust in the fabric of Berlin, and the daily lives of its citizenry becomes evident. The violence is revealed as continuing amongst the wider assemblages of everyday practices – catching public transport, navigating a city, transporting goods – and draws attention to how these practices were imbricated in these violences.

Conclusions

This chapter has sought to explore Teufelsberg as an unruly mass of vibrant matter, in the hope it might draw out the wider assemblage of the bombings to widen the scope of accountability in its cultural memory. Bennett's (2010) model of distributed accountability was applied to the assemblage of the bombings to expand this assemblage and to disrupt some of the assumptions of responsibility at the heart of Anglo-American cultural memory structures. At the outset, there are significant implications for questions of moral and even legal responsibility, questions which deserve more attention, expertise and nuance than can be afforded here. But it is enough (for me) simply for expansion, for radical inclusion. The effects on the dominant structures of the cultural memory of the air war can be profound if we are simply willing to expand the scope of who or what can be considered responsible for violence. While not offering any answers on the moral responsibility of non-human materials in violence, the radical expansion offered by a posthuman conceptualization of agency simply disrupts the framework through which we assign guilt and responsibility in common narratives about the air war, if not reversing or upending it to provide clear cut answers. This is after all the aim of this book, to bring complication and nuance to an area that has remained distinctly (if not totally) black and white.

The main disruption such a model of agency can engender is on the normal binary categories of 'victim' and 'perpetrator' that permeate Anglo-American cultural memory of the Second World War. In a related debate concerning German memory cultures, Moeller (2006) called for a deconstruction of the concept of 'German perspectives' in order to write a more nuanced and complicated history of the bombings. Moeller attempted to imagine a history of the war that might include a wider variety of stories: stories of Germans who denounced their Jewish neighbours alongside stories of Jewish Germans who dodged the camps because the Gestapo were interrupted by an air raid; stories of German intellectuals who welcomed the firestorm of Dresden because it saved them from the Gestapo alongside stories of Germans who moved from their bombed out houses to new 'Aryanised' homes they bought at reduced prices; or else stories of the women that the bombs killed, the women who cleared away the rubble and the women who shot down British and American pilots (Moeller 2006, p. 121). A similar argument might be made for Anglo-American memory cultures, deconstructing the concept of both German and Allied perspectives and instead widening the field of view to include additional – not replace existing – perspectives and stories, without forcing them into the binary categories of perpetrator and victim. Such a deconstruction would add the perspectives of the women who built the bombs, who worked alongside the pilots, who loaded bombs onto trucks and cooked meals for American GIs in small British towns and who waved to British and American pilots as they flew out over the English Channel to bomb a German town.

By widening the frame of reference, or 'widen[ing] the angle of vision on the action' (Bennett 2005, p. 458), we can bring into focus some of these other actors. This is enabled by dissolving the divide between the human and non-human that often still lingers when considering questions of responsibility, accountability and agency in Anglo-American cultural memory. The vibrant, vital materiality felt and seen at Teufelsberg holds potential as a way of dissolving this divide. The rubble, the very make-up of the hill, pushes back against the human observer, becomes an *actant* in its own right. The bombings, as a cultural, political, and technological phenomenon, can be remembered as an assemblage of many very agentic *actants*, some of which are human, but many of which are not.

Further positioning memory encounters in relation to wider systems of infrastructure and bureaucracy that implemented another violence – the Holocaust – draws attention to how chains of command, technology, bureaucracy, intelligence networks and policy themselves lengthen the emotional, psychological, moral, causal and conceptual distance between mechanized violence systems and the individuals responsible for their violence. But by a similar token, the everyday mechanisms of train networks became legitimate targets of the air war. Thus Gleis 17 and Anhalter serve to further complicate the cultural memory of area bombing, at once buttressing the idea they were necessary attacks against legitimate targets whilst simultaneously further entangling the cultural memory structures of the bombings with those of the Holocaust.

This conceptual distance is also often epitomized in the birds-eye view of aerial photography, which has seeped into dominant memory structures of the air war. The following chapter therefore looks to how these viewpoints elide the visceral and material violence of the bombings, and how bodily encounters with the vibrant matter of Teufelsberg's rubble might complicate this.

6

Aerial photography and bodily violence

Introduction

Walking Teufelsberg is an incredibly involved experience. Perhaps more than any site I visit in Berlin, it is a labour to visit Teufelsberg. One can drive to the spy station at the top of hill, but cars are rare on the road. Most visitors walk across, around and over Teufelsberg, ride their bikes up and down its slopes, hike through the deep forest or swim in the nearby lake. In mid-summer this is no easy feat – despite the dense vegetation it is hot in Berlin in May, the air is thick with mosquitoes, the woods thick with wild boars and birds. The slopes are steep in places, requiring effort, exertion, struggle. I slip and trip often on the uneven ground (the rubble), and curse the biting, burning sun on more than one occasion. There is a definite sense of struggle in many of my visits to Teufelsberg and some of the other *Trümmerberge*.

***

Encountering and remembering through Teufelsberg is a highly haptic, sensory and embodied affair, conveying the sense of agency, disruption and liveliness of the rubble that so intrigued me and which I discuss in the previous chapter. This chapter looks to the bodily encounters with Teufelsberg (and the Topography of Terror) as ways of complicating some of the distant and objective ways of understanding the violence of the bombings in Anglo-American cultural memory. This is first explored through the framework of the aerial viewpoint, so exemplified in the aerial photographs that became synonymous with aerial bombing during the war, which have continued to shape the dominant Anglo-American visual culture surrounding the bombing campaigns ever since. Many such photographs can also be found at sites in Berlin destroyed by the bombings or sites where they might be remembered by English-speaking visitors. One example is the Topography of Terror, and it is there that I begin my analysis of these viewpoints as positioned within wider ontological and epistemological understandings of aerial conflict in the English-language world, which has its roots in pre-war colonial conquest and stretches forward to contemporary drone warfare. These images help solidify and perpetrate the cultural memory of the air war that tends to keep the destruction 'on the ground' at a distance, whether through the images themselves or the objective techno-scientific-military language through which they are often described and comprehended. This framing has particular implications for understanding the scale of the bombings, the destruction of which has often been described as beyond comprehension in logical, cognitive terms. It also relates to understandings of safety and vulnerability associated with the subterranean, which came to characterize the wartime experiences of civilians in air raid shelters on both side of the conflict. Such experiences have contributed to the dominant Anglo-American narrative structures of cultural memory of the air war, often pointing to the overlap of seemingly separate perspectives of 'above' and 'below'. As well as imagery, the aerial viewpoint haunts the cultural memory of the air war as a way of knowing its violence, associated with distance, transcendence and power. This chapter explores bodily encounters with Teufelsberg, the other *Trümmerberge*, and

Figure 6.1 Forests at Marienhöhe, a *Trümmerberg* in Berlin. Photograph by Eloise Florence, 2017.

the Topography of Terror as a way of engaging the historical bodily violence of the bombings, which has so far been largely omitted from this cultural memory (with some notable exceptions). I also explore both the aerial viewpoint and bodily encounters with these sites as new ways one might be able to comprehend the sheer scale of the destruction. It is the entanglement of these two viewpoints, I argue, not the subversion of one with the other, that has the most potential to complicate the more rigid structures of Anglo-American cultural memory of the bombings, which tend to keep the two separate. By complicating this separation – above vs. below, perpetrator vs. victim, etc. – by encountering the sensory and material violence of the bombings through the aerial, distanced view point, we might begin to complicate these structures that continue to regulate who can and cannot be held responsible for mass deaths and destruction during the war.

Aerial photography and aerial bombing

The Topography of Terror contains several aerial photographs of the site, both before and after the war, showing the destruction of the site from aerial bombing and street fighting and Cold War urban regeneration and public memory works. The images on the boards accompanying the visitor around the Historic Site Tour contain several instances of aerial perspectives of the destruction, not just from the Allied planes that bombed them, but from reconnaissance missions surveying the damage they caused and from captures of reconstruction and denazification efforts during the Cold War. These images often have handwritten labels, arrows and other annotations written over them, relics of the Allied airforces identifying targets and points of interest, to bomb or to leave alone. Alongside these images of the destroyed site are aerial view diagrams positioning the visitor within the block (i.e. 'you are here').[1] The presence of these photographs evokes specific ways both of seeing and understanding the site of the Topography of Terror and of remembering the bombings.

At the Topography of Terror, photographs from an aerial perspective offer a perspective of the agents of destruction whilst simultaneously obscuring those agents. Many have credited this detached, distanced, aerial perspective as the very condition that made – and continues to make – aerial bombing of civilians possible (see Chapter 5). The destruction of entire cities is often more conceivable if it can be approached from an aerial perspective, looking down on the results without ever 'feeling' their reality. In terms of representation, Allied participants in the bombings are rendered somewhat invisible[2] at the

Topography of Terror, presenting the ruined city at a distance and from an elevated perspective. At the same time, dominant Anglo-American cultural memories of the war conceptualize the destruction Berlin suffered through a lens of 'aerial mastery' (Gregory 2011, p. 270), which is embodied in the perspective of the bombers.

Aerial bombing is by nature entwined with the aerial viewpoint, a perspective that has a rich and detailed history and which has also bled into public

Figure 6.2 Aerial photograph of bomb damage on information boards at the Topography of Terror, Berlin. Photograph by Eloise Florence, 2017.

consciousness of warfare, photography and ideas of nationhood. The British developed aerial bombing as a means of controlling foreign civilian populations in the inter-war years. Gregory (2011) called this tactic a 'specifically colonial doctrine of air control in the 1920s and 1930s that entailed bombing tribal peoples in a terrifying demonstration of its unassailable power' (p. 253). In mapping, managing and strategizing from the bird's-eye perspective inherent in aerial bombing, the British created spheres of control, surveillance and possession in its colonies, distinctly separated from the people and effects of this doctrine on the ground (Gregory 2011). 'The aerial viewpoints adopted and provided by the cartographers of state and empire', Adey, Whitehead, and Williams (2011) found, 'established the systems of legibility that were central to the formation of modern forms of terrestrial power' (p. 176). Aerial bombing is enacted through the mastery of this bird's-eye view, and has thus been regularly linked to technologies of surveillance and systems of power, but also to a certain techno-military separation of the aerial view and its grounded subjects.

As explored in relation to my methodology in Chapter 3, the historical development of photographs as a technology is entwined with the historical development of systems of surveillance and domination in warfare. Amad (2012) states that 'seeing in general is connected to the will to knowledge and the desire to control and act upon what one sees; and that the distanced, anonymous view, in particular, facilitates the will to power and the delivery of a dehumanised, abstracted view that makes killing easier and more efficient' (p. 71). Virilio (1989) examines the mutual relationship between war and cinema, drawing out the historical development of weapons and cameras as co-constitutive ocular technologies:

> Alongside the 'war machine', there has always existed an ocular ... 'watching machine' ... From the original watch-tower through the anchored balloon to the reconnaissance aircraft and remote-sensing satellites, one and the same function has been indefinitely repeated in the eye's function being the function of a weapon.
>
> (p. 3)

Specific to the context of this research, Matheson (2008) argues that aerial bombing, particularly night-time bombing, is quintessentially photographic:

> aeroplanes that light up a city at night with flares and that flash-photograph their own bomb drops; the sudden explosions in darkness; the searchlight and flak batteries tracing patterns against the blackness of the night sky; buildings

consumed by flames that illuminate their own destruction and imprint their incandescent image in the photograph.

(p. 264)

The marriage of bombing and photography also has clear links with the West's more contemporary aerial bombing in the two Gulf Wars and ongoing aerial engagement in the Middle East. This marriage has had direct impacts on the social, political and cultural understandings of this warfare in the publics of participating nations. As well as a technology of surveillance and state control, photography plays a key role in the development of visual culture in relation to warfare. The advent of drone photography and footage, scope cameras and body-cams during the Gulf War, for example, meant they were used liberally by the media and the public to circulate imagery of and gain and understanding of the conflict. Virilio (1989) pre-empted this leakage of weapon-vision into the public culture, stating 'a war of pictures and sounds is replacing the war of objects (projectiles and missiles)' (p. 4). Amad (2012) calls this 'cinema's military hardwiring' (p. 71), referring to the inherently entwined histories of technologies of video and photographic capture and technologies of destruction, surveillance and control. Speaking of the movement of drone targeting camera footage into the public consciousness, Stahl (2018) writes: 'what seemed only the by-product of our most advanced targeting systems began to flicker across the collective visual field via official military public relations, leaks, and fictional entertainment' (p. 2). The way warfare is documented has direct influence on how it is viewed by a public culture, and this is no less true of the Second World War.

The movement of these perspectives into cultural articulations of conflicts relates to wider trends of the militarization of public culture. Specific ways of seeing have moved from the strictly military and technology realm into public visual cultures. 'Militarized perception is always leaking into public culture, from the aerial prospect of balloon flight to the soldier's helmet camera' argues Richardson (2020, p. 858), focusing specifically on how drone vision has become firmly lodged in our visual culture, resulting in what he calls 'drone cultures'. This is part of a wider trend Richardson calls 'everyday militarisms' or how 'military histories, logics, technologies, ideologies, iconographies and practices become presences within the texture of the quotidian' (Richardson 2020, p. 859). Specific to the more automated aerial conflicts of the 1990s, Richardson identifies drone cultures as 'something distinct, a particular confluence of technics, bodies, aesthetics and modes of perception' (p. 859). This confluence draws on many technologies, modes of perception, narratives, histories and power relations, and can frame the ongoing cultural narratives surrounding a conflict.

The prevalence of the aerial, military gaze is by no means restricted to contemporary warfare. Military ways of seeing have always bled into the public screen from the beginning of television's rule:

> At first [in the inter-war years], mass audiences received only scattered glimpses, issued through newsreels and television broadcasts, shot from the perspective of the bombardier and gunner. By the Persian Gulf War of the early 1990s, an entire nation huddled around the television, like those who had come to witness the first television broadcast, to watch missiles close in on targets through nosecone cameras.
>
> (Stahl 2018, p. 2)

Drone vision and drone cultures therefore draw on a history of the aerial viewpoints that is inextricable from aerial bombing, extending 'a lineage of aerial views of war that extends back to the balloons first floated above the battlefields of Europe in the 1840s' (Richardson 2020, p. 859). Adey, Whitehead, and Williams (2011) identify this as a distinctly cultural process, calling the development of aerial targeting, reconnaissance and destruction part of 'violent epistemologies' (p. 177). These epistemologies 'saw the early modern practices of territorial legibility and consolidation replaced by an aerial epistemology devoted to locating sites that could be used to disrupt the territorial functioning of a community' (p. 177). We hear here echoes of the ethos of 'total war' that fed into the Allies' selection of targets during the Second World War, effectively rendering any target in Nazi Germany that contributed to the functioning of the Nazi state a 'legitimate target' (see Chapter 5). The epistemology of the air war developed out of the characterization of the entire Nazi apparatus as a legitimate target, drawing on narratives attached to aerial viewpoints to do so. And, as we saw with the 'total war' rhetoric, such military epistemologies can bleed into cultural framings of the war, and so too into cultural memory. This history of aerial viewpoints therefore remains entwined with that of the air war, and can still be found in its cultural memory.

Aerial photography in cultural memory

Stahl (2018) argues the aerial gaze has been moving into the public consciousness from the interwar period, tracing its history to footage played in American theatres in 1921. US Air Force head General Billy Mitchell played footage of an air raid on a German ship in Chesapeake Bay. 'This watershed moment played a role in shifting national faith from naval to air power', argues Stahl, 'but it also comprised a collective training exercise in reimagining national subjectivity through the eyes of this ascendant weapon' (p. 8). This 'collective training' saw representations of warfare come increasingly from military-technology sources. 'At a certain point', Stahl (2018) argues, 'perhaps through sheer force of numbers, the view through the weapon itself earned a primary place in the presentation of war in the postindustrial West' (p. 2).

With the increase of aerial bombardment as a key means of engagement with the conflict in Nazi-occupied Europe, much of the imagery of the war the Allied public received was from the perspective of the bomber (Connelly 2002). The aerial viewpoint of the bombers, the reconnaissance pictures and maps and statistics that can be found at the Topography of Terror have therefore moved into the visual culture surrounding the war to become part of cultural memory, filtered down from military officials into the (largely controlled and censored) wartime news media and so into visual culture and cultural memory. 'Coupled with the bombsight', Stahl (2018) argues, 'the newsreel camera came to deliver a view of strategic bombing runs that dappled the earth below, a perspective that structured the home front experience of war both at the time and later in collective memory as it replayed on the likes of the History Channel' (p. 9). Largely because of the difficulty of explaining and detailing the ins and outs of a raid, Bomber Command and the Ministry of Information usually used the 'user-friendly aerial photographs Bomber Command could produce showing huge areas of destruction and damage' (Connelly 2002, p. 44) to depict the war to British civilians.[3] Whilst it is difficult, as I explored in Chapter 2, to attribute the national or public perception of the event through press representations alone, it is clear that a significant way the British and American people saw and understood a conflict occurring miles away from them was populated by imagery from an aerial perspective. To understand the destruction of German cities during the war was to understand it through the lens of an aerial camera, and this imagery has lingered in the cultural memory of the war today.

Aerial perspectives have continued to frame cultural memory structures of the air war. Elżanowski (2012) argues 'the recent proliferation of online aerial photo archives from World War Two has encouraged a "photogenic" reading of destruction that reiterates and reinforces "the effects of modern industrialized warfare"' (pp. 120–2). This viewpoint is common in Anglosphere cultural memory texts, be they through aerial photography or accounts of the bombings from the perspectives of pilots, planners and military strategists.

A slightly less overt instance of the persistence of the aerial view is the continued framing of the cultural memory of Allied area bombing through dichotomous 'above vs. below' narrative structures. As already covered somewhat in the previous chapters (Chapters 5 and 1), these militarized aerial viewpoints draw on particular articulations of the relations between 'above' and 'below', perpetrator and victim, technology and bodies, objectivity and subjectivity. The viewpoints thus came to frame particular narrative perspectives of the conflict – less literal perspectives, more ways of knowing. Amad (2012) explains:

> whereas the view from below has come to signify an intimate, embodied, local perspective of those who are subjugated, that from above has acquired the status of a distant, dehumanising, transcendent perspective of those ultimately in power – or so this particular myth of vision goes.
>
> (pp. 66–7)

Similarly, Portelli (2006) describes this dichotomous framework as inherently limiting:

> The top down, outside, emic view from above possesses a *superior* (literally, higher) *power* to perceive the global context, the general picture. The bird's eye or bomber's radar view of the world sees farther, and retains the wholesome detachment, the capacity for abstraction, the rational ability to concentrate on the *objective* and the relevant (the target) and dismiss the irrelevant … On the other hand, the lower, (literally, *inferior*) point of view is narrowly focused, irretrievably bound to the detail, to the concrete – shall we say, down-to-earth, grassroots – immediacy of material experience, and is inevitably twisted into and limited by the personal, emotional identification and involvement.
>
> (p. 30, original emphasis)

While Amad and others (Mangold & Goehring 2019) have long since argued for a disruption of this binary understanding of views 'from above' and 'from below',[4] such a distinction and an association of aerial views with distance, transcendence, and power still lingers in dominant cultural framings of the air war (see Chapter 1).[5] As well as imagery, the aerial viewpoint haunts the cultural memory of the air war as a way of knowing violence.[6]

These ways of knowing the violence of the air war come not just from representations but from the systems of thought, policy, politics, command and bureaucracy through which they were conceived, some of which I explore in Chapter 5. The Allies' chains of command that brought about each bombing raid, Gregory (2011) argues, were each 'a concatenation of aerial views produced through a process of calculation that was also a process of abstraction' (p. 269). The historic and technical association with technologies of surveillance and domination directly influenced the ways historical aerial bombing was both imagined and carried out at the time and how it has been remembered since in the Anglosphere. Aerial bombing formulates 'the target' from an abstracted, critical distance. The physical distance between the ground and the plane carrying its payload distances both the perpetrator and the viewer of aerial bombing from the human subject being bombed on the ground. The systems explored in Chapter 5 perpetrate and inform this distance, even as it bleeds into the cultural memory of the air war.

The fact that the bombings are still largely mediated through reconnaissance photography taken from planes not only positions the audience of these images literally above the destruction but also within a certain position of power. Moshenska (2009) identifies the 'idea of bombers as inhuman, even godlike in their power [a]s a common theme in memories of war' (p. 49). Portelli (2006) similarly identifies this distinction between 'above' and 'below' at the heart of ongoing debates about the air war: 'There is a fatalistic perception of the war as destiny, of the bombs as a "bolt" from above, unleashed by an invisible hand' (p. 36). This ongoing dichotomy between 'above' and 'below' remains central to dominant Anglo-American cultural memory of the air war and in fact underpins many of the debates surrounding the memory of area bombing discussed in Chapter 1. As Lowe (2012) identifies, common traditional Anglo-American narratives reflect the view of the destruction on the ground when viewed from the air, as well as the power and ethical position of the bomber:

> After the bombs have been dropped, and the surviving bombers have returned home, the story tends to end. What happened on the ground, to the cities full of people beneath the bombs, is rarely talked about; even when it is discussed, it is usually only in terms of the buildings and factories destroyed, with a cursory mention of civilian casualties.
>
> (p. xv)

However, despite this focus on the viewpoint of the bomber in these structures, the agents of these bombings often remain nonetheless obscured. Much of this is enabled by extended and complex networks of technology and 'objective' military language that permeates Anglo-American cultural memory of the air war (discussed in Chapter 5), through which the perpetrator can become further obscured. Consider, for example, this account from military historian Davis (1991) describing Operation Thunderclap, one of the US air force's bombing campaigns over Berlin:

> On 3 February [1945] the Eighth struck Berlin. Of over 1000 B-17s dispatched, 932, employing mostly visual methods, dropped 2279 tons of bombs (250 tons

of them incendiaries). They lost 23 aircraft to flak ... the centre of the city industrial and residential property suffered severe damage, while government offices along the Wilhemstraße, including the Air Ministry, Reich Chancellory, Foreign Office, and Gestapo Headquarters (primary aiming point on the Thunderclap target list), received numerous hits. For the tenth time the Eighth had bombed the civil and military government area of Berlin.

(p. 106)

Whilst not positioned literally 'above' the destruction, this kind of language nonetheless positions the reader within the overarching 'objective' scientific perspective of the Allies. The site that would become the Topography of Terror can be identified as a target in this description – it is 'the government office along the Wilhemstraße'. The site that I visit, that I can feel and breathe and see – the rain drops, traffic sounds, the rough edges of the foundations and rubble poking through the leaf litter – and the violence that occurred on the ground, here simply 'received numerous hits'. In this description, the site is not really a place, but a target, a percentage of built-up areas, zones defined by their propensity to burn. The violence is quantified and categorized into military-scientific language, 'a highly approximated quantification of destruction that led to an abstraction of the ruin – and indeed its former and present inhabitants – so that all could be presented in increasingly intangible aerial views' (Elżanowski 2012, p. 120). The destruction of Berlin, in these accounts, is mostly articulated as the quantity of tonnes dropped, infrastructure neutralized or rates of detonation.

This objective detachment can also bleed into subjective, personal accounts of the war that are similarly often framed and enabled by the aerial viewpoint. One of the ways the bombings are often encountered by English-language populations is through biographical accounts from RAF and USAAF pilots.[7] Don Charlwood, an Australian navigator who flew for British Bomber Command, recounted a mission attacking a German city.[8] We can see here his use of his aerial perspective to frame his own subjective experience of the violence as 'unreal':

I felt the whole scene to be unreal. That there were men down there I could not believe ... I tried to tell myself that below in the darkness there were people, in their ears the drone of engines that was in my own. But even as I tried to visualize them, these people were unreal and, throughout my operational life, were to remain so.

(Charlwood 1987, p. 45)

Accounts like Charlwood's of a German city as 'unreal' have come to define Anglo-American cultural memory of the bombings and are mirrored in aerial perspectives. As Lowe (2012) argues, what happens 'when the bomb hits the ground is rarely shown' (p. xv). When it is shown, it is often depersonified, such as when the flood wipes away a German town in the culmination of *The Dam Busters*' (1955) *plot*. Combined with the scientific and military objectivity through which the bombings are habitually described in dominant Anglo-American cultural memory, the physical, material and bodily effects of Allied bombs remain abstract, non-concrete matter, unreal.

These Anglo-American narratives also take place in relation to German ones, and thus German cultural memory. Given it is inherently tied to the techno-military separation of the aerial view from its grounded subjects, much of the German victimhood debate pivots on these perspectives. One instance of this can be seen in the fact that many authors – especially German ones – have been accused of revisionism or self-pity because they featured vivid descriptions of the material effects of the bombings on humans' and cities' bodies, that is, 'from below'. Depictions of the effects of the bombings on the ground are therefore rare in Anglo-American depictions. But these criticisms, while valid in their wariness of revisionism, nonetheless fall afoul of restrictive dichotomies that see 'from above' as strictly separate from and antithetical to 'from below'. As I outline in Chapter 1, these dichotomous readings of the bombings only perpetuate and deeper other dichotomies that then continue to regulate who can and cannot be held responsible for mass deaths and destruction during the war. Because the oppositional dynamics between 'above' and 'below' perspectives become associated with those of 'perpetrator' and 'victim' respectively, for the Allies to be considered a perpetrator, the label of 'victim' must be assigned to those below the bombs – Nazi Germany. Given the risk of relativism and revisionism associated with assigning victimhood to Germans under Nazism (explored in Chapter 1), this is considered largely impossible, and the 'Allies' therefore can by and large avoid being labelled as 'perpetrator'.

It is perhaps for this reason that effects of the bombings are (or at least were, until a certain shift associated with Sebald (2004) and Friedrich's (2006) translations) rare in English language representations of the bombings, as I shall explore below. And it is for this reason that I argue for introducing the Anglo-American bodily encounter with sites of violence into Anglo-American framings of the cultural memory of that violence. It is my hope that by foregrounding the bodily encounter with sites like the Topography of Terror – and specifically the small bodily violence of encounters with Teufelsberg – we might begin to complicate some of this aerial attachment that is both a symptom of and props up the ongoing dichotomous restrictions in dominant Anglo-American cultural memories of the air war.

Bodily violence

'Official memory' and historical objectivity are often positioned in opposition to the subjectivity of personal memory. This antithetical relationship characterizes both sides of the German memory debate in the Anglosphere, pitting one against the other: subjective memory has been called both superior in its authenticity and inferior in its inaccuracy when compared to objective history or official memory projects. The German victimhood debate, particularly where it has been fuelled by Sebald's (2004) and Friedrich's (2006) controversial books as they were translated into English, similarly reflects this tension. Sebald and Friedrich have been both praised and condemned for their graphic depictions of the visceral impact of aerial bombing on German cities. Most famous is Sebald's (2004) unflinching depiction of Hamburg in the aftermath of a firestorm in the summer of 1943:

> Horrible disfigured corpses lay everywhere … clumps of flesh and bone or whole heaps of bodies cooking in the water gushing from bursting boilers. Other victims had been so badly charred and reduced to ashes by the heat … that the remains of families consisting of several people could be carried away in a single laundry basket.
>
> (pp. 26–8)

For such graphic descriptions, Sebald and Fredrich's books both received poor reviews from reviewers in Britain and America. One of the reasons these descriptions struck a chord with reviewers, Gregory (2011) argues, is because the reviewers 'privileged the objectivist language of Science … and the objectivist canons of a History aimed at a singular Truth' (p. 260) that have traditionally been used to describe the bombings. The visceral impact of the bombs remains a sticking point in the dominant ways Anglo-American audiences imagine area bombing raids, largely because it appears to run against the 'objectivity of history'. The Enola Gay controversy discussed in the Introduction, for example, shows how traditional Anglo-American representations of wartime aerial bombing tend to cringe away from graphic depictions of what the bombings felt like on the ground. This is often because the suffering of a victim who is an 'Other' – be it the residents of Hiroshima and Nagasaki or German civilian populations – poses a threat to the objectivity and accuracy that characterize military history and the 'militarised commemorative culture' at 'the heart of [US] national identity … designed to contain and control the death resulting from warfare' (Grant 2011, p. 305).

The normal dichotomies between 'above' and 'below' associated with aerial bombing can fit quite neatly into these dichotomous cultural memory structures. Amad (2012) points out how the aerial view has been historically characterized as distanced and separate to the bodily and sensory violence of war, not only in civilian air deaths but in trench warfare:

> Others have analysed the experience of the trenches as the epistemological and social other to aerial experience, based less on the elite pilot's sense of distanced sight than on the common soldier's sense of intimate tactility – 'the so called haptic way of knowing the immediate environment' through feeling it.
>
> (p. 85)

Adey, Whitehead, and Williams (2011) identify how the aerial viewpoint enables modern drone warfare by denying a full appreciation of its bodily effects:

> Indeed, the critique of the aerial target is the distance such an abstraction reinforces from the life it puts at threat. Without the fidelity of a Levinasian encounter with the *Other's* face, any possibility of ethical recognition will be gone.
>
> (p. 180, original emphasis)

Adey, Whitehead and Williams also identify how this process of abstraction is an act of violence itself in its erasure of the victim that becomes 'the target':

> it is undoubtedly performative of all kinds of violence that strip away the content of its subject and deliver it to 'ordnance' and 'kinetic' operations and other similarly abstract language that describes real violence upon real people and places.
>
> (p. 175)

The reduction of a series of violence, suffering, death, destruction and the sensory and material event of the bombings to figures of 'targets hit' and 'ordinance dropped' is therefore seen by many as an erasure of the violence bombings from the Anglo-American cultural memory of the bombings.

There are very few 'Levinasian encounter[s] with the Other's face' (Adey, Whitehead, & Williams 2011, p. 180) – the victims of area bombing – to be found at the Topography of Terror, such as that made possible by a portrait of a victim, or a graphic record of their experience of the attacks that we can find in Sebald (2004) or Freidrich's (2006) accounts. The aerial photographs of the bombings on parts of Berlin on the information boards only further distance a perpetrator from destruction and makes their destruction all the less 'real'. From this perspective, the violence is quiet and observed from a safe distance.

Figure 6.3 Open spaces at the Topography of Terror, Berlin. Photography by Eloise Florence, 2017.

In fact it finds echoes in the quiet and peace of the site itself, with large, empty, open spaces, and the soft hum of the city and birdsong in the trees. In this sense, it appears at first glance that the Topography of Terror perpetuates the dominant Anglo-American frames of cultural memory about the air war. There are some mentions of the victims of aerial bombing 'beneath' the bombs, a few photographs in the 'exhibition trench' and accounts of what life was like under both Nazism and the bombs. But I struggle to find the bodily violence of an air raid in the silent open space even as it evokes the specific bodies of Holocaust victims over of the bodies of bombing victims through imagery and signage. But there remains opportunity for bodily encounters with not only the Topography of Terror but also Teufelsberg and the other *Trümmerberge*, in which my own body might encounter other, less specified bodies.

The body at Teufelsberg

As I discussed in Chapter 5, the encounters with Teufelsberg and the other *Trümmerberge* are highly haptic and embodied.[9] The destruction of Berlin, as it is (or is not) evidenced by the rubble of the *Trümmerberge*, is anything but dormant, quietly lying underground, waiting to be 'uncovered', nor is it presented preserved behind glass like remnants at a museum. If the destruction of Berlin is evidenced by the rubble – whether as collections of remnants or simply a mark of the huge clean-up processes that followed the end of the war – then the hills imbricate the bodies of those who walk them with this destruction. Rather than this evidence of violence being merely seen, the rubble can be tripped on, picked up, held, examined. It can be touched, smelled, tasted, discarded, thrown at a tree, thrown into a lake, slipped into a backpack, rolled down a hill. Particularly at Teufelsberg, the rubble becomes part of the physical task of moving through and across the hill, rather than being critically appraised as relics of history. The remnants of a destroyed Berlin are felt with feet, hands, skin, legs. I trip and slide over pathways, scratch my knees and hands, and cover my skin with dirt. Walking Teufelsberg entwines human bodies into acts of remembering or forgetting. This has the potential to move the cultural memory I can produce at and with Teufelsberg beyond the purely cognitive or discursive appraisal, and thus disrupt the ordered, objectively distanced ways of understanding the war common in Anglo-American cultural memory of area bombing.

As discussed in Chapter 5, Teufelsberg is also both the evidence of and a participant in the material violence of the bombings. The rubble itself bears burn marks, cracks, rust and jagged edges, speaking to the material and sensory

Figure 6.4 Rubble in the forest at Teufelsberg, Berlin. Photograph by Eloise Florence, 2017.

violence inflicted on the city. In the same way that the stones reveal their agency in the destruction through the vibrant, material encounter between many actants explored in Chapter 5, the capacity and history of violence is contained in the stones' materiality. And embracing the stones' vibrancy through a sensory encounter allows for a more haptic understanding of this violence to emerge.

As well as a devastating impact on human bodies, the bombings also destroyed the stone, concrete, bricks, asphalt, motor, iron, wood, wire and steel that made up the very fabric of pre-war Berlin. The violence of the bombs transformed acres of built-up city landscapes into piles of rubble. From a detached perspective, Diefendorf (1993) provides a calculation of the cubic meters of rubble generated from the bombings in major German cities:

Berlin: 55 million
Hamburg: 35 million
Cologne: 24 million
Munich: 5 million
Stuttgart: 5 million
Dresden (estimated): 25 million
Leipzig (estimated): 8 million

But Diefendorf argues that the sheer scale of the destruction meant the sheer amounts of rubble the post-war Berlin had to contend with remained difficult to truly grasp. The flattened city blocks, the streets strewn with rubble, the incomprehensible landscapes devoid of any familiar landmarks or urban reference points – Germany's cities after 1945 seem to embody the '*Stande Null*' (Zero Hour), or the point after the war at which destruction was so complete and so incomprehensible and the horrors of the war and the Holocaust so complete that 'time was said to have ceased, leading to calls for a new beginning' (Anderson 2015, p. 77).

The term 'rubble generated' leaves out the violence of these raids on the ground. Sebald's (2004) description of a series of raids over Hamburg in July 1943 provides a glimpse of the violence that created those 35 million cubic meters of rubble:

> At its height, the [fire]storm lifted gables and roofs from buildings, flung rafters and entire advertising billboards through the air, tore trees from the ground, and drove human beings before it like living torches. Behind collapsing facades, the flames shot up as high as houses, rolled like a tidal wave through the streets at a speed of over a hundred and fifty kilometres an hour, spun across open squares

in strange rhythms like rolling cylinders of fire. The water in some of the canals was ablaze. The glass in the tram car windows melted; stocks of sugar boiled in the bakery cellars.[10]

(p. 27)

Berlin was by and large spared the devastating firestorms that struck Hamburg, Dresden and other German cities,[11] but the bombings nonetheless destroyed immense amounts of its buildings, turning almost an entire central business district into piles of rubble. And the reality of the sheer amount of this rubble, the sheer scale of the destruction, is another significant site through which the dominant Anglo-American cultural memory structures might be complicated with the inclusion of bodily encounters with the *Trümmerberge*.

Bodies and scales of violence

The aerial perspective is characteristic of Anglo-American framing of the scale of the bombings' destruction, which has often been described as 'incomprehensible' (Anderson 2015; Diefendorf 1993; Sebald 2004). Sebald (2004) called the 'total destruction' of the bombings 'experiences beyond our ability to comprehend' (p. 25). This occurred on both sides of the conflict – both German and the Allied soldiers, journalists, writers and politicians often struggled to find the language through which to describe the destruction of Germany's cities. This is exacerbated by the tendency of the Anglo-American discourse on the war to characterize the bombings as an appropriately and proportionately scaled response to Nazi aggression and atrocities. In Chapter 1, I established a discrepancy between the imagined and actual scale of the bombings in Anglo-American cultural memory (Ryan & Hewer 2016). Because of ongoing representations of the bombings as a response to the Holocaust and Germany's war aggression, the bombings are often depicted as reasonable in scale and proportionate in severity (Lowe 2012).

But the results of Ryan and Hewer's (2016) study might be the result not only of frames of cultural memory but also of the sheer difficulty in understanding the scale of such destruction as the result of human, or at least Allied, actions. It echoes what Portelli (2006) argues is the difficulty of the Allies to 'deal with the fact it was the "good guys," "our side," those with reason and humanity on their side, that destroyed your house and killed your family' (p. 36). The more the Fascists and Nazis are understood as absolute evil the more righteous the cause of the Allies appears, and the more difficult it becomes to consider the Allies capable of destruction of civilian areas on such an immense scale.

At the Topography of Terror, the scale of the bombings is mostly conveyed through images of a bombed and burnt-out Berlin on the information boards, taken from aerial reconnaissance missions of the very air forces who had destroyed the buildings they depict. There is one image in particular that shows a mid-range shot of the government quarter of Berlin in ruins, blown up to huge scale inside the documentation centre. Although dwarfing me in size, the image is wide enough that I can see the destruction on a comprehensible level – individual streets, train stations, parks and landmarks are all easily identifiable – but the photograph is tightly framed enough that it only hints at the utter scale of destruction that the city suffered. Some other images present at the Topography of Terror portray the destruction from a vantage point where the scale of the destruction is more apparent. Many of these aerial images have markers on them, or else are positioned next to diagrams and models, in an effort to orient the visitor as to where the buildings on Albrechtstraße once stood in this sea of ruins. And yet the sheer scale of the bombings still remains somewhat out of the field of vision and thus largely out of the field of comprehension, at the Topography of Terror. Imagery alone, it would seem, is not enough to fully grasp the sheer scale of the destruction, even though the elevated perspective of an aerial view would seem the best opportunity to do so.[12]

By drawing the body into this equation, the physicality of encounters with Teufelsberg might also affect how the bombings can be remembered in terms of scale. Beyond a photograph or a table of cubic feet of rubble, the scale and scope of the bombings can also be encountered at Teufelsberg through tangible, bodily exertion.

As well as tripping over stones, walking Teufelsberg entails toiling up a large, steep hill. Teufelsberg is 80 metres high, each metre added by several thousand tonnes of rubble. This is firstly evident when considering Teufelsberg from afar, rising out of the Teltow Plateau. From the top of the hill one can see back over the city, stretching away into a hazy horizon. Teufelsberg and its fellow *Trümmerberge* are some of the few places in the notoriously flat Berlin where one can view the city from an elevated position and appreciate the sprawling size of the capital. But getting to the summit of Teufelsberg is tough – the loose rubble and constantly shifting dirt and mud only make it more difficult to traverse and climb. Some paths wind gradually up the hill, others strike straight for the peak at a steep angle.

Struggling up these slopes, I am keenly aware that the hill is only as high as there are cubic metres of rubble that the bombings created. Walking up the hill engages the volume of this rubble, and therefore the scale of the destruction, but it does so through the body. In the exertion of climbing the hill, I feel the 55 million cubic yards of rubble, and, in a way, the 14,915 tons of bombs dropped each month (Diefendorf 1993). Rather than through a large aerial photograph or tables of cubic meters of rubble, the size and extent of the destruction are encountered through sweat, heavy breath, burning calf muscles, a heavy backpack, blisters, an elevated heart rate, a thrilling view from the top and jelly legs on the way back down.

The new materialist approaches to sites (explored in Chapters 2 and 3) have long argued for the better inclusion of knowledge produced by and through the body. Golanksa[13] (2020) identifies bodily, material encounters as a way of accessing 'the unrepresentable' (p. 75), arguing for the inclusion of 'an assemblage of embodied experiences, often eluding the processes of signification' (p. 76):

> Whereas the narrative memory can be consciously referenced and represented in figurative terms, the traumatic one can be activated only through mobilization of affects. Unlike the former, the latter mode of memory cannot be narrativized in any straightforward ways, yet it can be experienced and felt.
>
> (p. 75)

Golanksa approaches encounters with memory sites as 'bodily transaction which engages senses and sensibilities and produces sensations or affects, and so

Figure 6.5 An elevated view from the top of the spy station on Teufelsberg, Berlin. Photograph by Eloise Florence, 2017.

on' (p. 77). Golanska draws on the new materialists to move beyond the purely linguistic, representational or cognitive and draw in more material and bodily ways of knowing. As Grosz (2008) argues, 'sensation requires no mediation or translation. It is not representation, sign, symbol, but force, energy, rhythm, resonance' (p. 73). Foregrounding sensory encounters with sites pays 'attention to sensory perception and forms of knowledge that are not necessarily parsed in terms of cognitive categories' (Sumartojo 2019, p. 26), allowing not only for new ways of knowing but for different knowledges.

The well-documented difficulty in comprehending the scale of the bombing might be challenged by the sensory, material encounter precisely because it offers this potential for new ways of knowing. Destruction on this scale is difficult to comprehend purely cognitively, but the bodily exertion of climbing a hill articulates the scale of the bombings in a precognitive, bodily way. Perhaps where words and critical apprehension fail, bodily and sensorial comprehension of the scale of destruction might prevail. The sheer amount of the rubble at Teufelsberg might offer a material understanding of the destruction that contributed to it. In dominant Anglo-American constructions of the bombings, the destruction is commonly understood to be only a little worse than that inflicted on the UK by the Luftwaffe.[14] But the true scale of the destruction, the sheer volume of rubble generated from those years, becomes apparent to me each time the path twists upwards again.

Entanglement, or doing both

The body features heavily in the kind of remembering that can be done at Teufelsberg and the other *Trümmerberge*. The same can be said of the Topography of Terror, but that site draws the visitor's body into considerations of the bombings in a slightly different way. Whilst also holding the destruction at arm's length through the presence of aerial photographs, the Topography of Terror has very little opportunity to encounter the immediate, sensory violence of the bombings or their scale, preferring instead to focus on the remains, or the aftermath. One sign describes a picture of 'Pedestrians after an air raid … They covered their eyes, mouth and nose against the dust lingering in the air'.[15] Visceral encounters with the violence of the bombs, with explosions, firestorms and boiling canals, remain largely absent. The materiality of the Topography of Terror means physical sensations of the site are foregrounded: the touch of rain, sounds moving through trees, the roughness of a building's foundations.

But because of the nature of the site, the encounter is markedly different to that of the *Trümmerberge*. The Topography of Terror is less like a struggle and more an easy movement through a large, open space. There is a certain peacefulness and safety in the site. Its size ensures that although it may have a lot of visitors, it does not feel crowded. Birds sing in the copse of trees and the streets that surround the block buzz with a little traffic. The overall impression is one of peace and space, with few constraints on movement. It almost mirrors the experience of moving through an immensely large and sparsely furnished museum or art gallery. The silence and stillness of the empty lot, as well as the mundane and continual movement of the city surrounding it, are somewhat antithetical to the violence and terror of exploding bombs that were felt by Berlin's citizens and buildings. The silence of the site speaks more to the aftermath, the morning after the raid, the so-called 'moonscape', or what remained of many bombed out German cities after the war (Gregory 2011; Kanon 2015; Vonnegut 2000). The immediacy of the violence is nowhere to be found.

However, in the same way that the vibrancy of Teufelsberg's rubble brings the violence of the bombings to the fore somewhat, the empty space caused by the lack of buildings at the Topography of Terror makes the reality of the bombings as a sensory phenomenon much more apparent through the immense feeling of absence. The buildings that once stood here remain only visible in archival photos and documents presented on the information boards. The visitor feels some of the severity of the bombings by walking through the empty space created by the explosions that was once a city block tightly packed with buildings. What's more, I felt this to be accentuated by the presence of the aerial photographs, not downplayed. The empty space above one's head as you move across the large, shingled block of the site engenders a defined sense of vulnerability when one is simultaneously looking at the site destroyed by bombs from the air. These aerial images populate the Topography of Terror in the signs on the Historical Site Tour. Images of the site 'from above' are shown next to maps and models of the site today, and specifically place the spectator within both the absence and the destruction.

This creates a rather strange, slightly dissonant experience. When an Anglo-American visitor attends the Topography of Terror, she occupies the space depicted 'from above' in the aerial photographs at the site, simultaneously standing beneath and above those pictures. I view the aerial photographs whilst standing directly beneath the position from which they were taken. The ontological aerial mastery implicit in these images entangles with the grounded perspective I occupy when viewing them.

While I do not find personal accounts of suffering or what Adey, Whitehead, and Williams (2011) term the 'Levinasian encounter with the Other' (p. 180) at the site, I can nonetheless feel the vulnerability of a bombing target in a haptic sense, because of these aerial photographs and because I am explicitly 'placed within' them: 'You are here'. The perspectives of the photographs became the frame for my perspective on the ground. British novelist Kennedy (2007) describes what it is like to see your surroundings as though through the lens of a bomber aircraft:

> Walk anywhere and you'll catch yourself calculating out from where the first cookie [high explosive bomb] would fall and blast the buildings open, let the incendiaries in to lodge and play … And so you see targets beside targets: nothing but targets and ghost craters looping up from the earth, shock waves of dust and smoke ringing, crossing. *You feel the aerial photograph staring down at you where you stand*, waiting to wipe you away.
>
> (pp. 202–3, emphasis added)

At the Topography of Terror, I can place myself consciously in relation to the familiar perspective from above that is reflected in the aerial photographs on the information signs, specifically below the elevated viewpoint of the photographs. Through the act of visiting this site at the same time I view the destruction through aerial perspectives, this Anglosphere visitor can layer some of the assured distance and objectivity that normally colour my perspectives of the bombings with more a grounded perspective.

This evokes a kind of felt, physical vulnerability when it is layered with the sensation of the empty, open space of the block. The Topography of Terror is notably outdoors, only empty space stands between the ground and the sky. I can not only see the impact of the bombs, but can feel a kind of vulnerability to attack from above, feel metres of empty sky above me through which a bomb might fall. Entangling the aerial mastery of photographs taken from a bird's eye view with the grounded, physically vulnerable perspective of a visitor has potential to complicate the Anglo-American cultural memory of the war that tends to speak from a detached, aerial perspective. It does so not by subverting one with the other or replacing one with the other, but by entangling the two.

Aerials and burial

Such an entanglement relies in no small part on common notions of visibility. Visibility is central to subterranean narratives that are associated with aerial photography and its entanglement with practices of security and surveillance (and also with archaeology and burial, see Chapter 4). When considered as a burial ground in Chapter 4, remembering at Teufelsberg essentially becomes a question of optics – what is visible is present, what is invisible is absent. Berlin as a bombed city, as an 'untold' history, is said to lie beneath the surface and thus hidden from view. We can see here an acknowledgement of both the omnipotence associated with aerial viewpoints and the power dynamics they enact. In another similar study of Teufelsberg, Anderson (2015) expresses the desire to be able to see what is underneath his feet when he walks the hill: Speer's military facility. 'I imagine my film being a type of X-ray', he explains, 'sending electromagnetic waves through the hill's surface to reveal what lies buried. Yet, the film will show only what I see: dirt, grass, shrubs, trees and rubble' (p. 75). The surface of the ground is thereby linked with notions of resistance in the context of remembering aerial surveillance and warfare.

Aerial bombing is itself conceptually tied up with what is visible and what is not. Adey, Whitehead, and Williams (2011) identify how the surface of the ground is framed as resisting the optics of modern technologies of aerial bombing. They argue that 'the ground has provided one of the greatest forms of resistance to the aerial, the visible and the promise of omnipresent reach' (p. 181). In the same volume, Bishop (2011) describes the optical relationship between the aerial bomber and a surface thus:

> The triumph of the surface is unavoidable in the visual domain, and aerial surveillance and aesthetics are almost completely dominated by that which constitutes the visible. But the visible, like the tactile, can only engage surfaces … that which is graspable by hand and eye, predominate. Yet the surface also always presumes a depth underpinning it: the aerial view always implies and depends on the subterranean invisible.
>
> (p. 272)

The surface of the ground at Teufelsberg takes on this role of a resistant surface, what is 'graspable by hand and eye', but also, as Anderson (2015) found, implies the subterranean invisible: quantities of rubble and buried Nazi architecture. So too at the Topography of Terror do these themes of the (previously) subterranean invisible emerge in relation to buried Nazi prison cells, air raid shelters and remnants of state-sponsored genocide (see Chapter 4). Through this reading, the ground obscures the possibility of remembering the bombings in the same way the ground resists the omnipresent reach of an aerial bomber. The surface of Teufelsberg is a barrier between me and a hidden reality, maintaining the subterranean invisibility of a destroyed city and a history of destruction. Digging, like that I find at the Topography of Terror, would therefore probe beyond what I can see to reveal something underneath it by making it visible. Again, buried

Figure 6.6 A path cuts through the rubble that makes up the *Trümmerberg* Insulaner, Berlin. Photography by Eloise Florence, 2017.

rubble seems to bolster a key narrative in dominant Anglo-American cultural memory of the war circulating at both the Topography of Terror and Teufelsberg: that post-war German cultural memory projects initially repressed and attempted to forget Nazi atrocities, or in this case, the destruction of their capital.

But this discrepancy between the optical reach of the aerial view against the impenetrability of the ground at the heart of aerial bombing has been challenged. In the least sense, at Teufelsberg, this seemingly straightforward notion of buried equals forgotten, beneath ground equals invisible, and the aerial view as omnipotent over everything except the underground, is challenged by the reality of the hill itself. When walking Teufelsberg, the rubble is not buried. Walking Teufelsberg, as an act of remembering the destruction of Berlin, challenges what I perceive as the surface of the hill, and thus might be able to complicate not only the narrative that Berlin's wartime destruction is hidden and thus forgotten, but also the strict separation between aerial mastery and subterranean resistance. The 'surface' of Teufelsberg is not a solid, impenetrable one when I consider it beyond a barrier to sight. As I explored in Chapter 5, the ground at Teufelsberg is porous, changing and unstable. The barrier between contemporary Berlin and a ruined, past Berlin is therefore similarly dynamic. The ground does not exist as a barrier between me and the 'buried' city. The rubble hides the military school from view, but the rubble – and thus the ruination of Berlin and the labour of creating the hill – becomes evident as I walk on and over Teufelsberg. The hill is defined by the interaction of humans and rubble – pathways carved into its surface, bike tracks built out of and into it, a tourism destination and alternative arts space literally constructed out of the disassembled fragments of Berlin. The rubble becomes a space where I encounter a ruined Berlin as an ever-changing, interactive, almost animate object, defined by the task of traversing it.

So too emerges the dynamic, porous relationship between 'below' and 'above'. At first, Teufelsberg and the other *Trümmerberge* are known as hills, not buried below but rising up out of the Teltow Plateau, filling the otherwise empty kilometres of air between the ground and the realm of the bomber. Secondly, the hills' relationship with the bombings is inherently generative – the 'buried invisible', the masses of rubble at these hills, are not 'hidden' from the aerial mastery of the bombing, but were created by it. The aerial gaze in this instance created the millions of tonnes of rubble, dirt and stone, created a series of new surfaces and new subterranean fields. *Trümmerberge* evidences that the air, the ground and the underground are by no means inherently oppositional or even separate.

There are interesting overlaps here with what is today called 'aerial archaeology', a seemingly impossible bringing together of the aerial and the underground in order to better understand the past. The practice involves using aerial photography and photogrammetry to discover, survey and understand archaeology sites and traces from a largescale, bird's-eye perspective impossible on the ground. The practice is also entangled with the historical development of aerial warfare: 'aerial archaeology was born through the photographic reconnaissance of hidden and camouflaged military installations on the Eastern Front', point out Adey and colleagues (2011, p. 176). Such a practice points to the ability of the aerial and the subterranean to be entwined, rather than framed as antithetical. Adey and colleagues argue that this seeming contradistinction between the sky and the subterranean is in fact a key part of contemporary aerial targeting and bombing:

> aerial targeting has been as much about surfaces as it has been about getting to the below, cutting through the volumetric mediums of air, infrastructure, concrete and earth.
>
> (p. 181)

This enmeshment of the below-ground with the quite-far-above-ground can also be seen in the historical relationship in civilians' experiences of aerial bombing with subterranean safety, namely air raid shelters. As much safety as could be found in Berlin during an air raid was found beneath the ground in air raid shelters. In fact Merill (2015) argues that the experience of air raid shelters was one of the few shared experiences for European civilians during the Second World War across the boundaries of countries and across the Allied/Axis divide. Merrill (2015) argues that European civilian experiences of the air war are subterranean experiences, despite the fact that it was, in cities at least, the air that held the most threat (for non-Jewish and other Nazi-persecuted groups, of course). This experience subsequently bled into the cultural memory of aerial bombing in Allied countries (although to varying extents; see Chapter 1). In Britain in particular, subterranean spaces such as underground train stations and former air raids shelters have become wartime heritage sites. The projects of heritage around these sites largely conform with 'the wider theorisation of subterranean space as a paradoxical site and metaphor that encompasses contrasting notions of safety and danger in both real and imaginary terms' (Merrill 2015, p. 203). Mnemonic frames surrounding air raid shelters therefore can draw the aerial and the subterranean together and bring them into conversation with one another.

Thus Teufelsberg and the other *Trümmerberge* again emerge as sites of entanglement that might disrupt the dominant cultural memory of the area bombing of Berlin. By challenging another assumed dichotomy of above/below, the strange case of a *Trümmerberge* might challenge other dichotomies: victim/perpetrator, innocent/guilty, Allied/Nazi.

Conclusion

In his detailed exploration of the air war and its memory traces, Gregory (2011) explores the potential of shifting these narrative and visual positions that continue to hold the aerial, grounded and subterranean perspectives of the conflict apart. Gregory argues disrupting the solidity and apparent givenness of these positions' antithetical relationship can in turn challenge some of the restrictive cultural memory structures surrounding the war without succumbing to moral or representational comparisons with the Holocaust or other suffering. Gregory argues for a recasting of the 'usual separation between above and below, air and ground, bomber and bombed' (p. 271). He goes on:

> I understand the gesture of imaginatively crouching beneath the bombs and establishing an affinity with their victims, but I also believe that by the time we do so it is too late. Another critical response is necessary to precede, supplement, and reinforce this act of empathy and its mobilisation of memory: one that has the power to reveal and denaturalise the conceptual system through which the world is reduce to a target.
>
> (p. 271)

This chapter has offered visiting sites like Teufelsberg, the other *Trümmerberge*, and the Topography of Terror as one of these possible critical responses (which Gregory says 'can take many forms' (p. 271)). The vulnerability felt at the Topography of Terror and the physicality required to navigate Teufelsberg can complicate the normative separation of 'above and below' in Anglo-American cultural memory of the air war precisely because they are experienced through the normative frames of aerial photography, like those at the Topography of Terror. By bringing the sensory, material encounter with the material effects of the bombings – the rubble, and the empty space over the Topography of Terror – into direct contact with the detached, aerial viewpoints that are commonplace in dominant cultural framings of the bombings, encounters with these sites can denaturalize this conceptual separation, and therefore complicate and nuance these frames of cultural memory. It might even be what Amad (2012) argues should be a 'less polarised approach that displays the complicated material and ideological networks within which aerial images were produced, circulated, interpreted and acquired meaning' (p. 67). Amad argues for reintroducing the relationality of the aerial view, 'its fluid sites of production, influence, interpretation, and dissemination' (p. 86). This could even arguably be done by engaging the relational, networked sites of aerial bombing that are captured in the expanded networks of agency explored in Chapter 5. Regardless, entangling the bodily encounter with the effects of the bombings with aerial imagery at Teufelsberg and the Topography of Terror offers a further opportunity in which the distant, rational, objective understanding of the bombings might be complicated, entangled and therefore seen through the more haptic effects of the bombing on the ground. More specific to the objective of this book, the photography present at the Topography of Terror reinforces the importance of perspectives in political negotiations of Anglo-American cultural memory of the bombings. The optical position of the tourist on the ground can be imagined within the photographs of the city taken from the safety of an aircraft. This complicates the established aerial detachment of aircraft reconnaissance photographs that has so strongly characterised Anglo-American cultural memory of the bombings. So too can the bodily encounter – even small violences – of walking and wrestling with the stones of Teufelsberg engage the bodily violence of the bombing through the all-encompassing, aerial views that continue to dominate the cultural memory of the air war and which accompany the Anglo-American visitor to these sites.

7

Bodies in the stones

Introduction

The first note on my field work simply says 'Rubble everywhere. So surprised'. The first time I walked Teufelsberg, I was struck but how the rubble was abundant, just lying on the ground waiting to be picked up and examined. The shock at seeing relics of pre-war Berlin quickly turned to scepticism: 'Could just be rocks', I wrote. But no, 'Can tell they are manmade: right angles, not "natural shapes". Incredible'.

Later that day I found a small piece of tile. It was sitting in the grass slightly off the path – I had only found it because I had walked over to examine and photograph a large piece of rubble I spotted from the path. On one side, it has an intricate blue and white pattern depicting what looks to be a windmill in a field. The piece is about ten centimetres long, and five centimetres wide. It has obviously been broken in half – one side is a long uneven curve, breaking off half of the windmill pattern. On the underside there is dirt, the traces of grout, and more chips and cracks than on the front side. There are letters etched in the back: ERNST G.m.b.H.

In the May sunshine of 2017, as I held this tile in my hand, history of destruction I had been studying felt the closest it ever would. In my hand, I thought, was the trace of something long gone by, processes we are still remembering to this day, events that continue to shape culture and politics after nearly eight decades. And yet I also felt deep scepticism and doubt: was this tile really, *really*, from the bathroom of a house exploded by bombs in 1944? Was it really a relic of a time gone by? How could it be? If it was, what was it doing here?

What struck me later, after examining the hundreds of pictures of rocks and rubble pieces I had taken that day, was the difficulty in telling them apart. I had picked up the piece of tile because it was so obviously manmade, the white and blue so obviously different to the 'natural' materials of soil and trees and

Figure 7.1 A shard of tile found in the forest at Teufelsberg, Berlin. Photograph by Eloise Florence, 2017.

grass surrounding it. The other pieces I focused on were similarly marked: right angles, grooves, layered and different materials, even text. At Prenzlauerberg, another *Trümmerberge* in the city, I notice 'No real sign of rubble … Odd rock here or there'. At Volkspark Friedrichshain, I write 'A few stones, again can't be sure'. What, I thought days later, was the difference between rocks and rubble? And why does it matter?

✢✢✢

This final analysis chapter looks at various ways of approaching Teufelsberg that engage the rubble as evidence and remnants of violence. I begin by approaching the remnants at Teufelsberg as forensic evidence of destruction. However, as relayed in my field notes above, taking the rocks seriously as forensic traces of the bombings proved difficult. This is because, I will argue, of the lack of materials at the site that might designate the site as a collection of forensic traces. I therefore explore how seemingly 'objective' 'material traces' still rely heavily on processes of codification in order to have cultural and political effects. These stones, in other words, did not speak for themselves (Kühnl-Sager 2013, p. 20). Using other sites in Berlin – the Schwerbelastungskörper and the Topography of Terror – I then show how the notions of forensic traces can in fact be used as discursive devices to serve a commemorative function – much like archaeological digging explored in Chapter 4. Just as much as forensic evidence then, Teufelsberg could be considered through several other narrative devices that are used to describe objects like rubble and stones, with different effects. This chapter therefore explores the possibility of reading Teufelsberg alternatively as a collection of historic remnants and as trash or waste, and how the question of forensics relates to the assignation of value that accompanies these categories of matter. If, despite the lack of materials at the site that encourage us to do so, English-language visitors do consider Teufelsberg as a kind of forensic record of the bombings, there are then certain implications for the Anglo-American cultural memory of the bombings that can be developed there.

Such a forensic approach also introduces the disturbing possibility of human remains entangled with the dirt, rubble, rocks and tree roots of the hill, and by extension with the very materiality of Berlin's urban landscape, further implicating bodies and bodily violence in the cultural memory of the bombings English-language visitors can form there. Could walking the hill, engaging the bodily violence of the bombings, be an act of literally engaging other bodies caught up in the violence? Combined with posthuman theory, themes of haunting, and the engagement with the bodily violence of the bombings explored in the preceding chapters, the possibility of human remains in the soil of Teufelsberg seems an uncomfortably literal instance of Gordon's (2008) 'ghostly matter': 'the lingering past', 'the seemingly invisible' (p. 205). Climbing Teufelsberg begins to feel like a literal encounter between the walker's body and other bodies, entangling the visitor with both the 'lost beloveds and the force that made them disposable' that Gordon evokes (2008, p. 205), but also with an assemblage of the nature, culture, architecture and history of Berlin.

I therefore also explore Teufelsberg as a site of the Anthropocene, embodying the blurred lines between humans' and machines' effects on the planet that become apparent in geology, and the implications this has for the kinds of entangled cultural memory that can be formed there. Geological studies of the hill tend to focus on its perceived toxicity, the ability of the soil to hold and filter water, and the depth to which tree roots can penetrate the soil and entangle themselves in the fine cracks of bricks. But, as I have explored above, the site is also one of (if only imagined) archaeology. Anthropocene imaginings of Teufelsberg allow the realms of archaeology to overlap with those of geology, blurring the relationship between humans and the planet and exploring the bombings as an entanglement of both. This final analysis chapter considers what it means for Anglo-American visitors to remember the bombings and the effects they had on human bodies, culture and the earth's crust and atmospheres in the age of the Anthropocene.

The findings of the previous three chapters coalesce and overlap in this chapter to explore the overlapping implications of considering Teufelsberg as a collection of fragments and a site of the Anthropocene on dominant frameworks of cultural memory. We begin by considering the scattered objects on the hill – bricks, tiles, safes, iron bars, glass bottles, steel mesh, wire, concrete – as a collection of remnants, some of the last remaining traces of a city destroyed by the Allies.

Forensic traces of violence

A pile of remnants

Rather than being buried and then uncovered, as in the more traditional forms of archaeology explored in Chapter 4, the remains of Berlin have been collected and drawn together into piles dotted across the city. Rather than as unmarked graves for a buried city, it is perhaps more fruitful to consider Teufelsberg and the other *Trümmerberge* as collections of historical remnants.

Figure 7.2 Rubble in the forest at Teufelsberg, Berlin. Photograph by Eloise Florence, 2017.

Viewed through a more forensic framework, the pieces of stone, metal, ceramics, brick, glass and wood that make up Teufelsberg and the other *Trümmerberge* can be read as material records of the violence committed against Berlin: burns, jagged edges, fragmentation, bent metal. There is also evidence of the rubble's age, of the passing of time: moss, mould, dirt, edges smoothed by water and wind. These objects could be read as material witness to the destruction, tangible relics of pre-war Berlin, the destruction of Berlin, and the massive clean-up effort after the war (which itself was imbricated in wider projects of often politicized remembering and forgetting). One might encounter the burn mark on a brick as evidence of a terrible fire on Friedrichstraße one night in May 1944, or the jagged edges of a cracked piece of tile a tangible relic of an exploded blockbuster bomb. Walking Teufelsberg, one can run their fingers along the tiny marks along the edge of a chunk of masonry, which might be all that is left of the taps of a *Trümmerfrauen's* trowel as she worked to clear the streets a lifetime ago.

Through this view, the violence of the bombings, the time that has since passed and the massive clean-up effort after the war, feel and seem quite close. They are not distanced, objectively and safely behind glass, like in a museum or at the documentation centre of the Topography of Terror. The destruction is close, immediate, tangible, albeit still viewed from the safe distance of seventy years.

However, viewing the matter of Teufelsberg in this forensic way – the rocks, rubble, cracks, moss and dirt as forensic evidence of the past – proves difficult in practice. At first glance, the sheer variety of materials at Teufelsberg, and the absence of any obvious signifiers to mark it as a site of archaeology or heritage, means the rubble's status as 'forensic evidence' or 'historical remnants' is unclear and uncertain. The historical, archaeological, forensic 'value' of these rubble pieces is called into question, by the lack of text, signage or glass cases. There are marble busts at the spy station that might be from Alexanderplatz during the 1920s or might have been carved in a home studio yesterday. The twisted piles of concrete and metal could be from the Reichstag Building's dome or they could be the remains of a hotel built on the Unter den Linden in 2007 and torn down last week. Looking for material, tangible, forensic traces of Berlin's past as I walk these hills, I therefore treat everything with a kind of suspicion. Ladd (1997) argued that every pre-1933 building in Berlin bears witness to Nazi terror – could the same be said about that worn glass Coke bottle on the side of a walking track? What role did this shard of tile play in the history of Berlin? Could this brick be from the Gestapo buildings, the home of a resistance fighter, the Berliner Dom?

Figure 7.3 A twisted piece of metal in the forest at Teufelsberg, Berlin. Photograph by Eloise Florence, 2017.

Rhetorical uses of remnants

As I established with regard to archaeology in Chapter 4, objects like pieces of rubble are almost always already positioned within discursive frameworks that are then caught up in negotiations of cultural memory. Seemingly objective things like a rock or piece of glass, or even objective concepts like 'forensic traces', 'material witness', 'archaeological remnants', are not only already laden with their own rhetorical meanings, but can also be put to work as narrative and representational tools, both in heritage projects and in visitors' processes of making sense of them (see Florence 2019). Memorial spaces, argue Micheli-Vitsinas and Cavvichi (2019), often 'employ the affective power of nonhuman actors to reproduce ... narratives' (p. 504). Because of their common positioning within frameworks of 'authenticity', 'evidence' and 'traces', objects like the rubble pieces of Teufelsberg can be co-opted into existing narratives that relate specifically to memory cultures of the bombings and the war, both through commemoration and heritage projects and how the sites can be 'read' or encountered.[1]

A more explicit example of the kinds of rhetoric frames associated with remnants can be found at the Topography of Terror. Visiting the site in 1995, Czaplicka said 'moving from site to site on [the Topography of Terror's] topography, absorbing clue and fragment, trace and document, induces the informed viewer to reconstruct history in place' (p. 183). The scattered fragments (which one can still find today) at the Topography of Terror create the impression that these are remnants of history that have been left at the site to be found by a visitor. The empty block littered with rubble, foundations and remnants of the buildings that once stood there suggest that I might encounter history here outside of the stabilized narratives of history in museums or curated heritage sites. The rigid, commodified, museum-like interior of the documentation centre is juxtaposed against the raw material remnants of the Nazi prison outside that can be touched, smelled, listened to, tasted. Remnants are often considered as a way of providing unmediated encounters with the past, free from commodification or explicit codification (Edensor 2005b). Finding remnants at a site of trauma like the Topography of Terror suggests that these remnants exist in spite of or even directly in opposition to the wishes of an official power centre or deliberate projects of heritage. The remnants I find scattered around an abandoned lot in the middle of the city appear to represent a Benjaminian 'stockpile of forgotten junk and detritus that can be reconfigured in the image of those forgotten or trampled by the victors of history' (Bullock 2012, p. 35).

Because of its archaeological origins, the Topography of Terror often evokes discussions regarding the inherent dichotomy between official memory projects and counter-memorials. In its early life as a memorial, the site that is now the Topography of Terror was even less a centralized, homogenized site, and merely a collection of loosely related relics. After the archaeological dig, what is now the permanent display in the documentation centre was intended as a temporary exhibition, haphazardly put together and shown on wooden fences in the open air. In 1999 Till (2004) saw the fence marking off the temporary exhibition as a mark of 'contested social identities' (p. 73), reflecting the dramatic shifts in German cultural memory that occurred following reunification. Nazi remnants uncovered in the central government sector of Berlin appeared a way of encountering the past as 'untouched' by German official or state bodies. As covered in Chapter 4, this has particular meaning in Berlin, a city where the country's task of grappling with its difficult past has often played out on the streets, not in the least in response to and a site of Cold War politics and memory cultures divided by the Iron Curtain. In 2002 Till (2004) described the creation of the permanent site as the result of 'citizens' initiatives formed to make visible the post-war history of official denial' (p. 80). Remnants were framed as a counter measure to official memory projects.

As 'raw' and 'untouched' evidence, the authority of remnants as unmediated points of access to the past can be utilized by political actors to bring capital to their narrativizations of the past. Remnants can actually lend their assumed authenticity to state-sponsored expressions of remembering and forgetting. So whilst the Topography of Terror is itself one of these public projects of political remembering and forgetting, the archaeological remnants present at the site also render it a forensic record of the past, a past of urban destruction, mass atrocities and genocide, as well as post-war and Cold War memory politics. Official memorial projects and material traces of area bombing are entangled in one another at the Topography of Terror. I cannot therefore separate out the activism dig from the establishing of the Topography of Terror Foundation as oppositional, as counter- vs. official memory. Rather, they both emerge as continuations of the task of negotiating political acts of remembering, using the streets of Berlin as a technology for this negotiation.

Back at Teufelsberg, the awareness of these ongoing negotiations over the meaning of rubble renders the status of the pieces on the ground all the more uncertain. Are these rubble chunks, like at the Topography of Terror, the uncovered evidence of an official program of forgetting?

Another site at which these negotiations play out is the Schwerbelastungskörper. The structure is touted, even by its own signage, as one of the last remaining remnants of Nazi urban planning in Berlin. As a brief reminder: the Schwerbelastungskörper is a large concrete pillar (literally 'load-bearing structure'), built to test the possibility of a structure that would be a key piece of Albert Speer's 'Germania' – what he and Hitler envisioned as the renewed capital of the Third Reich that would be built after a German victory over Europe. Today the structure stands in an obscure spot near a railway in the residential suburb of Tempelhof, with a small visitor centre attached with information on the structure and the proposed megacity of Germania.

Inside the structure it is cold, that particular, clear cold that often gets stuck in seldom used rooms with concrete walls, or underground. The chill feels like it has sat in these stones and concrete walls for decades, almost lurking. The summer wind pushing through the door feels like an intrusion. The overwhelming impression is of stillness and silence. The holes in the walls appear to be gaping, staring. The place appears tired, beat down.

A few old, formless and nameless machines scatter the interior. The effect of the remnants makes the Schwerbelastungskörper seem less intentional than the Topography of Terror; the place gives the impression of an abandoned workshop,

Bodies in the Stones 193

Figure 7.4 The Schwerbelastungskörper in Berlin. Photograph by Eloise Florence, 2017.

Figure 7.5 Interior of the Schwerbelastungskörper in Berlin. Photograph by Eloise Florence, 2017.

much in the same way as the interiors of the spy station at Teufelsberg. Like at Teufelsberg, the remnants of the place aren't put behind glass or explained. Like at Anhalter, there are wooden beams that look recent, holding up the old concrete and stone. Despite the surfeit of signage, information and diagrams in the 'information point', inside and around the structure there is a distinctly abandoned feel. The signage and 'information point' are only recent editions. Until recently, the remnants at the site remained, like those at Teufelsberg, notably unmarked and therefore largely unrecognizable as traces of a Nazi past. When Schwab and Beshty (2005/6) visited in 2005, they found 'a mute grey lump', resistant to their efforts to remember Berlin's Nazi past through it:

> Eager efforts to experience this as something more than an abandoned mass of concrete meet with unexpected resistance. If only it offered some trace of Nazi insignia, or some odious corner suggesting atrocious acts – instead of a mute grey lump, not nearly huge enough to overwhelm its surroundings, let alone a curious traveller.
>
> (para. 8)

Because of the lack of signage or 'small plaque', Schwab and Beshty call the Schwerbelastungskörper 'altogether useless' (para. 8), 'rejected by history, ignored by tourism, indigestible by nature' (para. 9). Others have written about

Figure 7.6 Ground level at the Schwerbelastungskörper, Berlin. Photograph by Eloise Florence, 2017.

the structure as a rare instance of Nationalist Socialist architecture remaining in Berlin that hasn't been demolished or 'coded' into particular narratives of Berlin's history:

> Without a purpose, the structure's status as a relic of National Socialist excess has not been mitigated through its incorporation into other narratives, through physical transformation or through integration into the surrounding city. In a stark shift from its purely functional origins, the *Schwerbelastungskörper* now serves primarily as an unintended yet enduring monument to National Socialist megalomania, dislocated from the city it was designed to reshape.
>
> (Copley 2019, p. 220)

Copley in 2019 offers a reading of the site as perhaps what Schwab and Beshty were searching for in 2005, an ominous reminder of the city's fascist history and megalomaniac architecture. The signage helps to position the remnants within particular narrative frameworks, in this case one that Copley (2019) calls the 'common rationale' of attitudes towards making heritage of Nazi traces, which has been informed, 'shaped and mediated by myriad factors not necessarily relating to the trace itself' (p. 220). Like at the Topography of Terror and unlike at Teufelsberg, the remnants of the Schwerbelastungskörper have been positioned within recognized frameworks of 'archaeological remnants', 'material witness', 'historic traces'. And with this position come implications for the cultural memory of the air war for Anglo-American visitors, explored in part in Chapter 4 in relation to archaeology.

Waste

Teufelsberg and rubble generally both have an intersecting history with trash, waste or rubbish. One of the other names of the *Trümmerberge* across Germany is *Schuttberge* – 'trash mountains' or 'rubbish mountains'. Teufelsberg was, at one point, a tip, landfill. There remains a large amount of uncertainty about the true nature of the material that makes up Teufelsberg. Whilst not explicitly endowed with the social and cultural capital of 'archaeological remnants', it is neither dismissed as 'trash'. But what then of the empty Coca-Cola bottle, the rusted and broken safe half buried in the forest, the shard of blue and white tile I find at Teufelsberg? Trash, or remnant?

Of course, the distinction between a rubbish tip and a pile of archaeological remnants is, as I explored above, a distinction to be made largely by culture and politics. Rubble continues to carry notions of waste and un-usefulness because it is often held in regard to ruin, as Elżanowski (2012), drawing on Helmut Puff, explains:

> Ruins in post-war Europe were most often termed 'rubble,' dispossessed of any site-specificity, cultural or historic value. Whereas ruin 'evokes traditions, visual codes and a wealth of significations', rubble, writes Helmut Puff, 'is material without significance, it is matter destined to be removed'.[15] Denying the ruin 'form' cancels the possibility of indexing it in memorial terms.
>
> (p. 118)

The distinction between archaeological remnant and waste, like that between ruin and rubble, hinges largely on value; an object can be deemed waste because it no longer has a function, or 'archaeological remnant' because its function has been identified as an important relic of the past. The permeability of this boundary between 'waste' and 'archaeological remnant' is evidenced by the overlap of the fields of 'contemporary archaeology' and 'garbology' (Graham 2016). Both fields look to recently discarded and discovered material evidence as an indicator of a culture; both designate what might otherwise be called 'waste' as a valuable source of knowledge; both do so through cultural and political processes of assigning value. The same might be said of Teufelsberg: what has been alternatively called a 'debris landfill' (Schonsky et al. 2013) and a 'dump' (Edgeworth 2017) has also been called a site of potential archaeology (Anderson 2015), 'a contemporary and spectacular ruin' (Cocroft & Schofield 2019, p. xix), and 'the dark ruins of verticalized total war' (Graham 2016, par. 2).

A truly fascinating example of the transformation of matter through cultural and political processes can be found with regard to the material remains of the World Trade Centre in New York after the 9/11 attacks, much of which was moved to a landfill site in New Jersey called Fresh Kills. Because of the nature of the destruction of the Twin Towers, most of the victims' remains were never recovered. 'Of the 2753 people killed in the Trade Towers' collapse', Micieli-Voutsinas and Cavicchi (2019) explain, only '176 bodies were recovered from the rubble "relatively intact," classifying the remaining 94% of victims as "missing"' (p. 505). Much of the remains of these victims were therefore moved with the remains of the buildings to Fresh Kills, what is essentially a landfill site. 'In an effort to provide families with some material trace, or remnant, of their loved ones' Micieli-Voutsinas and Cavicchi (2019) explain, 'small urn-like vials were filled with WTC ash, or "dust," as popularly referred, and given to victims' family members in October 2001' (p. 515). I discuss Fresh Kills in more detail below in relation to the presence (or the possibility of the presence) of human remains in rubble fields in Berlin, but it also relates to this socio-cultural process in which materials at a landfill site are transformed into the sacred matter of human remains, matter with value. Indistinguishable from the matter of the buildings, which had by and large been deemed 'waste', the remains of victims of 9/11 were placed at risk of being rendered 'waste', even if only by the act of moving them to a landfill site. To prevent this, a kind of transformation of the landfill site itself also took place, 'transforming [Fresh Kills] into the sombre burial grounds of these now "sacred remains"' (Micieli-Voutsinas and Cavicchi 2019, p. 515). Through acts of memorialization, including the redesign of the landfill site into a public memorial park, the garbage of Fresh Kills was 'unmade' as garbage and re-made into material with memorial and historic value, 'instilling narrative specificity into unidentifiable dust' (Micieli-Voutsinas & Cavicchi 2019, p. 517).

The mostly unidentifiable material at Teufelsberg and the other *Trümmerberge* again evidences how the status of an object as a 'historical remnant' or 'waste' is cultural and political, and therefore evidences how the forensic materials that evidence the destruction of Berlin can remain, mostly, unacknowledged as such. The pieces of rubble that make up and scatter the surface of Teufelsberg are, for the most part, unrecognizable. The rubble pieces are not especially identified as remnants, placed behind glass or carefully cordoned off with signage. Teufelsberg's status as an unmarked collection of dirt, trees, rocks and rubble also indirectly suggests how the material evidence of the Allies' destruction remains largely unacknowledged in dominant Anglo-American memory cultures.

We can therefore approach Teufelsberg as both forensic evidence of destruction and the outcome of post-war projects of remembering and forgetting. Elżanowski (2012) argues that the cultural currency we afford to ruins should be further extended to things like rubble and waste, which entails accepting the cultural value of architectural material beyond its intended use and looking to how it is used after its destruction. Elżanowski calls for the refiguring of the material remains of architecture as culturally productive in their own right, beyond their role as evidencing past and destroyed architecture. Teufelsberg, if approached as the material evidence of destruction that has been swept under a carpet of trees and topsoil on the outskirts of town, therefore speaks to similar narratives of burial and forgetting explored in Chapter 4.

But encountering the rubble of Teufelsberg as forensic evidence of destruction also offers an opportunity to complicate the dominant Anglo-American cultural memory frames of the air war by further evidencing the material violence of the campaigns that is so often left out of hegemonic narratives. This continues the trend identified in previous chapters in which bringing the material, tangible violence of the bombing campaigns to the fore offers an opportunity to complicate the cultural memory of the war that often keeps it at an objective distance, and therefore somewhat minimizes its effects on how the historical responsibility of the Allies is remembered. Just as an Anglo-American visitor feeling, seeing and comprehending the material effects of the bombings at Teufelsberg through the stones herself might readjust her understanding of the bombings as objective, military necessities, she might also do so by framing the hill on which she walks as a pile of broken remnants of a pre-war and wartime Berlin, a place where she can see and feel the traces of destruction Allied bombs wrought on the bricks and iron of the city.

The marks on the rubble therefore also evidence social, political, military and even natural processes. But another, more peculiar reading of Teufelsberg can also emerge if we perhaps look even more forensically at the actual matter of the hill, beyond rhetoric of forensics.

Human remains

Engaging the forensic potential of Teufelsberg introduces the disturbing possibility of actual bodies – human remains – beneath my feet and mixed with the dirt, rubble, rocks and tree roots. Just as I examine in Chapter 5, considering Teufelsberg through a vibrant materiality lens figures walking Teufelsberg as an interaction between several agents or *actants*. But walking Teufelsberg could also be a *literal* encounter between my body and other bodies.

The presence of human remains in Teufelsberg is not beyond the realm of possibility. The explosions and firestorms of Allied area bombing of other German cities, for example, were immense. Overy (2013) wrote that people in Hamburg's air raid shelters were 'burnt so completely that doctors afterwards had to estimate the number of dead by measuring the ash left on the floor' (p. 435). Berlin was notable in that it 'would not burn' (Moorhouse 2010) when it was bombed: its wide avenues and sprawling suburbia made the capital less conducive to firestorms than the densely packed streets of Dresden, Cologne and Hamburg. But the explosions in Berlin have still been described as 'disintegrating' (Friedrich 2006, p. 319), and the bodies of many victims of the bombing raids were never recovered. Friedrich describes the search for bodies buried under the 'mountain of debris a 5-story building creates' in Berlin:

> The people lie within the mountain; some were never found. Russian prisoners of war carefully cleared away one stone after another and they were getting

nowhere. Down in the cellar the people were banging and not a single one of them could be rescued.

(p. 320)

Between 1997 and 2006, Hollman and colleagues (2008) surveyed 290 collections of bones from 257 sites across Berlin and found most of them were fragmented and co-mingled due to the violences of the war. The buildings of Berlin, once destroyed by Allied bombs, were therefore almost certainly suffused with human remains.

We might also look again to more recent violence for evidence of such co-mingling of bodies and architecture. When the towers of the World Trade Centre collapsed on 9/11, the forces of explosion, combustion, collapse and gravity were so immense that many victims, as well as the material of the buildings themselves, simply disintegrated:

> Bodies were hurtled through space, vaporized without a trace, or transformed into bits and pieces. Two 110-story buildings were inconceivably pulverized in their descent to the ground, reduced to atom-sized bits of debris. Massive objects and emergency vehicles were crushed as if they were children's toys. Powerful steel beams were bent and twisted into strange shapes.
>
> (Sturken 2016, p. 14)

Micieli-Voutsinas and Cavicchi (2013) point out that 'nearly 22,000 bone fragments and pieces of organic matter were collected from the debris … Of those 22,000 remains, approximately 13,000 (1600 victims) have been positively identified and returned to victims' family members' (p. 515), with the remainder sent to Fresh Kills landfill site. Scandura (2008) attempts a catalogue of the '107,000 truckloads carrying 1.62 million tons of rubble' (p. 2) that were shipped out to Fresh Kills:

> 4100 body parts, 1350 crushed vehicles, clumps of human hair, the engine from one of the hijacked planes, dozens of Gap bags and Fossil wristwatches, chicken bones from restaurants, silver police shields, Blue Cross/Blue Shield insurance cards, leather shoes, firefighters' boots, diamond engagement rings, American Express cards, corporate IDs, sets of keys, fragments of keyboards, broken photographs, charred photo slides, baseball memorabilia, stuffed animals, and a few battered but intact Rodin sculptures.
>
> (Scandura 2008, p. 2)

Debates continue to this day over the content of the dust created by the collapsing towers that spread across the city and entered the lungs of Manhattan's citizens (Micieli-Voutsinas & Cavicchi 2019).

Similar examples of this kind disintegrating destruction were spreading across Europe during and after the Second World War. Elżanowski (2012) documents the massive clean-up effort that followed the end of the war in Warsaw (a city deliberately bombed into near oblivion by the Nazis) that echoed that of German (and indeed almost all European) cities. The possibility of human remains in the rubble took on a gruesomely practical element because much of these materials (including those of Berlin) were then used as and transformed into building materials for reconstruction efforts:

> One can be reasonably sure that corpses were disinterred during the clearing work. What protocol did clearing crews follow for this unpredictable exhumation? Were they able to separate bodies from the inorganic contents of rubble before it was turned into granulate, ready for reuse in *gruzobeton* [rubble-concrete]? How was it even possible to imagine recycling rubble if it was known that it could contain human remains? Or did the scope of wartime objectification of the human body go so far beyond peacetime imagination, that the proximity of corpses became an integral part of life in the city?
>
> (Elżanowski 2012, p. 119)

Elżanowski follows these questions to their logical conclusion: if these materials were used to reconstruct Warsaw, are there human remains suffused within the architecture today? 'Are there crushed bones and human ashes in the rubble-concrete walls and even in the precise architectural ornamentation made of *gruzobeton* that adorns the facades of Warsaw's buildings?' (Elżanowski 2012, p. 140). It is therefore not only conceivable that some kind of human matter is mixed with the dirt and stone and metal of Teufelsberg, but that this matter is mixed with the urban fabric of Berlin itself.

Actually determining whether there are human remains in Teufelsberg is a difficult matter. Several investigations into the geological make up of Teufelsberg and other *Trümmerberge* have been undertaken (Abel et al. 2015; Wessolek & Toland 2017; Zalasiewicz et al. 2016), but little or no indication of the presence or absence of human matter has been studied. Perhaps it is not possible: Sturken (2016) notes how after 9/11 the dust was so fine and spread so far that it was likely impossible to determine definitively whether there were human remains in it.

But any empirical certainty about the existence of human remains at Teufelsberg is almost beside the point. 'Confirmation is both impossible and unnecessary', argues Elżanowski (2012), 'for even the slightest, undocumented possibility of truth means a total re-evaluation of the material relationship between humans and their built environment, between body and architecture'

(p. 140). As Elżanowski argues, it is enough to imagine the commemorative implications of the *possibility* of human remains at Teufelsberg and the other *Trümmerberge*, because of the shift it might entail in the relationship between the hill and the Anglo-American visitor in terms of the cultural memory of the bombings that might emerge there. Just as I interrogated the effects of the rhetoric impact of the pieces of rubble at Teufelsberg being trash or archaeological remnant, it is the commemorative implications of human remains in the soil and Teufelsberg that are our main concern. What would change, conceptually, discursively and experientially, if the interaction between the walker's body and the hill were an interaction between actual bodies? What shifts in the way Anglo-American visitors might remember the air war if Teufelsberg – and indeed the concrete, roads, runways, walls of the city – are made up of the victims of area bombing by the Allies?

The possibility of human remains might complicate Anglo-American cultural memory of the air war at Teufelsberg and the other *Trümmerberge*. Firstly, as Elżanowski (2012) has already highlighted, the possibility of human remains in the rubble of Berlin and in the matter of Teufelsberg entails a transformation of the seeming 'waste' of rubble into something more akin to 'sacred remains', in the same way that the waste dump at Fresh Kills was transformed. Entertaining the possibility of human remains at Teufelsberg might, in a more extreme sense, mean that the entire hill quite suddenly becomes a burial site for the thousands of victims of Allied bombings. It is perhaps the reluctance and even danger of recognizing the victimhood of German civilians during the war – because of the associated revisionism and denialism – that renders the likelihood of Teufelsberg being rendered a burial site like Fresh Kills extremely unlikely. Similarly, Teufelsberg's physical proximity to Gleis 17 and the other *Trümmerberge*'s proximity to other Holocaust memorials pose the risks of moral comparison and detracting from Holocaust memory discussed in Chapter 2. Conversely, such proximity might also offer the disruptive effect detailed in Chapter 4 when exploring the uncomfortable notion of Jewish remains mingled with a mass grave of air raid victims and even Nazi officers at the memorial cemetery on Grosse Hamburger Strasse.

Secondly, the implications of this on the dominant frames of cultural memory surrounding area bombing are similar to those explored in previous chapters regarding ideas of haunting and buried history. For one, there is the implication of buried and forgotten history, which has impacts on the cultural memory of the air war similar to those of archaeological remnants explored above: namely that long-buried and therefore forgotten truths are being brought to life, and that these truths are free from prescriptive and potentially suppressive narrative influence of state and official sources. Anderson (2015) argues for an archaeological dig at Teufelsberg to bring the 'unheard story' of Berlin's destruction 'to the surface'. But he makes no mention of the uncovering, acknowledgement or memorialization of the human remains, these 'lost beloveds and the force that made them disposable' (Gordon 2008, p. 205). Therefore, entertaining this notion, even briefly, also frames an encounter with Teufelsberg as one of encountering hidden, ghostly and so far largely unheard voices, if not material traces. Furthermore, the (possible) presence of human remains evokes ideas of haunting, which offers the opportunity for a sense of temporal entanglement, whereby the sites make evident the complicated and non-linear nature of Berlin's history. Both these potential impacts of Teufelsberg as a site of human remains can therefore complicate the dominant Anglo-American cultural memory structures explored in Chapter 1.

Thirdly, and perhaps most evident to me as I climbed the hill, acknowledging the possibility of human remains means that climbing Teufelsberg begins to feel like an encounter between my body and other bodies. As much as the rubble's agentic qualities were made evident through my bodily struggles with the rubble (Chapter 5), scrambling over the hill, using my hands, arms and legs, made me uncomfortably close to the bodily nature of the hill and the destruction contained therein. It was, occasionally, deeply unsettling. The occasional glimpse of small, almost recognizable objects – porcelain tile with a blue and white pattern of a windmill, a bent and buckled piece of lacquered iron – left me fearing I would find something horrifying like a shoe, a scrap of clothing, a pair of glasses. Perhaps it was simply the domesticity of many of these objects – the tile of someone's bathroom, the iron bar of someone's bedhead – that made the thought of those 'someones' come quite close. The hill drew the possibility of these humans close, in quite an illogical (pre-cognitive, emotive, perhaps bodily) way; humans like me caught up in the bombings' violence years ago, and now caught up in this mess of rubble and dirt that I was climbing.

Whether literally or through ghosts of domesticity, the bodies of Berlin's victims of area bombing are present at Teufelsberg. Whether or not I am interacting with actual human remains, I can encounter some of the highly visceral and bodily impacts of the bombings through and *because of* my own bodily labour of traversing Teufelsberg (see Chapter 6), but also by taking seriously the forensic nature of its materials.

As I covered in detail in Chapter 6, the bodily violence of the bombings has been by and large removed from Anglo-American cultural memory of the campaigns, instead being covered mostly in numbers and figures of targets hit, pay loads dropped and air crew survival rates. This objectification of destruction also applied to deaths, not just over the course of the campaigns but in the aftermath and the clean-up programs of those on the ground, below the bombs:

> A semantic divorce between architecture and violence can be extended to people. Histories of urban destruction ignore the 'material dimension' of human annihilation. Humans are totalized in similar numbers to architecture and corpses are analogously often described only in relation to the perpetrators of murder and the mechanics of industrialized killing. Human remains distributed throughout the post-catastrophic city – of necessity outside cemeteries – defy accepted peacetime narratives of culture and challenge normative definitions of urban space and place.
>
> (Elżanowski 2012, p. 117)

Elżanowski's assertion that empirical evidence of bodies within the building blocks of both Teufelsberg and Berlin is *unnecessary* runs alongside this acknowledgement of the potential for human remains to disrupt how these histories ignore the 'material dimension' of annihilation.

This view on the possibility of human remains in Teufelsberg is congruent with the posthuman and new materialist expansion of knowledge beyond only cognitive, objective, reasoned knowledge, to incorporate bodily, subjective and sensory knowledges as well. Alaimo (2016), for instance, suggests 'the enmeshment of place with flesh' allows 'a mode of being that deviates from the pre-dominate Western mode of distancing the human from the material world' (p. 1). Foregrounding my own bodily encounters with the possibility of bodies in the sands of Teufelsberg is an allowance for this 'mode of being', a mode I have explored above as a potential to disrupt the often rationalist and objective knowledges that continue to frame dominant memory cultures of the war. By foregrounding and making space for these knowledges, a more complex cultural memory of the air war can emerge, one in which the bodily, human violence of the bombs complicates the otherwise sanitized, objectively distanced accounts that continue to shape dominant cultural memory of the campaigns.

Teufelsberg as a site of the Anthropocene

The acknowledgement of human remains means Teufelsberg and the other *Trümmerberge* might be considered as sites of entanglement of human and non-human matter. This brings us to the final consideration of Teufelsberg for this chapter: as a site of the Anthropocene. Even without this possibility of human remains, the sheer scale of rubble at Teufelsberg and the other *Trümmerberge* evokes the question of humans' relationship with architecture and the environment more generally. While now largely discussed in relation to effects, causes and responses to the climate crisis, the relationship between human actions and the forces of nature became a significant question after the wholescale destruction that characterized the Second World War, particularly in Europe and Japan. In this more than any preceding conflicts, Europe and Japan's biospheres were destroyed on unprecedented scales. Beyond that war, twentieth-century conflicts have left deep scars on the geologic depths of the earth (Zalasiewicz & Zalasiewicz 2015) and the highest levels of the atmosphere (Scott & Major 2018). Forests were stripped, hills flattened, rivers dried up. Trench warfare, for example, left some of the most notable and lasting geomorphic traces of the twentieth century (Gregory 2015), with Valjavec and colleagues (2018) calling them 'geoheritage' and 'the last witness' to the conflicts. Warfare of the twentieth century is nothing if not a strong indication of humans' ascension to a planetary, geological force.

As a human-made geological formation, Teufelsberg in particular is perhaps an overt instance of humans' impacts on the planet and its geosphere, but it also speaks to the challenging of the perceived divide between human and planet that accompanied the wholescale destruction of the Second World War. Before exploring the implications of this on the dominant Anglo-American narratives of the air war, however, I will first briefly turn to the entanglement of geology, archaeology, environmental humanities and anthropology that have coalesced into a discussion of humans' historical role in the geo – and bio- sphere of the planet – otherwise known as the debate over the 'starting point' of the Anthropocene – and its relationship with the Second World War and with Teufelsberg.

Even though it was first raised as a potential new geological epoch by Paul J. Crutzen in 2002, the Anthropocene has continued to vie for recognition for the past twenty years. Geologists looking to prove the geological legitimacy of the Anthropocene are searching, in part, for 'ground zero' (Suberamanian 2019, p. 168). Also known as the 'golden spike', this globally synchronous moment marks when – and where, as time in geology is a matter of location in strata – humans' physical, chemical and biological processes 'amounted to the irreversible crossing of a geological threshold from the Holocene to something altogether different' (Suberamanian 2019, p. 8). The Anthropocene Working Group (AWG), one group of geologists dedicated to having the Anthropocene formally recognized as a geological epoch, argue that this spike is located at 1945, when the 'Great Acceleration' in industrialization that followed the end of the Second World War, as well as the associated spike in nuclear activity, created the first marks of human civilization on the earth's geological strata, satisfying the requirements to be recognized as a legitimate geological period.[2] The 1945 golden spike is the moment-location of 'a vast transformation after the Second World War when the growing population began consuming resources and creating completely new materials at an exponential rate, eclipsing even the Industrial Revolution' (Suberamanian 2019, p. 8). The 'spike' the AWG and others are searching for may take various forms: research teams around the world are examining fly ash deposits from coal burning, micro plastics, testate amoeba, ice cores, coral reefs and peat bogs for the signal. The front runner, however, is nuclear signals, 'most probably carbon-14 and the long-lived isotope plutonium-239' (Suberamanian 2019, p. 8). This obviously lends credence to the 1945 argument, where-when nuclear energy and bombs became ubiquitous. 'Nuclear bomb blasts left a fingerprint of radioisotopes in the atmosphere, rocks, trees and even humans', argues Suberamanian (2019, p. 8). This is also the timepoint at which Teufelsberg began to rise.

Teufelsberg is therefore an obvious site at which the Anthropocene becomes evident. I found only a few geological studies of the hill itself, but much of the scientific and geological interest in Teufelsberg is around its obviousness as a site of the Anthropocene and a possible 'golden spike' location. Abel and colleagues (2015) have interest in the hill as a 'rubble-composed artificially constructed urbic technosol' (p. 3), identifying it as an instance of the 'technosphere', a term designating parts of the environment influenced by humans. Graham (2016) (citing Denizen (2013)) looks to Teufelsberg as a site at which we can comprehend the reality that 'the city [is] a thing that makes geology' (Denizen 2013, p. 29). Cities have long been geologic forces, Graham argues, and Teufelsberg is an example of how cities can variously arise 'on ground of their own making' (2016 para. 7).

Teufelsberg is exemplary of a site at which the boundary between geology and archaeology becomes blurred, in a way epitomizing the Anthropocene. As Wesslock and Trond (2017) argue, Teufelsberg 'is part of the cultural landscape of the Anthropocene, its parent materials of rubble and ash are studied objectively, as if they were natural bedrock' (p. 4). The Anthropocene marks the ascendance of humans to a geologic force, and yet the study of human traces on the planet is a realm usually consigned to archaeology. Instances like Teufelsberg, which

Graham (2016) calls 'manufactured ground', therefore offer sites at which the two are somewhat indistinguishable:

> Geology is the study of the stratigraphic accumulation of rocks and material through 'natural' processes. Archaeology is the study of the evolution of human societies through their preserved material legacies. Which raises a pertinent question: is manufactured ground the purview of the geologist or the archaeologist?
>
> (para. 15)

Graham has a simple answer: 'Well, both'. Precisely the point of the Anthropocene enquiry is to take seriously humans forces as planetary forces, rendering the divide between archaeology and geology less salient. For Graham (2016), Teufelsberg provides a fertile ground for such an 'Anthropogenic geology' rather akin to archaeology, but draws in the cultural and political implications of the term as well:

> Teufelsberg serves as a powerful reminder of the capacity of humans to forget the very ground beneath our feet – to manufacture our own geological history.
>
> (para. 4)

Teufelsberg, Graham argues, is a site at which we might encounter the somewhat unsettling notion that humans are changing the ground beneath their feet in similar ways to tides, gravity and tectonics, which means archaeology, in its search for human traces, must turn at times to geology.

Anthropocene violences

As explored in previous chapters, the bombings, and the sheer scale and devastation they brought, were thus part of a shift in understandings of the relationship between humans and the planet. This was not restricted to geology. One pan-European phenomena in which the industrialized destruction of the war altered how this relationship is perceived was that of ruderal ecologies. In the summer months following Germany's defeat, vegetation began to creep into the empty spaces left by destroyed buildings in German cities. The term 'ruderal ecologies' was developed to describe communities that 'emerged spontaneously in disturbed environments usually considered hostile to life: the cracks of sidewalks, the spaces alongside train tracks and roads, industrial sites, waste disposal areas, or rubble fields' (Stoetzer 2018, p. 297). The plantlife of these ecologies was deeply entwined with humans and our cities; some of

Bodies in the Stones 207

Figure 7.7 Rubble pieces in the forest at Teufelsberg, Berlin. Photograph by Eloise Florence, 2017.

the plants in Berlin's ruderal ecologies had not been seen in the capital before, but they had been carried in on the boots of foreign soldiers and in the treads of enemy tanks. Elżanowski (2012) even argues that such verdancy was in part facilitated by the destruction of *humans*: 'drawing nutrients from the decomposing organic matter – by the summer of 1945 [ruderal ecologies] had covered much of the landscape of devastation' (p. 118). As the plant life crept into human paces, so too did human matter creep into plants. Ruderal ecologies set about re-writing the spaces of Europe's cities as sites where the relationship between 'man-made' and 'natural' became further shattered by the violence of bombing.[3]

Teufelsberg's blurring of the boundary between human and nature therefore both draws on and has implications for our understanding of the violence of the bombings in relationship to the planet, or the non-human. One of the results of the conflict was a dramatic shift in this relationship. This is not only evidenced through *Trümmerberge* but also through the phenomenon of ruderal ecologies, or the traces of nuclear pollutants on the earth and human bodies, or the changes the bombings left on the ionosphere (Scott & Major 2018). The relationship between humans and the planet, and the history of the Anthropocene, is therefore inherently a history of destruction and violence.

Anthropocene assemblages

What is clear, from both the limited studies of its geology and my fieldwork encounters with it, that the relationship between geology and humans at Teufelsberg is neither straightforward nor linear. It cannot be conceived simply as the techno- or archeosphere, in which humans are present as an intrusion, a force acting upon the otherwise pure and free geology of the planet (Edgeworth 2014). My findings in the chapters above are of both a material and conceptual entanglement of visitor, rock, earth, memory, archaeology, bricks and history, findings that are in the very least supported by the nature of the hill itself. In Chapter 5 I mentioned the sense of churning in the make-up of the hill, of constant movement, unsettledness, a constant re-uncovering of rock, rubble and remnants. This was affirmed in one geologic study of the hill, in which Wesslock and Trond (2017) found that 'artifacts such as tile fragments, bricks, and glass shards are readily brought to the surface by burrowing animals and isolated points of erosion due to recreational activities and natural weathering processes' (p. 2). This sense of entanglement, of mixing and minglement, should similarly be applied to exploring Teufelsberg as a site of the Anthropocene.

Abel and colleagues (2015) specifically investigate the 'eco-services' function of rubble fields. Rather than looking – as geologists in search of the Anthropocene do – for the impacts of humans *upon* the geosphere, eco-services studies look to the impact geosphere and soils can have on humans. It is, perhaps unintentionally, a somewhat posthuman approach, looking to the capacity of the rocks and soil beneath and around us to act back, and act against or with us. Rubble piles, for example, vary enormously in their geological, soil and artificial material substances, and so vary enormously in their capacity to service or 'disservice' humans. The geological make-up of these rubble fields can lead to unexpected impacts upon human populations looking to live on and around them. Rubble from Berlin, for example, has led to high levels of sulphate leaching into the water supply and risking the quality of drinking water for Berliners (Abel et al. 2015), but at the same time, the cultural and recreational benefits of green spaces such as the Grunewald for urban populations have been well-documented, and would be counted as a 'service'. Furthermore, Wessolek and Trond (2017) argue for more acknowledgement of soils' service to humanity as a cultural text, a performer of a kind of heritage (this is explored in Chapter 4 as stratigraphical history). Soils have a function for and on humans, beyond merely being records of human activity.

The Anthropocene is inherently about humans' *entanglement* with earth. The Anthropocene layer, the 'golden spike', speaks to an inherent interconnection with the earth's crust, not simply our effects upon it. As the sulphate of rubble – an anthropogenic geological formation – leaches into Berliners' water supply, the radioactivity of the 'bombing spike' during nuclear testing in the 1950s and 1960s leaches into the isotopic traces in our bodies (Hopkin 2005). The planet, in this sense, acts back, not against or with us, but simply within the same network of agency as us. If nothing else, the Anthropocene will show that we are not separate from nature; we are not apart from something that we then impact upon. Zalasiewicz (2009) explores how our traces on the earth will look from 100 million years in the future, and suggests the distinction between human fossils, trace fossils and technofossils might fade (see also Tien & Florence 2022). To future geologists, the 'trace fossils' of humans, such as roads, megacities, glass, will be indistinct from 'body fossils', such as teeth and bones, implants, plastics. Zalasiewicz and Zalasiewicz (2015) compare the mud of Verdun – the final resting place of over 290,000 unidentified soldiers killed there during the First World War – to 'bone beds', geological strata in which concentrations of vertebrate fossils can be found in prehistoric rock. And beyond geology, Zalasiewicz and Zalasiewicz explore the effects nuclear testing and fly ash deposits from fossil fuels are having on today's plant and animal life; not as a present-day ecological crisis, but through the effects they might have on the preservation and markers of what they see as 'future palaeontology' (p. 39). Zalasiewicz (2009) demonstrates how thinking about humans as a geological force renders 'the gulf between us and all other creatures [as] a chasm, an irreversible threshold in our (and the 'our' is emphatically possessive) planet's history' (pp. 2–3). Geological forces – most notably time – will prove we are not distinct from the non-human world. Somewhat paradoxically, while we might be planetary, geological forces, so too are geologic forces able to act with, against us – act back.

With this in mind, Edgeworth and colleagues (2015) argue against naming 1945 as the 'beginning' of the Anthropocene, instead suggesting we look at geologic indicators of humans less as humans acting upon the earth and more along the lines of an assemblage. Edgeworth and colleagues argue this in part because the 'boundary' between the Holocene and the Anthropocene will not be synchronous across the earth. Rather, it will be diachronous, uneven and contingent on very local processes. Edgeworth and colleagues instead argue for the acceptance of an 'anthrozone' within what geologists call the archeo-sphere, or the sphere within the geosphere where human activity is present. This anthrozone, they argue:

> thus includes cumulative events and processes on local and regional scales as well as the measurable global effects of human impact. Despite the 'anthro' in its suggested name, it need not necessarily be defined in terms of *Homo sapiens* alone. It could be characterized as an 'assemblage biozone' or 'ecozone', which recognizes 'a set of dependent ecological relations among species and between organisms and their environment' (MacLeod, 2005). While acknowledging the role of humans as a driving force, it would also acknowledge the interconnected participation of other actants (such as domesticated animals and plants, and microbial organisms in soils) in formation of the archaeosphere.
>
> (pp. 53–4)

Beyond the disciplinary boundaries of geology, environmental humanities and cultural studies scholars (Povinelli 2016; Yusoff 2013; 2018) have similarly begun to challenge the Anthropocentric, extractive and indeed white and Western formulations of geology that continue to frame the planet as something separate from humans that can be acted upon (see Tien and Florence 2022). In particular, many (Whyte 2018) are turning to Indigenous environmental studies and sciences to provoke rich critical discussion in approaches to the climate crisis and the human/planet relationship based in Indigenous and First Nations People's cosmologies, epistemologies and ontologies. These knowledges are long-standing ways of comprehending this inherently entangled relationship between humans and the planet. Our relationship with the planet – with the rock strata, with the earth's crust – these scholars argue, is always-already deeply entangled and enmeshed.

It is a fact I brush against when contemplating the possibilities of human remains in the soil at Teufelsberg, and one that begins to slowly emerge when considering the site as one of the Anthropocene. The possibility of human remains in the soil holds potential for this kind of entangled reading of human-planetary relations. Considering, even fearing, the presence of a shoe, a scrap of clothing, a watch, allows for a further opening of this relationship, even if only obliquely. And because of its entanglement with histories of violence, Teufelsberg offers the opportunity for a similarly entangled form of cultural memory.

Bombing memory for the Anthropocene

What does this Anthropocene understanding of Teufelsberg mean for the Anglo-American cultural memory of area bombing?

Firstly, it might make evident the non-human nature of the bombings' cultural memory itself, and what can emerge once the distinction between nature and culture is dissolved somewhat. Clara de Massol (2019) asserts that:

> Memory in the Anthropocene is therefore not only legible through human archives but also through non-human traces of extinction – flood lines and drowned islands, extinct species and future fossils, CO_2 levels in the atmosphere and plastic particles contaminating bodies and landscapes.
>
> (p. 5)

By problematizing the dualism of nature/culture, new materialist enquiries in memory studies are expanding the act of 'reading the past from the earth' to account for more complex understandings of the relationship between nature with culture. Memory in the Anthropocene requires the continual teasing out of this relationship between humans and their environment as a way of remembering. The depths of the earth's crust, ice cores, the state of plant and animal life, even the edge of the atmosphere, can then emerge as books from which we might read the memory of the bombings, and that memory would be one of destruction.

Encountering the traces of the bombings left in and on the earth means taking seriously their material effects beyond the human. But somewhat paradoxically, because of the sense of entanglement at Teufelsberg, this may actually make more space for the very human bodily violence often left out of common re-tellings of the air war. The non-human aspects of destruction might be taken more seriously, allowing more space for the material effects on human bodies in cultural memory frameworks. Like Zalasiewicz's comparison of the trenches of Verdun with the 'bone beds' of palaeontology, acknowledging or even considering the bombings as a geological force in which geology and humanity are entwined places the bodily material damage along the same lines as the deep and devastating material damage the war did to the planet. If the two are inseparable, then the bodily violence of the air raids might be foregrounded alongside the violence on the city's materiality.

Which brings us to the second potential implication of the Anthropocene for the Anglo-American cultural memory of area bombing, that of scale. Endowing the destruction of the war with the qualities of a 'natural' process has potential to endow the Allied bombers with the power and, crucially, the lack of responsibility, of natural forces. In an investigation into the ways German- and English-speaking populations understand aerial bombing, Gregory (2011) illustrates how area bombing is often described in ways akin to natural disasters, inevitable occurrences that were without human blame or responsibility. Dehumanizing the destruction was a necessary part of understanding the completely altered world Europe faced at the end of the war: it was otherwise impossible to reconcile this level of carnage on that scale and severity with *human* capabilities. In the absence of a human perpetrator, accountability is referred 'higher', often endowing the Allied bombers with the awesome and indifferent power of nature (or God, see Süss 2014; Bell 2012). This is somewhat problematic, of course, because there is no responsibility to be assigned for the damage of natural destruction, no feet at which to lay blame. It is perhaps for this reason such readings of the bombings have often taken up a place within dominant understandings of the air war, as they elide historical responsibility being placed on the shoulders of the Allies.

But just as walking the slopes of Teufelsberg engages the sheer scale of the bombings through a bodily encounter (see Chapter 6), embracing the geologic and planetary forces of the bombings might make evident the scale of the bombings beyond what is commonly told in dominant articulations of their cultural memory in Anglo-American spheres. Again as explored in previous chapters, the scale of the bombings and of their destruction is often greatly diminished in these dominant frameworks, so appreciating the immense impact they had upon the earth offers potential to disrupt and complicate these frameworks. This also draws on elements of time and permanency: if the bombings can be thought of geologically, as leaving deep, irreversible and lasting marks on the planet, they can be thought of in the same serious terms as tectonic plates shifting and shaping the planets; in short, large, devastating and much more significant than 'a little like Coventry, or perhaps slightly worse' (Lowe 2012, p. xii).

Third, and most importantly, is the offering of entanglement and minglement suggested by an Anthropocentric view of Teufelsberg. As I argue above in line with Edgeworth and colleagues (2015), as well as many others in the environmental humanities and feminist Anthropocene studies, the Anthropocene can be thought of as an assemblage of various agentic actors – of which humans are only one. Teufelsberg as an Anthropocentric site might therefore suggest a similar cultural memory of the bombings. This sense of entanglement, engaged in a networked model of agency and accountability, as I've argued above, is key to disrupting the linear, cause-and-effect frameworks underpinning cultural memory of the air war. Furthermore, the minglement of the human with nature similarly disrupts the over-reliance on objective, rationalist and military-scientific knowledges and language to tell the story of the destruction, further making room for the inclusion of more bodily, sensory and even non-human accounts of the destruction. By decentring the human from understandings of the violence of the bombings, we can make space for a fuller, more comprehensive account of the destruction in its cultural memory. This, in turn, disrupts and complicates the cultural memory that continues to regulate who can and cannot be held accountable for mass civilian deaths and destruction during the war.

Conclusions

This chapter explores the assignations of value we give to different kinds of matter, particularly those that are caught up in violence. Whether as a forensic trace of violence, trash or a natural landform, Teufelsberg's meaning for cultural memory depends in no small part on the ways it is framed, just as much as it is experienced. This chapter has drawn on findings from the previous chapters about archaeology, burial, digging, remnants, bodies, ghosts and nature, to explore how these intersecting framings of the matter of Teufelsberg might reshape or at least disrupt common retellings of the bombings. What emerges is a hill that is made up of human-made materials and destruction deeply entangled with that of nature – the two are largely impossible to tell apart, and should in fact be considered as thoroughly entwined. I propose it is vital to lean into this entwining, this confusing in-between the human and the 'natural'. At Teufelsberg, the violence of the bombings can be understood to similarly bridge this divide, which in turn allows for a form of cultural memory that more comprehensively engages this destruction. Encountered as a collection of forensic remnants, Teufelsberg acknowledges the destruction of area bombing was deeply material, not only the rationally and objectively distanced campaigns that are so commonly depicted in Anglo-American re-tellings. At Teufelsberg, they can be considered on a scale and severity that rival that of shifting tectonic plates, as geological. The area bombing campaigns also enacted a minglement of the human and non-human, an assemblage of actors that included phosphorous and metal and radar and bricks and fire, but also pilots and navigators and commanders and politicians and drivers and factory workers. In the following, final chapter, I will draw these disparate ways of framing and understanding Teufelsberg as a site of cultural memory and explore the implications this might have for the underlying assumptions of the former Allies' national and historical guilt and responsibility, which remain beneath some extremely contemporary debates.

8

Conclusions

Unfinished business

Curtis Le May, the infamous mastermind behind the US air force's firebombing of Japanese cities during the final years of the war, famously said of his campaigns that killed hundreds of thousands of civilians: 'I suppose if I had lost the war, I would have been tried as a war criminal. Fortunately, we were on the winning side' (in Rhodes 1995, par. 3). Fellow air force veteran Robert McNamara agreed with Le May years later, but added: 'What makes it immoral if you lose and not immoral if you win?' (*The Fog of War* 2003).

The answer is more complex than the simple adage that 'history is written by the winners'. While their strategic and moral victory in the war has no doubt allowed the Allies to shape and guide the enduring narratives about the conflict, the adage ignores the complexity of the intersecting political and cultural reasons for doing so: the urgency of defining the West as a democratic force against evil during the Cold War, for example, or the very real need to internationally condemn the Nazi atrocities that came to light after the war, and ensure they were never repeated.

What's more, the dominant cultural articulations of the 'story' of the war are involved in more than simply writing history. As well as history, the present continues to be written by the victors, continually proving how very current articulations of the former-Allies' sense of self in cultural artefacts still draw on particular framings of those years between 1939 and 1945. Particular narratives of the war – which after all is actually quite a 'good story' (Reynolds 2017) – continue to regulate not only who can be held accountable for death and destruction historically, but to regulate the self-image of former combatant nations today. The social, cultural and political upheavals of the recent decades in these nations regarding race relations, public space and national identity are all in some way grounded in self-images that draw in no small part on the roles these countries played in the Second World War and how this is articulated in cultural texts. For example, the uproar at the toppling of Edward Colston's statue in 2020 (discussed in Chapter 1) demonstrates how specific cultural narratives about history continue to shape British national identity with so much potency that the vandalism of a statue of a slave merchant causes vitriolic counter-protests and the literal protection of the figure of Winston Churchill. The controversy caused by the mere hint of challenging established narratives about Britain's historical role in Europe and the world shows how little space there is for cultural accounts of aspects of the past that fall outside this 'good war', heroic, morally righteous and victorious mythology. What's more, these accounts are often seen to be challenging or replacing, rather than adding to or expanding this mythology.

In short, there is unfinished business in the dominant Anglo-American cultural framings of the Second World War, and the cultural memory of area bombing is a key example. A well-grounded fear of historical relativism and a similarly legitimate wariness of perpetrator narratives have meant that cultural memory of the *effects* of the bombings on civilians and cities has been too long excluded from English-language cultural memory of the war. While this does ensure the primacy and exceptionalism of the memory of the Holocaust remain protected – an always necessary function, given the continued threats Holocaust memory faces – it has simultaneously prevented proper interrogation at the cultural level of the culpability of the Allies' actions during the war.

This is a significant omission, given the continued centrality and even reverence of narratives about the war in the combatant nations' national identities – even nearly eighty years later. This book adds to the continued struggle to complicate those narratives and offer additional, more nuanced accounts of the war by encountering their effects 'in person' in Berlin. It is my hope that engaging these sites in Berlin as sites of memory might offer new and additional cultural perspectives on the Second World War, and open the possibility for a renewed cultural memory of historical responsibility on behalf of the former Allies.

While this seems like a small contribution, it is nonetheless difficult to achieve. To illustrate how difficult, I will return briefly to the Enola Gay controversy outlined at the beginning of this book. When speaking to the press about the controversy, a curator of the exhibit identified that it was not the omission of the Holocaust, victims of Pearl Harbour, victims of Japanese war crimes or the suffering of the American air crewmen, that drew criticism: 'I think what fundamentally bothers people about the show is that it attempts to tell the fullest story possible. In other words, it doesn't end when the bomb leaves the bomb bay' (in Neiman 2015, p. 16). One of the sources of the controversy was that the exhibition simply suggested that there was more than one story to tell about the Second World War, and that the one the former Allies had been telling themselves for fifty years might not be the whole story, or even the only story. Simply including other perspectives, the grounded experience of victims of the bombings, was deemed 'anti-American' (Engelhardt & Linenthal 1996, p. 2). Some of this tapped into very personal fears, particularly of war veterans. Thelen (1995) identifies how the veterans (somewhat legitimately) feared their desire to commemorate their sacrifices 'would allegedly be diminished by a questioning of the need to drop the bombs or an exploration of the suffering those bombs caused civilians' (p. 1031). But the vitriol that the Smithsonian faced evidences the ongoing potency of these narratives in a much wider, cultural sense.

The Enola Gay exhibit was so controversial, I argue, not because it outright attacked the sacredness of veteran perspectives or tried to indict them, but for the simple reason it suggested other perspectives of the war might exist. Again, it has served us well to be wary of those perspectives; when discussing the controversy, the *Los Angeles Times* (1995) was careful to add that questioning the decision to drop the bomb and placing moral responsibility on the United States for the suffering they caused have both 'been staples of revisionist history for more than three decades' (par. 3), and I've established how this revisionism can slide easily into factual inaccuracy, denialism, racism and anti-Semitism. But the outrage from including these perspectives if nothing else shows the rigidity of dominant Second World War cultural narratives and their centrality to the sense of self of many post-war nations, and how disruptive the cultural memory of area bombing in Europe on the ground can be. In the critics' eyes, including stories about the bombing of Hiroshima and Nagasaki *as well as* than those of the US air crews was so offensive simply because it implied that there were more perspectives than those of the veterans. The multiplicity of these perspectives, the possibility that the story does not end when the bomb leaves the bomb bay, questioned the accepted perspectives of those who planned and implemented the attack. Those perspectives – victor perspectives – not only hold the justification and reasoning for the violence the Allies caused that Le May so keenly identified, but are also formative of what Grant (2011) calls the 'militarised commemorative culture' at 'the heart of [US] national identity', which is 'designed to contain and control the death resulting from warfare' (p. 305) (see Chapter 1).

Much the same can be said about the reluctance of the memory cultures of former Allies to interrogate the true effects of the Allies' actions in Europe. As well as similar subject matter, the Enola Gay controversy holds significant parallels with the tension surrounding the English-language cultural memory of area bombing German cities in that they both reveal the characteristics and contradictions of the normative cultural framings through which Anglo-American populations form and reform cultural memory of the war. What Hughes (2021) calls 'veterans' extreme sensitivity to any hint of criticism' (p. 3) points to both the (well-founded) fear of revisionism as well as the strength of the war myth and deification of military sacrifice in national identities.

By offering a differing perspective, the sensory subjective encounters with the urban fabric of Berlin explored in this book have been shown to reveal some of the characteristics and contradictions of the normative framings through which Anglo-American populations form and reform cultural memory of area bombing. This is possible because Anglo-American visitors can encounter the more sensory, visceral and embodied effects of the bombing *through* these very normative framings that accompany them. In what remains of this chapter, I will outline three significant elements upon which underlying assumptions of the former Allies' national and historical guilt and responsibility are built: a linear model of cause and effect, in which area bombing is accepted to have occurred in direct response to (and was thus ultimately caused by) Nazi war atrocities; a dichotomous moral framework that is incapable of identifying a person, group or nation as simultaneously a victim and a perpetrator; and the objective distance of the perpetrators of the bombings from their material impacts and violence, most often epitomized in the aerial perspective of the bomber and aerial reconnaissance photographs. Drawing on the findings of the four analysis chapters, I demonstrate how encounters with the sensory and experiential realities that the bombs left behind in Berlin, at Teufelsberg and several other sites of violence, can disrupt and complicate these assurances, in turn making room for more a complex English-language cultural memory of the air war.

Underlying pre-conditions

Objective distance

The study reveals dominant Anglo-American productions of the cultural memory of the air war are underpinned by, perhaps somewhat obviously, the perspectives of the perpetrators of area bombing.

These perspectives most often appear from the elevated viewpoint of the aerial bomber, as well as the aerial reconnaissance photographs of the damage.

Such viewpoints work to distance the reality of the damage from the viewer. This distance is also afforded through the typically objective, scientific, military or technological language used to describe it. In many cultural representations, the violence of the bombings is reduced to a series of measures of ordnance dropped, targets hit, pay loads delivered, citizens 'de-housed'.

As I discussed in Chapter 6, the aerial perspective does also offer potential to complicate some of these assurances in that it shows the sheer scale of the bombings. Some aerial photography common in cultural representations of the bombings does convey the large amount of damage they wrought on Germany's cities and thus challenge the assumption that the bombings were proportional and strategic, rather than over-wrought, indiscriminate or punitive. But the scale of the bombings is more often than not conveyed in numerical terms, and is therefore often less likely to be truly comprehended. More on this below.

The objective distance is also reaffirmed by the strong position of veteran narratives and perspectives. For example, one instance in which the cultural memory of the air war was challenged and discussed wasn't around the lack of representation of the victims of area bombing but of the perpetrators: the RAF had long been left out of commemorative honours in postwar Britain, only receiving a statue of Bomber Command's leader Arthur Harris in 1992, and a memorial to the flight crews in 2012 (Connelly 2004). This is in spite of the disproportionately high casualty rates of bombing air crews.

Cumulatively and as I covered in Chapter 6, this has the effect of making the violence somewhat 'unreal', an exercise in targeting and the delivery of ordnance, rather than the taking of lives and the material violence of bombing cities.

The site encounters of my fieldwork therefore hold potential to complicate these assurances by bringing the sensory, visceral violence of the bombing attacks to the fore. In Chapter 6, I showed how engaging the bodily task of navigating Teufelsberg and the other *Trümmerberge* brings the body to the fore, generating a kind of affective connection to the material violence of destruction otherwise largely depicted from a safe distance. I feel vulnerable to attack at Topography of Terror, feel the scale of the destruction by climbing Teufelsberg, feel the power of the bombs in the cracks and crumbling masonry at Anhalter. Encountering the visceral effects of the bombing campaigns complicates the 'objectivist canons of a History aimed at a singular Truth' (Gregory 2011, p. 260) that are normally privileged in British and American representations of the air war. Visiting the sites introduces bodily, sensorial and material subjectivities to these objectivist canons, further complicating dominant productions of cultural memory.

Such a focus on the bodily struggle with the *Trümmerberge* also challenges the reduced scale of the bombings represented in dominant cultural memory of the air war. The true scale of the destruction, the 55 million cubic meters of rubble generated by Allied bombs falling on Berlin, becomes most evident through the bodily exertion required to climb Teufelsberg and the other *Trümmerberge*: straining calf muscles, elevated heart rate, sweat under the hot Berlin sun. By engaging the scale of the destruction through the body, encounters with the *Trümmerberge* offer the opportunity to sidestep the well-documented difficulty in comprehending the scale of destruction in a rational, cognitive sense. The affective encounter with the site is further engaged when considered on a more forensic level. Teufelsberg, as a site of both a collection of evidence of the violence of the bombings as well as the bodily remains of their victims (see Chapter 7), further challenges the normative scientific objective detachment through which retellings of the air war are often framed.

Finally, these perspectives can become complicated because they are layered with these more affective, emplaced, 'on the ground' perspectives offered by a visit to sites of aerial destruction. In aerial photographs present at the Topography of Terror, for example, I can feel the vulnerability of bombed subjects at the same time I can view the destruction from a bird's-eye perspective. I can orient myself within the scenes depicted in the aerial photographs, and position myself amongst the effects of the bombs on the ground, at the same time. The layered perspectives afforded by these site-encounters indicate the critical distance through which the bombings are generally considered in Anglo-American discourses, refracting a reading from above through one from below. These aerial images do not simply show the aerial viewpoint of the Allied planes, they allow an Anglo-American visitor to orient herself within an aerial photograph and thus imagine herself beneath an aerial vantage point, that is, 'feel the aerial photograph staring down at you where you stand, waiting to wipe you away' (Kennedy 2007, pp. 202–3, see Chapter 6). Viewing these photographs of destruction whilst standing at the place depicted in them encourages a cultural memory that includes *both* the grounded perspective of the bombing victim and the aerial viewpoint of the bomber. Visiting these sites therefore critically engages the material impacts of the bombings from and therefore through the perspectives of the systems that implemented them and that continue to frame the possibilities around cultural reproductions of them.

Moral framework: Either-or

The site studies also revealed the fundamental moral framework that underpins and structures negotiations of the Anglo-American cultural memory of the air war, a framework that is above all else dichotomous. The 'good story' of the war that features in common Anglo-American re-tellings hinges in no small part on a moral code in which a person, group or nation is either wholly good or wholly evil. This emerged, as I mention above, partly out of the necessity of condemning Nazi Germany completely for its conduct during the war. But it has also led to a rigid, inflexible form of cultural memory, which continues to prohibit accountability being assigned to the Allies for mass civilian deaths and destruction.

A perfect example of this can be found again in the Enola Gay Smithsonian controversy, when chief supervisor of the exhibit Tom Crouch wrote a memo to Director Harwit:

> Do you want to do an exhibition intended to make veterans feel good, or do you want an exhibition that will lead our visitors to think about the consequences of the atomic bombing of Japan? Frankly, *I don't think we can do both.*
>
> (qtd. in Washburn 1995, p. 42, emphasis added)

Much of the reason for the Enola Gay controversy and, I argue, the notable lack of accountability for the damage and deaths of area bombing is because they are positioned on the other side of a simple, dichotomous moral framework: good vs. evil, victim vs. perpetrator, winner vs. loser, Allied vs. Nazi. Under this model it is not possible to discuss the results of area bombing without them being posited as directly *opposing* respect, witness and justice for the victims and survivors of the Holocaust, the ongoing deification of military sacrifice, the absolute moral righteousness of the Allies' cause (posited in no small part in opposition to the absolute immorality of the cause of the Nazis, see Chapter 1), and the rigid, well-worn, and well-known 'script' of the war ('the good guys won'). Under this model it is also impossible to be a victim and a perpetrator simultaneously. The model relies on a zero-sum notion of morality: there is danger, this model states, in designating the Allies as perpetrators, as this would then depict those under the bombs – many of whom were Nazis, many of whom were involved in the Holocaust and other atrocities – as *victims*. If being a victim precludes you from being a perpetrator, then, *ipso facto*, the Germans under the bombs might be considered 'less guilty' for their role in the Holocaust.

The moral philosophy questions raised by waging a war of area bombing against at genocidal regime and its civilian population are not a topic of this book. But it remains important to lay out how this framework allows limited accountability to be taken for the destruction of area bombing by the former Allies on a cultural and social level. Common expressions of this model can be found in the cultural depiction of the Nazi as the absolute evil Other, against which the Allies' absolute moral righteousness can be juxtaposed. Another is the focus on the terror and reprehensibility of Nazi Germany's actions, similar to the way this is framed in Le May and McNamara's quotes above. Again, I am not arguing for *less* focus on the historical legacy of Nazi terror, but for a model of cultural memory where more attention on one set of mass violence by no means entails less attention on another. I do this to demonstrate the centrality of this zero-sum narrative to articulations of the historical guilt and responsibility of the Allies, or rather the lack thereof, in dominant articulations of cultural memory. Rather than subverting or challenging the centrality of the Holocaust and German historical guilt in normative Anglo-American cultural memory, I have shown how these dominant accounts of area bombing in a way *rely* on these frameworks. The storying of the war that focuses on the Holocaust allows area bombing to continue to be characterized as justified (see below).

To complicate this model somewhat, I examined how the sites of my study could evoke a more distributed model of agency like that developed by Jane Bennett. Through the lens of vibrant materiality and posthuman theory, engaging the vibrant materiality of the sites widens the scope of actions and actors that can be implicated in the deaths and destruction caused by the bombs, particularly those sites at which the lines between natural and human matter are blurred. A more dispersed model of accountability creates space for considering the Allies as involved in the deaths and destruction caused by area bombing without alleviating German collective responsibility for Nazi atrocities, somewhat disrupting the dichotomous moral framework at the heart of dominant Anglo-American cultural narratives on the war.

In particular, the sites where the boundary between the human and non-human became blurred expanded the network of actors involved in the area bombing campaigns, further dispersing accountability and stretching beyond a good vs. evil moral framework. In Chapter 5, the active, unruly rubble of Teufelsberg encouraged visitors to think of the material participants in the violence of the bombings beyond the human: electricity, earth, paper, plastic, wind, metal, roof tiles, radio waves, propellers, cameras, uniforms, thermite, magnesium, phosphorous, air pressure, gravity. This also worked to expand the network of *human* actors involved in the bombing campaigns, incorporating the factory workers, delivery drivers, cooks, pilots, administrative assistants, navigators, chemists, physicists, train drivers. This was also evoked at the two train stations included in my site visits – Anhalter Bahnhof and the Gleis 17 memorial – which evoked the widespread networks of violence that became incorporated in the Nazis' genocide machine. By engaging the bureaucratic distance that lengthened between the decision to bomb a city and the actual explosion on the ground, the possibilities of accountability widened, and left room for the inclusion of Allied actors.

Again keeping in mind the more sinister applications of such models – such as that of total war, in which all citizens of a nation are involved in the war effort, and thus are considered 'legitimate' targets of violence[1] – it is through such a widened, networked model of accountability that accountability can be attributed to Allied actors *without* detracting from the accountability of German and Nazi actors. Taking such a widened approach to cause-and-effect can simultaneously expand the actors involved and held accountable for the destruction of the air war in cultural memory structures – including making room for Allied actors – and expand the moral framework that designates an actor as *either* perpetrator *or* victim, but never both.

Linear model of cause-and-effect

Finally, my study revealed dominant Anglo-American productions of the cultural memory of the war are underpinned by a linear model of cause-and-effect: area bombing is accepted to have occurred in direct response to (and was thus ultimately caused by) Nazi aggression and war atrocities. This is related to the central role of the Holocaust and Nazi terrors as a narrative pillar discussed above: the narrative of the moral reprehensibility of the Nazis' cause only furthered the moral righteousness of the Allies'. But it also indicates more specifically a certain linear model of history and widespread acceptance of chronology that permeates common retellings of the war, discussed in Chapter 4 in relation to strata and haunting. Under such a model, the 'true' cause of the violence of area bombing can be traced backwards in a straight line, not to the Allied bombers and decision-makers, but beyond them, to the war of aggression, tyranny and racial superiority that was begun by the Nazis.

The causal logic that links the devastation of the bombings to the Nazis can be found at another site in Berlin marked by bombing: the Kaiser Wilhelm Memorial Church. The church, bombed heavily by the Allies, has been left in its partially ruined state as a memorial to all victims of war and bombing. German philosopher Anders' (trans. and qtd. in Zill 2011) rumination on the ruined spire of the memorial church in 1953 demonstrates a common billiard ball causality, whereby the bombings are framed as caused by the war, and thereby ultimately caused by the Nazis, not the Allies. When he saw the church in 1946, Anders wondered what Berliners might think when they raise their eyes to it:

> When they lamented, did they accuse him, him and themselves? And when the sky above them turned red, from the fire that engulfed their world, did they recognize the fire of the torchlight processions of the year of '33? And *themselves* as the arsonists?
>
> (trans. and qtd. in Zill 2011, p. 819, emphasis added)

This narrative chain of cause-and-effect not only rightfully maintains the historical guilt of wartime Germany, it also deflects responsibility from former Allied governments. It links the ruins of the church to the exploded bomb, the exploded bomb to the planes overhead, to the airfields in East Anglia, to Bomber Command, to the *Luftwaffe* over London, to Goring and Hitler plotting in Berlin and so on and on, all the way back to 'the fire of the torchlight processions of the year of '33'. It continually 'passes the buck', so to speak, beyond the Allies, back to Hitler invading Poland, Austria and Czechoslovakia, and, by extension, back further to those torchlight processions.

We can see here again the linear sense of history, ostensibly embodied in the strata of Teufelsberg, that I aimed to complicate in Chapter 4. This linearity is most commonly expressed in cultural memory texts as the assurance of the justifiability, necessity and proportionality of the area bombings in relation to Nazi atrocities. The central role of the Holocaust in Anglo-American cultural narratives of the war (see above) means that any violence enacted by the Allies can be linked back – in causality and in responsibility – to the Nazis.

In Berlin, the continued presence of texts referring to the Holocaust and other horrors at the four sites reveals the importance of these narratives of justified and necessary violence in the dominant cultural memory of area bombing. At Anhalter, I view the marks of the bombs on the facade literally alongside a sign detailing the deportations of the Holocaust. At the Topography of Terror, the bombings are visible as the force that destroyed the bureaucratic heart of Nazi terror and genocide. The information signs ensure the historical responsibility of wartime Germany remains central to the cultural memory of the bombings that can be performed at and through the site. Traces and mentions of the bombing are almost always accompanied – whether by accident or design – by traces and mentions of the Holocaust and other Nazi crimes.

Encountering the traces of the bombing in Berlin means encountering them alongside traces of the Holocaust and other atrocities. Through analysis, I explored this in a literal and more ephemeral sense: through the entangled geological and archaeological remains of Berlin's past in the ground of the Teufelsberg, the other *Trümmerberge*, and the Jewish memorial cemetery (Chapters 4 and 7), and through haunting at Teufelsberg's spy station, the memorial cemetery and Anhalter, where the linearity of time becomes disrupted, allowing the simultaneity of the Holocaust and the bombings to be considered.

The simultaneous presence of material traces and ghostly presences of both the bombings and the Holocaust at these sites – in the interwoven traces and ghosts of area bombing victims, Holocaust victims, Nazi officers, Cold War spies and post-reunification artists – disrupt this linear sense of cause and effect and thereby confront the well-documented practice of remembering the bombings as *a response to* the Holocaust. Encountering traces of the Holocaust simultaneously with traces of area bombing challenges the linear logic of causality that underpins dominant Anglo-American cultural representations of area bombing, which suggests the bombs were dropped on German civilians in response to – and therefore following – the Holocaust. Through these sites, a more complex form of cultural memory can emerge, one in which the bombings can be considered as interconnected with more accepted and widely discussed episodes of the war.

Notes

Introduction

1. For more detail on the differing campaigns from the two Allies, see Gregory (2011), Davis (1991), and Grayling (2007). Grayling (2007) places great importance on the difference between 'less precise' night-time bombing and 'more precise' daytime bombing as a moral question, and Gregory writes that despite their differing approaches, what is important is how the two Allies differed on the way they viewed the justifiability of their campaigns. However, Davis (1991) points out that the United States 'judged themselves on their motives, rather than their results' (p. 435), drawing attention to the continued focus of the perspective of the bombers over the bombed in questions of morality, responsibility and accountability.
2. See Groehler (1992) for more on the difficulty calculating these figures. Estimating these numbers is also encapsulated in the German Historian's Debate in which Groehler himself was a key participant. See Chapter 1 for more on the political and cultural controversy that continues to surround estimating such numbers.
3. As noted above, this book explores Anglo-American cultural memory of the war and the bombings, rather than that of Germany. Scholarship on post-war German memory cultures is of course prolific, but for a starting point on the cultural memory of area bombing in the German sphere see Azaryahu (2011); Assmann (2006); Childers (2005); Confino (2000); Cook and van Riemsdijk (2014); Czaplicka (1995); Forest, Johnson, and Till (2004); Friedrich (2006); Giesen (2004); Kettenacker (2010); Preußer (2007); Schmitz (2007); Sebald (2004); Taberner and Berger (2009); Till (2004); Zehfuss (2007).

Chapter 1

1. The US Air Force dropped approximately 6.7 million tons of bombs on South East Asia during the Vietnam War (Grant 2012, p. 55).
2. For more on this debate, in which the memory of victims of area bombing played a pivotal role, see Habermas (2018). As this debate is primarily concerned with constructions of victimhood and guilt of and in Germany, it thus falls outside the scope of this book, which is concerned primarily with Anglo-American debates and historical memory.

3 Sol Goldstein's date of publication means their analysis missed several notable English-language films released since 2017, including *Jojo Rabbit* (2019), *Greyhound* (2020), and *Operation Mincemeat* (2022).
4 Such a persistent depiction of Nazis as the ultimate evil other has arguably led to the subversive trend of so-called 'Nazi comedy', or media that mocks and depicts Hitler and Nazis as farcical characters – see for example *The Producers* (1968), *Iron Sky* (2012), and *Jojo Rabbit* (2019). Both lauded for its subversion of the terror of Nazis and criticized for trivializing the very real evil of Nazis, Nazi comedy continues to be a contested and controversial artform.

Chapter 2

1 I do not agree with this straight line, preferring instead the history of the present discussed in Chapter 1 and expanded upon in Chapter 4. But Knittel and Driscoll's awareness of the legacy of the war on memory studies as a discipline cannot be ignored, specifically the distinctly humanist form of the war and the Holocaust.

Chapter 3

1 A prime example of this is the opening of The Documentation Centre for Displacement, Expulsion, Reconciliation in 2021, four years after my fieldwork took place. Situated directly adjacent to the Anhalter Bahnhof and the Topography of Terror, the Centre has been in planning stages for nearly thirteen years, plagued by controversy and imbricated in the related debates on German memory cultures and the German victimhood debate discussed in Chapter 1.
2 Gunter Grass immortalized the *Trümmerfrauen* in his poem 'Die grosse Trümmerfrauen spricht' or 'The Great Rubble Woman Speaks'.
3 Renamed Brandenburg Airport terminal 5 in 2020.
4 When I visited in 2017, the spy station at the top of Teufelsberg was fenced off, and required an 8 Euro entrance fee.
5 The definition of accessible is of course up for debate. It would be difficult to access Teufelsberg with reduced mobility, for example, and it would be less than safe for those whose access to public space is often restricted at night – that is, women, people of colour, LGBTQI individuals – to remain in the forests surrounding Teufelsberg and the greenery around Anhalter after dark.

Chapter 4

1. See also the so-called German Historian's Debate, in which the memory of victims of area bombing played a significant role (see Ladd 1997; Habermas 2018).
2. See Florence (2019) for discussion of the cultural memory text of the Kaiser Wilhelm Memorial Church using a similar methodology.
3. See Moshenka (2006; 2015) for a discussion of the deliberate utilization of ruin imagery in memorialization projects, also known as 'curated ruins'.
4. See Florence (2019) for a discussion of the ethics and narrative impact of exploring the air raids as 'religious' destruction.
5. https://www.youtube.com/watch?v=pUxVJEocME8&ab_channel=lucabronzi
6. In her fascinating account of the processes of dealing with the dead in Berlin during the war, Black (2010) highlights how while city officials were trying to create a sense of normalcy and respect for some of Berlin's dead, they went to great lengths to disrupt and destroy the normal spiritual and cultural practices surrounding deaths of other Berliners: the Jewish community. Black (2010) writes: 'By definition, members of German society – the racial community – could not be handled in the same way as those unfortunate enough to count as Germany's enemies. Distinctions between Germans and Jews and slave labourers had to be maintained even, or perhaps especially, in death' (p. 121).
7. It should be noted that zero raids took place over Berlin for the entirety of 1942 (Grayling 2007), yet deportations continued from Anhalter for the last six months of that year. Deportations also continued the entirety of 1942 from Platform 17 of Grunewald station, adjacent to Teufelsberg and home of the Gleis 17 memorial. See Chapter 5 for more on Gleis 17.

Chapter 5

1. This kind of language is the reason for much criticism of Friedrich's book: that he was drawing comparisons between, even equating, the suffering of victims of area bombing with that of the Holocaust. Friedrich similarly used words like 'extermination' and 'annihilation' to describe the deaths, and evoked imagery of 'ovens' and 'gas chambers' when describing air raid shelters. See Chapter 1 for more.
2. This cutting loose from time, the non-linear experience of history, is also key to the entangling effects of haunting explored in Chapter 4.
3. Bennett (2010) is keen to point out (and I explore further below) how these networks are characterized by uneven topographies of power, that 'capacity to act' is held by some actors more than others.

4   The translation of Rothberg's book *Multidirectional Memory: Remembering the Holocaust in the Age of Decolonization* (2009) into German in 2021 sparked an ongoing and often heated controversy about the position of the Holocaust in German memorial culture that has been described as a 'Historikerstreit 2.0', or the next wave of the German victimhood debate.
5   Of course, the Holocaust has been described in similar ways.
6   By means of further expansion, Gregory traces this logic 'back to the public sphere itself', to the set of political and cultural conditions in Britain and America at the time that facilitated and even necessitated the area bombing campaign. Thus so too do the politicians, the commentators, the civilian campaigners, the peace lobbyists and more become captured in this ever-expanding network of agency that forms the bombings. An account of the air war, Gregory argues, 'it is also necessary to take the measure of the ground in Britain, in its conventional, geographic sense and in the sense of a conceptual order – where German cities were busily being transformed into targets' (p. 274).
7   This has also been identified as owing in no small part to the scale of destruction caused by bombing. See Florence (2019; 2021).
8   For a deeper exploration of the relationship between the Holocaust, the war, bureaucracy and modernity, see Burleigh and Wippermann (1991); Aly and Heim (2002); O'Kane (1997).
9   See Chapter 4 for a discussion on the cultural memory impact of such events occurring simultaneously. Deportations occurred at Anhalter during all the months that saw bombing raids on Berlin with the exception of March 1943 and April 1945 (Grayling 2007). Deportations occurred from Gleis 17 from June 1941 to March 1945, meaning all the bombing raids on Berlin between these dates (Grayling 2007) fell as deportations occurred.

Chapter 6

1   Notably, each sign has two diagrams; one positioning the visitor within the site as it stands today, the other within the site as it was in 1945, a form of site-based time-travel, through a bird's-eye view.
2   Air crews of Bomber Command missions were often excluded from post-war memory cultures (Hughes 2021), despite their disproportionate casualties rates (Werrell 1986). See Chapter 1 for more on this.
3   Connelly adds that Arthur Harris may have released these photographs precisely because they were difficult for the general public to understand and interpret, and would therefore avoid uncomfortable questions about the nature and intent

of Bomber Command's raids on civilian areas: 'Even Service Officers in many cases have not the vaguest idea what they are looking at when viewing an air photograph … one never knows whether they are vertical photographs of air damage or the south end of a bathing beauty looking north!' (Harris 1942, in Connelly 2002, p. 44).

4   Amad (2012) writes 'For all the allure of transcendent vision they promise, it is more accurate to describe aerial images as exemplifying the blindspot of western rationality' (p. 83).
5   Mangold and Goehring (2019) write: 'The boundaries of this privileged status are changing. Citizen-operated drones, publicly available mapping software, and other access points to aerospace have loosened the state's historical control over the viewing position' (p. 29).
6   Not necessarily to the detriment of adequate representations of Allies destruction: the aerial viewpoint remains one of the only ways of representing the true immense scale of the bombings (see below).
7   These accounts remain largely excluded from many representations in collective memory of the Second World War; see Hughes (2021).
8   Charlwood's account also appeared in Chapter 5 for its reference to the non-humanness of his target.
9   The new materialist approach to memory studies suggests all site visits are haptic, and therefore takes notice of the bodily as much as the cognitive at any site.
10 Whilst the violence of the bombings is often abstracted and distanced, by no means is there a lack of accounts of this violence, even in the English language. But as I covered in Chapter 1, these accounts are often the subject of significant debate, if not controversy.
11 Freidrich speaks of the difficulty of the Allies to achieve the 'Hamburgization of Berlin' (p. 97), or to create the kind of firestorm that so devastated the city. Due largely to its older stone buildings and wide thoroughfares, 'Berlin would not burn' (Freidrich 2006, p. 98).
12 See, for example, the so-called 'blue marble effect', wherein the earth's insignificance in the scale of the universe was conveyed (perhaps for the first time) in the public sphere through the famous photograph taken by astronaut William Anders in 1968, during the Apollo 8 mission (Mangold & Goehring 2019).
13 Golanska's approach crucially calls for a combining of both the representational and the non-representational: 'I consider memorial art a complex assemblage, interweaving the natural *and* the cultural, the matter *and* how it matters, the sensation/affect *and* the complex work of signification processes' (p. 77).
14 Any attempt at a 'balance sheet' of victims killed, homes destroyed, bombs dropped or rubble created between the exploits of the air forces on each side of the conflict has of course been labelled as morally deficient. This is not in the least because it

is the argument often utilized by far-right groups and Holocaust deniers, looking to exculpate Germany by comparing their suffering to that of the Allies and by extension, the victims of the Holocaust and other Nazi atrocities.
15 Behind these pedestrians struggling with their luggage are the remains of Anhalter Bahnhof.

Chapter 7

1 This is not to say, of course, that remnants or even signage in heritage projects dictate or control the meaning of a space. The cultural memory model outlined in Chapter 2 instead looks to how things like remnants and rubble might circulate within existing frames of references for visitors, frames that are patterned and recurring, but are by no means fixed or uncontested.
2 Others argue the Industrial Revolution is this golden spike; others the advent of agriculture, when humans began terraforming, shifting soils and remaking landscapes in order to form advanced civilizations. Still others argue the spike can be found at the point at which humans wiped out the megafauna of Australia and North America, some 11,000 years ago. Some (Edgeworth et al. 2015) even argue that this point, boundary layer, 'ground zero of the Anthropocene', is not synchronous but diachronous, unevenly distributed across the crust of the earth in accordance with local context and actions and actors.
3 Ruderal ecologies in bomb sites also came to represent the material evidence of time passing. In the bombed-out streets of Germany's cities, German novelist Heinrich Böll (1995) wrote that one could tell how old a bomb site was by the kinds of wildflowers growing in it:

> It was a question of botany. This heap of rubble was bare, naked, all rough stones and recently shattered masonry … while in other places trees were already growing, charming little trees in bedrooms and kitchens, close by the rusty shell of the burned-out stove (p. 86).

Chapter 8

1 Tony D'Amato (2005) recalls a former US Airforce officer at a panel arguing the victims of US firebombing campaigns over Japan were not non-military targets because 'the women were darning socks and mending army uniforms' (par. 6).

References

Abel, S., Peters, A., Nehls, T., & Wessolek, G. (2015). Long-term release of sulfate from building rubble–composed soil. *Soil Science*, 180, 1. https://doi.org/10.1097/SS.0000000000000127

Adey, P., Whitehead, M., & Williams, A. J. (2011). Introduction: Air-target: Distance, reach and the politics of verticality. *Theory, Culture & Society*, 28(7–8), 173–87.

Alaimo, S. (2010). *Bodily Natures: Science, Environment, and the Material Self*. Indiana University Press.

Alaimo, S. (2016). *Exposed: Environmental Politics and Pleasures in Posthuman Times*. University of Minnesota Press.

Allen, M. J. & Brown, S. D. (2011). Embodiment and living memorials: The affective labour of remembering the 2005 London bombings. *Memory Studies*, 4(3), 312–27.

Alone in Berlin. (2016). [Film] Dir. Perez, Vi. Alititude Film Distribution.

Aly, G., & Heim, S. (2002). *Architects of Annihilation: Auschwitz and the Logic of Destruction*. Princeton University Press.

Amad, P. (2012). From God's-eye to camera-eye: Aerial photography's post-humanist and neo-humanist visions of the World. *History of Photography*, 36(1), 66–86.

Anderson, B. (2010). Morale and the affective geographies of the 'war on terror'. *Cultural Geographies*, 17(2), 219–36.

Anderson, B. (2015). Trümmer Geographies: Teufelsberg as a site of forgetting. *Performance Research*, 20(3), 75–82.

Anderson, B. (2017). *Buried City, Unearthing Teufelsberg: Berlin and Its Geography of Forgetting*. Routledge.

Arnold, J. (2011). *The Allied Air War and Urban Memory: The Legacy of Strategic Bombing in Germany*. Cambridge University Press.

Arnold-de Simine, S. (2015). The ruin as memorial–the memorial as ruin. *Performance Research*, 20(3), 94–102.

Assmann, A. (2006). On the (in)compatibility of guilt and suffering in German memory. *German Life and Letters*, 59(2), 187–200.

Azaryahu, M. (2011). The critical turn and beyond: The case of commemorative street naming. *ACME: An International Journal for Critical Geographies*, 10(1), 28–33.

Barad, K. (2007). *Meeting the Universe Halfway*. Duke University Press.

Barad, K. (2014). Diffracting diffraction: Cutting together-apart. *Parallax*, 20(3), 168–87.

BBC News. (2020). Black Lives Matter: "Much more that we need to do" to tackle racism – PM. *BBC News*, June 15. https://www.bbc.com/news/uk-53045349

Bell, A. (2012). Landscapes of fear: Wartime London, 1939–1945. *Journal of British Studies*, 48(1), 153–75.

Bell, D. S. (2003). Mythscapes: Memory, mythology, and national identity. *The British Journal of Sociology*, 54(1), 63–81.

Bella, M. P. D. (2012). Walking Memory: Berlin's 'Holocaust Trail'. *Journeys*, 13(2), 55–70. https://doi.org/10.3167/jys.2012.130205

Bennett, J. (2005). The agency of assemblages and the North American blackout. *Public Culture*, 17(3), 445–66.

Bennett, J. (2010). *Vibrant Matter*. Duke University Press.

Bennett, M. M. (2020). The making of post-post-Soviet ruins: Infrastructure development and disintegration in contemporary Russia. *International Journal of Urban and Regional Research* 45(2), 332–47.

Berger, S., Scalmer, S., & Wicke, C. (2021). Memory and social movements: An introduction. In Stefan Berger, Sean Scalmer, and Christian Wicke (Eds.), *Remembering Social Movements: Activism and Memory*, 1–25, Routledge.

Biddle, S. (2010). Military effectiveness. In *Oxford Research Encyclopedia of International Studies*.

Biddle, T. D. (1995). British and American approaches to strategic bombing: Their origins and implementation in the World War II combined bomber offensive. *The Journal of Strategic Studies*, 18(1), 91–144.

Bielenberg, C. (1984). *The Past Is Myself*. Corgi Books.

Binns, D. (2017). *The Hollywood War Film: Critical Observations from World War I to Iraq*. Intellect.

Bishop, R. (2011). Project 'Transparent Earth' and the autoscopy of aerial targeting: The visual geopolitics of the underground. *Theory, Culture & Society*, 28(7), 270–86.

Black, M. (2010). *Death in Berlin: From Weimar to Divided Germany*. Cambridge University Press.

Boll, H. (1995). *The Silent Angel*. St Martins Press Special.

Bond, L., Craps, S., & Vermeulen, P. (2016). *Memory Unbound: Tracing the Dynamics of Memory Studies*. Berghahn Books.

Branscome, E. (2021). Colston's travels, or Should we talk about statues? *ARENA Journal of Architectural Research*, 6(1).

Brett, D. W. (2015). *Photography and Place: Seeing and not Seeing Germany after 1945*. New York: Routledge.

Brian, A. M. (2020). The Strange afterlife of Adolf Hitler in American popular culture. *The Journal of Popular Culture*, 53(2), 363–83. https://doi.org/10.1111/jpcu.12899

Brown, S. (2013, October 31). Mystery of Gestapo chief's fate is "solved", shocking German Jews. *Reuters*. https://www.reuters.com/article/us-germany-gestapo-idUSBRE99U0XY20131031

Bullock, M. (2012). *Memory Fragments: Visualizing Difference in Australian History*. Intellect.

Burleigh, M., & Wippermann, W. (1991). *The Racial State: Germany 1933–1945*. Cambridge University Press.

Calder, A. (1995). Britain's good war?. *History Today*, 45(5), 55.

Cammaerts, B. (2020). The neo-fascist discourse and its normalisation through mediation. *Journal of Multicultural Discourses*, 15(3), 241–56. https://doi.org/10.1080/17447143.2020.1743296

Captain America: The First Avenger. (2011). [Film] Dir. J. Johnston, Paramount Pictures.

Chapman, A. (2016). It's hard to play in the trenches: World War I, collective memory and videogames. *Game Studies*, 16(2). http://gamestudies.org/1602/articles/chapman

Charlwood, D. (1987). *No Moon Tonight*. Penguin Australia.

Childers, T. (2005). "Facilis descensus averni est": The Allied bombing of Germany and the issue of German suffering'. *Central European History*, 38(1), 75–105.

Clark, L. B. (2015). Ruined landscapes and residual architecture: Affect and palimpsest in trauma tourism. *Performance Research*, 20(3), 83–93.

Cocroft, W. D., & Schofield, J. (2019). *Archaeology of the Teufelsberg: Exploring Western Electronic Intelligence Gathering in Cold War Berlin*. Routledge.

Cole, T. (2014). 'Nature was helping us': Forests, trees, and environmental histories of the Holocaust. *Environmental History*, 19(4), 665–86.

Cole, T. (2020). Expanding (Environmental) histories of the Holocaust. *Journal of Genocide Research*, 22(2), 273–9.

Confino, A. (2000). Traveling as a culture of remembrance: Traces of National Socialism in West Germany, 1945–1960. *History & Memory*, 12(2), 92–121.

Connelly, M. (2001). *Reaching for the Stars: A New History of Bomber Command in World War II*. I.B. Tauris.

Connelly, M. (2002). The British People, the press and the strategic air campaign against Germany, 1939–45. *Contemporary British History*, 16(2), 39–48.

Connelly, M. (2004). *Britain and the debate over RAF Bomber Command's role in the Second World War* (p. 28 06 2004-492). H-Soz-Kult. http://www.hsozkult.de/debate/id/diskussionen-492

Cook, M., & Riemsdijk, M. (2014). Agents of memorialization: Gunter Demnig's Stolpersteine and the individual (re-) creation of a Holocaust landscape in Berlin. *Journal of Historical Geography*, 43, 138–47.

Copley, C. (2019). 'Stones do not speak for themselves': Disentangling Berlin's Palimpsest. *Fascism*, 8(2), 219–49. https://doi.org/10.1163/22116257-00802006

Craps, S., Crownshaw, R., Wenzel, J., Kennedy, R., Colebrook, C., & Nardizzi, V. (2018). Memory studies and the Anthropocene: A roundtable. *Memory Studies*, 11(4), 498–515. https://doi.org/10.1177/1750698017731068

Crew, D. F. (2007). Sleeping with the enemy? A fiction film for German television about the bombing of Dresden. *Central European History*, 40(1), 117–32.

Crownshaw, R. (2017). Speculative memory, the planetary and genre fiction. *Textual Practice*, 31(5), 887–910.

Czaplicka, J. (1995). History, aesthetics, and contemporary commemorative practice in Berlin. *New German Critique*, (65), 155–87.

D'Amato, T. (2005). History's two worst war criminals. *Opinio Juris*. http://opiniojuris.org/2005/08/09/history%e2%80%99s-two-worst-war-criminals/

Dam Busters (1955), [Film] M. Anderson, Associated British Pathé.

Darian-Smith, K., & Hamilton, P. (2013). Memory and history in twenty-first century Australia: A survey of the field. *Memory Studies*, 6(3), 370–83.

Davis, R. G. (1991). Operation 'Thunderclap': The US army air forces and the bombing of Berlin. *Journal of Strategic Studies*, 14(1), 90–111.

Deleuze, G., & Guattari, F. (1988). *A Thousand Plateaus: Capitalism and Schizophrenia*. Bloomsbury Publishing.

Dellenbaugh-Losse, M. (2020), *Inventing Berlin*. Springer International Publishing. https://doi.org/10.1007/978-3-030-29718-3_1

Dempsey, A. M. (2007). Berlin's Hackescher Markt: Gentrification, cultural memory and the new public square. In *Local/Global Narratives*, 255–79, Brill.

Demshuk, A. (2012). *The Lost German East: Forced Migration and the Politics of Memory, 1945–1970*. Cambridge University Press.

Denizen, S. (2013). Three holes: In the geological present. In E. Turpin (Ed.) *Architecture in the Anthropocene: Encounters among Design, Deep Time, Science and Philosophy*, 29–46, Open Humanities Press.

Der Spiegel. (2007). Director buys Berlin mountain: David gets lynched over 'Invincible Germany' medita- tion center plan'. *Der Spiegel*. https://www.spiegel.de/international/zeitgeist/director-buys-berlin-mountain-david-gets-lynched-over-invincible-germany-meditation-center-plan-a-517873.html

Der Untergang. (2004). [Film] Dir. O. Hirschbiegel, Momentum Pictures.

Derrida, J. (1994). Spectres of Marx. *New Left Review*, 205, 31–58.

DeSilvey, C. (2007). Salvage memory: Constellating material histories on a hardscrabble homestead. *Cultural Geographies*, 14(3), 401–24.

DeSilvey, C., & Edensor, T. (2012). Reckoning with ruins. *Progress in Human Geography*, 37(4), 465–85.

Deutsche Bahn, A. G. (2019). The Track 17 memorial at Grunewald railway station. *Deutsche Bahn AG* [Online]. https://www.deutschebahn.com/en/group/history/topics/platform17_memorial-1210934

Diefendorf, J. M. (1993). *In the Wake of War: The Reconstruction of German Cities after World War II*. Oxford University Press.

Dillon, B. (2005). Fragments from a history of ruin. *Cabinet Magazine*, 20.

Dittmer, J. (2013) *Captain America and the Nationalist Superhero: Metaphors, Narratives, and Geopolitics*. Temple University Press.

Dittmer, J. & Waterton, E. (2019). 'You'll go home with bruises': affect, embodiment and heritage on board HMS Belfast. *Area*, 51(40), 706–18.

Dobraszczyk, P. (2017). *The Dead City: Urban Ruins and the Spectacle of Decay*. I.B. Tauris.

Driscoll, K. (2019). Perpetrators, animals, and animality. In Susanne C. Knittel and Zachary J. Goldberg (Eds.) *The Routledge International Handbook of Perpetrator Studies*, 192–205, Routledge.

Drozdzewski, D., & Birdsall, C. (2019). Sensory impact: Memory, affect and sensory ethnography at offcial memory sites, In D. Drozdzewski & C. Birdsall (Eds.), *Doing Memory Research*, 21–37, Palgrave Macmillan.

Drozdzewski, D., De Nardi, S., & Waterton, E. (2016). Wrecks to relics: Battle remains and the formation of a battlescape, Sha'ar HaGai, Israel. In M. Azaryahu (Ed.), *Memory, Place and Identity*. Routledge (pp. 88–106).

Drozdzewski, D., Waterton, E., & Sumartojo, S. (2019). Cultural memory and identity in the context of war: Experiential, place-based and political concerns. *International Review of the Red Cross*, 101(910), 251–72. https://doi.org/10.1017/S1816383119000110

Dunkirk. (2017). [Film] Dir. C. Nolan, Warner Bros. Pictures.

Edensor, T. (2005a). *Industrial Ruins: Spaces, Aesthetics, and Materiality*. Berg Publishers.

Edensor, T. (2005b). The ghosts of industrial ruins: Ordering and disordering memory in excessive space'. *Environment and Planning D: Society and Space*, 23(6), 829–49.

Edgeworth, M. (2017). Humanly modified ground. *The Encyclopedia of the Anthropocene*, 157–61.

Edgeworth, M., de Richter, D., Waters, C., Haff, P., Neal, C., & Price, S. J. (2015). Diachronous beginnings of the Anthropocene: The lower bounding surface of anthropogenic deposits. *The Anthropocene Review*, 2(1), 33–58. https://doi.org/10.1177/2053019614565394

Elcott, N. M. (2004). Tattered snapshots and castaway tongues: An essay at layout and translation with WG Sebald. *The Germanic Review: Literature, Culture, Theory*, 79(3), 203–23.

Eley, G. (2001). Finding the people's war: Film, British collective memory, and World War II. *The American Historical Review*, 106(3), 818–38.

Elkins, D. (2005). *Berlin: The Spatial Structure of a Divided City*. Routledge.

Elżanowski, J. (2012). Ruins, rubble and human remains: Negotiating culture and violence in post-catastrophic warsaw. *Public Art Dialogue*, 2(2), 114–46. https://doi.org/10.1080/21502552.2012.717838

Engelhardt, T., & Linethal, E. T. (1996). *History Wars: The Enola Gay and Other Battles for the American Past*. Henry Holt and Company.

Erll, A. (2008). Literature, film, and the mediality of cultural memory. In S. B. Young, A. Erll, & A. Nunning (Eds.), *Cultural Memory Studies*, 389–98, de Gruyter.

Erll, A. (2011). Travelling memory. *Parallax*, 17(4), 4–18.

Erll, A. (2022). The hidden power of implicit collective memory. *Memory, Mind & Media*, 1, e14. https://doi.org/10.1017/mem.2022.7

Eyerman, R. (2001). *Cultural Trauma: Slavery and the Formation of African American Identity*. Cambridge University Press.

Eyerman, R. (2015). Social movements and memory. In A. L. Tota & T. Hagen (Eds.), *Routledge International Handbook of Memory Studies*, 101–5, Routledge.

Fallada, H. (1947). *Jeder stirbt fur sich allen*. Melville House Publishing.

Falzon, C. (2013). *Making History*, (C. Falzon, T. O'Leary, & J. Sawicki, Eds.), Blackwell Publishing Ltd.

Fischel, J. (2007). The crimes of my enemy. *Virginia Quarterly Review*, 83(1), 289–94.

Flanner, J. (1945). Letter from Cologne. *The New Yorker*, 58–63.

Florence, E. (2016). The July 20 plot: Reading news as myth in the imagining of the British nation. *Communication, Politics & Culture*, 49(2), 111–32.

Florence, E. (2019). *Entangling Pasts: Remembering the Bombing of Berlin from the Air through Sites on the Ground* [RMIT University]. RMIT University Research Repository. https://researchrepository.rmit.edu.au/esploro/outputs/doctoral/Entangling-pasts-remembering-the-bombing-of-Berlin-from-the-air-through-sites-on-the-ground/9921893411501341

Florence, E. (2021). Entangled memories: Complicating the memory of area bombing through the Haunted ruins of Anhalter Bahnhof. *Cultural Studies ↔ Critical Methodologies*, 21(3), 251–63.

Foley, M., & Lennon, J. J. (1996). JFK and dark tourism: A fascination with assassination. *International Journal of Heritage Studies*, 2(4), 198–211.

Forest, B., Johnson, J., & Till, K. (2004). Post-totalitarian national identity: Public memory in Germany and Russia. *Social & Cultural Geography*, 5(3), 357–80.

Fornet-Betancourt, R., Becker, H., Gomez-Müller, A., & Gauthier, J. (1987). The ethics of care for the self as a practice of freedom: An interview with Michel Foucault on January 20, 1984. *Philosophy & Social Criticism*, 12(2–3), 112–31.

Foucault, M. (1977). Neitzsche, genealogy, history. In *Language, Counter Memory, Practice: Selected Essays and Interviews by Michel Foucault*, 138–64, Cornell University Press.

Foucault, M. (1979). *The History of Sexuality, Volume 1: An Introduction* (R. Hurley, Trans.), Allen Lane.

Franklin, S. (2019). Nostalgic nationalism: How a discourse of sacrificial reproduction helped fuel Brexit Britain. *Cultural Anthropology*, 34(1), 41–52.

Freeman, L. A., Nienass, B., Daniell, R., & Friedrich, J. (2016). Memory, materiality, sensuality. *Memory*, 9(1), 3–12.

Friedrich, J. (2006). *The Fire: The Bombing of Germany, 1940-1945*. Columbia University Press.

Frith, J., & Kalin, J. (2016). Here, I used to be: Mobile media and practices of place-based digital memory. *Space and Culture*, 19(1), 43–55.

Fulbrook, M. (1994). Aspects of society and identity in the New Germany. *Daedalus*, 123(1), 211–34.

Fulbrook, M. (2009). Historical tourism: Reading Berlin's doubly dictatorial past. In *Memory Culture and the Contemporary City*, 126–44. Springer.

Fussell, P. (2009). *The Great War and Modern Memory*. Sterling Publishing Company, Inc.

Gallup, S. (2015). *Dresden bombed in the Second World War: Then and now—In pictures*. The Guardian. https://www.theguardian.com/world/gallery/2015/feb/13/dresden-bombed-second-world-war-then-and-now-in-pictures

Garland, D. (2014). What is a "history of the present"? On Foucault's genealogies and their critical preconditions. *Punishment & Society*, 16(4), 365–84.

Giesen, B. (2004). The trauma of perpetrators: The Holocaust as the traumatic reference of German national identity. In J. C. Alexander, R. Eyerman, B. Giesen, N. J. Smelser, & P. Sztompka (Eds.), *Cultural Trauma and Collective Identity*, 112–54, University of California Press.

Giroux, H. A. (2016). Donald Trump and neo-fascism in America. *Arena Magazine*, 140, 31–2.

Golańska, D. (2015). Affective spaces, sensuous engagements: In quest of a synaesthetic approach to 'dark memorials. *International Journal of Heritage Studies*, 21(8), 773–90.

Golanska, D. (2020). Bodily collisions: Toward a new materialist account of memorial art. *Memory Studies*, 13(1), 74–89.

Goldstein, C. S. (2017). Good kill? US soldiers and the killing of Civilians in American film. In C. Hellmich & L. Purse (Eds.), *Disappearing War: Interdisciplinary Perspectives on Cinema and Erasure in the Post 9/11 World*, 16–33, Edinburgh University Press.

Goldstein, R. (1999). World War II chic'. *Village Voice*, 44, 42–7.

González-Ruibal, A. (2008). Time to destroy: An archaeology of supermodernity. *Current Anthropology*, 49(2), 247–79.

Gordon, A. (2008). *Ghostly Matters: Haunting and the Sociological Imagination*. University of Minnesota Press.

Gordon, A. (2011). Some thoughts on haunting and futurity. *Borderlands*, 10(2), 1–21.

Gould, M. R., & Silverman, R. E. (2013). Stumbling upon history: Collective memory and the urban landscape. *GeoJournal*, 78(5), 791–801.

Graham, S. (2016). City ground. *Places Journal*. https://doi.org/10.22269/161107

Grant, R. G. (2012). *The Vietnam War*. Encyclopedia Britannica Arcturus Publishers.

Grant, S.-M. (2011). Constructing a commemorative culture: American veterans and memorialization from Valley Forge to Vietnam. *Journal of War & Culture Studies*, 4(3), 305–22. https://doi.org/10.1386/jwcs.4.3.305_1

Grayling, A. C. (2007). *Among the Dead Cities: The History and Moral Legacy of the WWII Bombing of Civilians in Germany and Japan*. Bloomsbury Publishing.

Grayson, K. (2016). *Cultural Politics of Targeted Killing: On Drones, Counter-Insurgency, and Violence*. Routledge. https://doi.org/10.4324/9781315627755

Gregory, D. (2011). "Doors into nowhere": Dead cities and the natural history of destruction. In P. Meusburger, M. H. Ernan, & E. Wunder (Eds.), *Cultural Memories*, 249–83, Springer.

Gregory, D. (2016). The natures of war. *Antipode*, 48(1), 3–56.

Greyhound (2020), [Film] A. Schneider, Zhengfu Pictures.

Groehler, O. (1992). The conduct of the air war in the Second World War: An international comparison. In H. Boog (Ed.), *Proceedings of the International Conference of Historians in Freiburg im Breisgau, Federal Republic of Germany, from 29 August to 2 September 1988*, 279–97, Berg.

Grossberg, L., Wartella, E., Whitney, D. C., & Wise, J. M. (2006). *Media Making: Mass Media in a Popular Culture*. SAGE Publications.

Guggenheim, M. (2009). Building memory: Architecture, networks and users. *Memory Studies*, 2(1), 39–53.

Habermas, J. (2018). *The New Conservatism: Cultural Criticism and the Historians Debate*. John Wiley and Sons. Halbwachs.

Hacksaw Ridge (2016). [Film] Dir. M. Gibson, Lionsgate.

Hake, S. (2012). *Screen Nazis: Cinema, History, and Democracy*. University of Wisconsin Press.

Halbwachs, M. (1992). *On Collective Memory*. University of Chicago Press.

Hansen, R. (2008). *Fire and Fury: The Allied Bombing of Germany 1942–45*. Doubleday Canada.

Haraway, D. (1988). Situated knowledges: The science question in Feminism and the privilege of partial perspective. *Feminist Studies*, 14(3), 575–99. https://doi.org/10.2307/3178066

Haraway, D. J. (2016). *Staying with the Trouble*. Duke University Press.

Hassapopoulou, M. (2018). Playing with history: Collective memory, national trauma, and dark tourism in virtual reality docugames. *New Review of Film and Television Studies*, 16(4), 365–92. https://doi.org/10.1080/17400309.2018.1519207

Hastings, M. (2013). *Bomber Command*. Zenith Press.

Hedetoft, U. (1993). National identity and mentalities of war in three EC countries'. *Journal of Peace Research*, 30(3), 281–300.

Hitchens, C. (2003). The wartime toll on Germany. *The Atlantic Monthly*, 291(1), 182–9.

Hoelscher, S. (2012). 'Dresden, a camera accuses': Rubble photography and the politics of memory in a divided Germany. *History of Photography*, 36(3), 288–305.

Hohn, U. (1994). The Bomber's Baedeker – target book for strategic bombing in the economic warfare against German towns 1943–45'. *GeoJournal*, 34(2), 213–30.

Hollmann, T., Byard, R. W., & Tsokos, M. (2008). The processing of skeletonized human remains found in Berlin, Germany. *Journal of Forensic and Legal Medicine*, 15(7), 420–5. https://doi.org/10.1016/j.jflm.2008.02.010

Hopkin, M. (2005). Carbon in teeth helps to identify disaster victims. *Nature*. https://doi.org/10.1038/news050912-7

Hoskins, A. (2017). The restless past: An introduction to digital memory and media. In A. Hoskins (Ed.), *Digital Memory Studies*, 13–36, Routledge.

Hughes, H. (2021). Memorializing RAF Bomber Command in the United Kingdom. *Journal of War & Culture Studies*, 0(0), 1–23. https://doi.org/10.1080/17526272.2021.1938840

Huyssen, A. (2003). Air war legacies: From Dresden to Baghdad'. *New German Critique*, 90, 163–76.

Illustrated London News. (1943). The glory on their wings. *Illustrated London News*, 23(ue 5414), 2.

Ingold, T. (1993). The temporality of the landscape. *World Archaeology*, 25(2), 152–74.

Ingold, T. (2010). Ways of mind-walking: Reading, writing, painting. *Visual Studies*, 25(1), 15–23.

Jackson, M. (2007). *Excursions*. Duke University Press.

Jackson, P. (2020). *Transnational neo-Nazism in the USA, United Kingdom and Australia*. George Washington University.

Jacobs, J. (2008). *Houses of Life: Jewish Cemeteries of Europe*. White Lion Publishing.

Jojo Rabbit. (2019). [Film] Dir. T. Waititi, Fox Searchlight Pictures.

Jordan, J. A. (2006). *Structures of Memory: Understanding Urban Change in Berlin and Beyond*. Stanford University Press.

Judt, T. (1992). The past is another country: Myth and memory in postwar Europe. *Daedalus*, 121(4), 83–118.

Kanon, J. (2015). *The Good German*. Little Brown.

Kansteiner, W. (2017). The Holocaust in the 21st century: Digital anxiety, transnational cosmopolitanism, and never again genocide without memory. In *Digital Memory Studies*, 110–40, Routledge.

Kaplan, C. (2017). *Aerial Aftermaths: Wartime from above*. Duke University Press.

Kelsey, D. (2013). The myth of the "Blitz spirit" in British newspaper responses to the July 7th bombings. *Social Semiotics*, 23(1), 83–99.

Kennedy, A. L. (2007). *Day*. Jonathan Cape.

Kennedy, R., & Radstone, S. (2013). Memory up close: Memory studies in Australia. *Memory Studies*, 6(3), 237–44.

Kettenacker, L. (2010). The German debate. In I. Primoratz (Ed.), *Terror from the Sky: The Bombing of German Cities in World War II*. Berghahn Books.

Klemperer, V. (2013). *To the Bitter End: The Diaries of Victor Klemperer 1942–45* (M. Chalmers & H. UK, Trans.). Preface by Martin Chalmers.

Knittel, S. C., & Driscoll, K. (2017). Introduction: Memory after Humanism. *Parallax*, 23(4), 379–83. https://doi.org/10.1080/13534645.2017.1374507

Kolk, H. A. (2020). Negative heritage: The material-cultural politics of the American haunted history tour. *Journal of Cultural Geography*, 37(2), 117–56.

Korte, B. (2019). *In the Brexit mood: Film critics and British World War II cinema after 2016*. Conference: Writers and Intellectuals on Britain and Europe, 1918–2018', Northumbria University, 2018.

Kühnl-Sager, C. (2013). 'Steine reden nicht von selbst': Enthüllung weiterer historischer Informationsstelen auf dem Tempelhofer Feld. *Aktivesmuseum Mitgliederrundbrief*, 69.

Kysela, J., & Štorková, P. (2015). Using augmented reality as a medium for teaching History and Tourism. *Procedia - Social and Behavioral Sciences*, 174, 926–31. https://doi.org/10.1016/j.sbspro.2015.01.713

Ladd, B. (1997). *The Ghosts of Berlin: Confronting German History in the Urban Landscape*. University of Chicago Press.

Landsberg, A. (2003). Prosthetic memory: The ethics and politics of memory in an age of mass culture. In P. Grainge (Ed.), *Memory and Popular Film*, 144–61, Manchester University Press.

Langenbacher, E. (2010). Still the unmasterable past? The impact of history and memory in the Federal Republic of Germany'. *German Politics*, 19(1), 24–40.

Latour, B. (2004). *Politics of Nature: How to Bring the Sciences into Democracy* (C. Porter, Trans.). Harvard University Press.

Lee, J. (2020). *The Media and the Normalisation of Right-Wing Violence in the Age of Brexit and Trump*. Rowman & Littlefield. https://dora.dmu.ac.uk/handle/2086/20321

Lekan, T. M. (2009). *Imagining the Nation in Nature: Landscape Preservation and German Identity, 1885–1945*. Harvard University Press.

Lekan, T. M., & Zeller, T. (2005). *Germany's Nature: Cultural Landscapes and Environmental History*. Rutgers University Press.

Lennon, J. (2017). Dark tourism. *Oxford Research Encyclopedia of Criminology and Criminal Justice*. https://doi.org/10.1093/acrefore/9780190264079.013.212

Levi, N., & Rothberg, M. (2018a). Memory studies in a moment of danger: Fascism, postfascism, and the contemporary political imaginary. *Memory Studies*, 11(3), 355–67.

Levy, D., & Sznaider, N. (2002). Memory unbound: The Holocaust and the formation of cosmopolitan memory. *European Journal of Social Theory*, 5(1), 87–106.

Lewis, T. (2015). One city block at a time': Researching and cultivating green transformations. *International Journal of Cultural Studies*, 18(3), 347–63.

Lipstadt, D. E. (1993). *Denying the Holocaust: The Growing Assault on Truth and Memory*. Simon and Schuster.

Los Angeles Times. (1995, February 1). *Wrong place for anti-nuclear message: Smithsonian scotches Enola Gay exhibit amid a controversy that shouldn't have happened. Los Angeles Times.* https://www.latimes.com/archives/la-xpm-1995-02-01-me-26610-story.html

Lowe, K. (2012). *Inferno: The Devastation of Hamburg, 1943*. Penguin.

Maier, C. S. (1988). *The Unmasterable Past: History, Holocaust, and German National Identity*. Harvard University Press.

Mangold, E. B., & Goehring, C. (2019). The visual rhetoric of the aerial view: From surveillance to resistance. *Quarterly Journal of Speech*, 105(1), 25–41.

Marschall, S. (2015). Touring memories of the erased city: Memory, tourism and notions of 'home'. *Tourism Geographies*, 17(3), 332–49.

Massol, C. de. (2019). The Anthropocene memorial: Recording climate change on the banks of the Potomac river in Washington D.C. *Sanglap: Journal of Literary and Cultural Inquiry*, 5(2), 5–18.

Matheson, N. (2008). National identity and the melancholy of ruins: Cecil Beaton's photographs of the Blitz. *Journal of War & Culture Studies*, 1(3), pp. 261–74.

McClancy, K. (2018). Winter soldiers and Sunshine patriots: World War II and the Cold War in Captain America. *ImageTexT: Interdisciplinary Comics Studies*, 9(3), 10.

McRae, L. (2002). The Postmodern Prometheus: Collective experience and the carnivalesque. *Transformations*, 3.

Merrill, S., Keightley, E., & Daphi, P. (2020). *Social Movements, Cultural Memory and Digital Media: Mobilising Mediated Remembrance*. Springer Nature.

Micieli-Voutsinas, J., & Cavicchi, J. (2019). Toxic landfills, survivor trees, and dust cloud memories: More-than- human ecologies of 9/11 memory. *Environment and Planning D: Society and Space*, 37(3), 504–22.

Miller, L. (2020). 'Wolfenstein II'and MAGA as fandom. *Transformative Works and Cultures*, 32.

Moeller, R. G. (2005). Germans as victims?: Thoughts on a post-Cold War history of World War II's legacies. *History & Memory*, 17(1–2), 145–94.

Moeller, R. G. (2006, March). On the history of man-made destruction: Loss, death, memory, and Germany in the bombing war. In *History Workshop Journal,* 61(1), 103–134. Oxford University Press.

Mondon, A., & Winter, A. (2020). *Reactionary Democracy: How Racism and the Populist Far Right Became Mainstream*. Verso Books.

Moorehead, A. (1968). *Eclipse*. Harper & Row.

Moorhouse, R. (2010). *Berlin at War*. Basic Books.

Morris, B. (2004). What we talk about when we talk about 'walking in the city'. *Cultural Studies*, 18(5), 675–97.

Morris, E. (2004). *The Fog of War*. Sony Pictures Classics.

Moshenka, G. (2006). Scales of memory in the archaeology of the Second World War. *Papers from the Institute of Archaeology*, 17, 58–68.

Moshenska, G. (2009). Resonant materiality and violent remembering: Archaeology, memory and bombing. *International Journal of Heritage Studies*, 15(1), 44–56.

Müller, R.-D., Schonherr, N., & Widera, T. (2010). *Die Zerstörung Dresdens 13. bis 15. Februar 1945: Gutachten und Ergebnisse der Dresdner Historikerkommission zur Ermittlung der Opferzahlen* (Vol. 58). V&R unipress GmbH.

Neiman, S. (2015). Forgetting Hiroshima, remembering Auschwitz: Tales of two exhibits. *Thesis Eleven*, 129(1), 7–26.

Noakes, L., & Pattinson, J. (2013). *British Cultural Memory and the Second World War*. A&C Black.

Noon, D. H. (2004). Operation enduring analogy: World War II, the war on terror, and the uses of historical memory. *Rhetoric & Public Affairs*, 7(3), 339–64.

Nora, P., Olick, J., Vinitzky-Seroussi, V., & Levy, D. (1989). Between memory and history: Les lieux de memoire. *The Collective Memory Reader*, 26(1), 7–24.

O'Kane, R. H. (1997). Modernity, the Holocaust and politics. *Economy and Society*, 26(1), 43–61.

Olick, J., Vinitzky-Seroussi, V., & Levy, D. (2011). Introduction. In J. Olick, V. Vinitzky-Seroussi & D. Levy (Eds.) *The Collective Memory Reader*, 3–62, Oxford University Press.

Operation Mincemeat (2022), [Film] J. Madden, Warner Bros. Pictures.

Osborne, T. (2019). *A Critical Reflection on Doing Memory Research through the Body*. In D. Drozdzewski & C. Birdsall (Eds.), *Doing Memory Research*, Palgrave Macmillan.

Overy, R. (2013). *The Bombing War: Europe, 1939–1945*. Penguin UK.

Overy, R. (2014). *The Bombers and The Bombed: Allied Air War over Europe 1940–1945*. Viking.

Parker, J. (2013). 'This is our Armageddon': Berlin in postwar American fiction. *Amaltea. Revista de mitocrítica*, 5, 129–39.

Pastor, D., & Kent, A. J. (2020). Transformative landscapes: Liminality and visitors' emotional experiences at German memorial sites. *Tourism Geographies*, 22(2), 250–72.

Pirro, R. (2011). Luftkrieg and alien invasion: Unacknowledged themes of German wartime suffering in the Hollywood blockbuster Independence Day. *European Journal of American Culture*, 30(1), 19–42.

Portelli, A. (2006). So much depends on a red bus, or, innocent victims of the liberating gun. *Oral History*, 29–43.

Povinelli, E. A. (2016). *Geontologies*. Duke University Press.

Presner, T. S. (2001). Traveling between Delos and Berlin: Heidegger and Celan on the topography of 'what remains'. *The German Quarterly*, 74(4), 417–29.

Preußer, H.-P. (2007). Regarding and imagining. Contrived immediacy of the Allied bombing campaign in photography, novel and historiography. In Helmut Schultz (Ed.) *German Monitor*, no. 67, 141–159, 264. Brill. https://brill.com/display/title/29843.

Primoratz, I. (2010). *Terror from the Sky: The Bombing of German Cities in World War II*. Berghahn Books.

Reading, A. (2014). Seeing red: A political economy of digital memory. *Media, Culture & Society*, 36(6), 748–60.

Reynolds, D. (2017). Britain, the two World Wars, and the problem of narrative. *The Historical Journal*, 60(1), 197–231.

Rhodes, R. (1995, June 11). The general and World War III. *The New Yorker*. http://www.newyorker.com/magazine/1995/06/19/the-general-and-world-war-iii

Richardson, M. (2020). Drone cultures: Encounters with everyday militarisms. *Continuum*, 34(6), 858–69.

Rigden, I. (2020). The battle of Berlin, April–May 1945. In G. Fremont-Barnes (Ed.), *A History of Modern Urban Operations*, 151–83, Springer International Publishing. https://doi.org/10.1007/978-3-030-27088-9_6

Rigney, A. (2017). Materiality and memory: Objects to ecologies. A response to Maria Zirra. *Parallax*, 23(4), 474–8. https://doi.org/10.1080/13534645.2017.1374517

Rosenberg, Y. (2017). "Jews will not replace us": Why white supremacists go after Jews. *The Washington Post*, 14.

Ross, T. (2016). Boris Johnson interview: We can be the 'heroes of Europe' by voting to Leave'. *The Telegraph*. https://www.telegraph.co.uk/news/2016/05/14/boris-johnson-interview-we-can-be-

Roth, M. S. (1981). Foucault's 'history of the present'. *History and Theory*, 20(1), 32–46.

Rothberg, M. (2009). *Multidirectional Memory: Remembering the Holocaust in the Age of Decolonization*. Stanford University Press.

Rothberg, M. (2013). Preface: Beyond Tancred and Clorinda: Trauma studies for implicated subjects. In Gert Buelens, Sam Durrant, and Robert Eagelstone (Eds.), *The Future of Trauma Theory: Contemporary Literary and Cultural Criticism*, xi–xviii, Routledge.

Ryan, J. F., & Hewer, C. J. (2016). What did we do to Germany during the Second World War? A British perspective on the allied strategic bombing campaign 1940–45. *Papers on Social Representations*, 25(1), 10 11–10 28.

Saunders, N. (2020). *Trench Art: Materialities and Memories of War*. Routledge.

Scandura, J. (2008). *Down in the Dumps: Place, Modernity, American Depression*. Duke University Press.

Schaffer, R. (1980). American military ethics in World War II: The bombing of German civilians. *The Journal of American History*, 67(2), 318–34. https://doi.org/10.2307/1890411

Schaffer, R. (1988). *Wings of Judgment: American Bombing in World War II*. Oxford University Press, USA.

Schwartz, B. (1982). The social context of commemoration: A study in collective memory. *Social Forces*, 61(2), 374–402.

Schmitz, H. (2007). *A Nation of Victims?: Representations of German Wartime Suffering from 1945 to the Present*. Rodopi BV.

Schonsky, H., Peters, A., Lang, F., Abel, S., Mekiffer, B., & Wessolek, G. (2013). Sulfate transport and release in technogenic soil Substrates: Experiments and Numerical Modeling. *Journal of Soils and Sediments*, 13(3), 606–15.

Schwab, E., & Beshty, W. (2005). Stumped. *Cabinet*, 20.

Scott, C. J., & Major, P. (2018). The ionospheric response over the UK to major bombing raids during World War II. *Ann. Geophys*, 36(5), 1243–54.

Sebald, W. G. (2000). *Vertigo* (M. Hulse, Trans.). Penguin.

Sebald, W. G. (2001). *Austerlitz*, (A. Bell, Trans). Penguin.

Sebald, W. G. (2002). *The Rings of Saturn* (M. Hulse, Trans.). Vintage.

Sebald, W. G. (2004). *On the Natural History of Destruction*. (A. Bell, Trans.). Penguin.

Sebald, W. G. (2006). *Campo Santo*. (A. Bell, Trans.). Penguin.

Smith, C. L., & Shand, B. J. (2016). Architectural wounds: Teufelsberg. *Architecture and Culture*, 4(2), 185–92.

Sontag, S. (1979). In Plato's cave. In S. Sontag (ed.), *On Photography*, 3–24, Penguin.

Speer, A. (1970). *Inside the Third Reich* (R., C. Winston, & Macmillian, Trans.) Macmillian.

Spinoza, B. (1992). *Ethics*. Hackett.
Stahl, R. (2018). *Through the Crosshairs: War, Visual Culture, and the Weaponized Gaze*. Rutgers University Press.
Stanley, J. (2020). *How Fascism Works: The Politics of Us and Them*. Random House Trade Paperbacks.
Stoetzer, B. (2018). Ruderal ecologies: Rethinking nature, migration, and the urban landscape in Berlin. *Cultural Anthropology*, 33(2), 295–323.
Stöver, B. (2013). *Berlin: A Short History*, trans D. Stonecipher. CH Beck.
Stuckey, M. E. (1992). Remembering the future: Rhetorical echoes of World War II and Vietnam in George Bush's public speech on the Gulf War. *Communication Studies*, 43(4), 246–56.
Sturken, M. (1997). *Tangled Memories: The Vietnam War, the AIDS Epidemic, and the Politics of Remembering*. University of California Press.
Sturken, M. (2020). Containing absence, shaping presence at ground zero. *Memory Studies*, 13(3), 313–21. https://doi.org/10.1177/1750698020914015
Sturken, M. (2016). The objects that lived: The 9/11 Museum and material transformation. *Memory Studies*, 9(1), 13–26. https://doi.org/10.1177/1750698015613970.
Sturken, M., & Cartwright, L. (2018). *Practices of Looking* (3rd ed.). Oxford University Press.
Subramanian, M. (2019). Humans versus Earth: The quest to define the Anthropocene. *Nature*, 572(7768), 168–71.
Sumartojo, S. (2015). National identity and commemorative space: Connections to the nation through time and site. *Landscape Review*, 15(2), 7–18.
Sumartojo, S. (2019). Sensory impact: Memory, affect and sensory ethnography at official memory sites. In D. Drozdzewski & C. Birdsall (Eds.), *Doing Memory Research*, 21–37, Springer.
Süss, D. (2014). *Death from the Skies: How the British and Germans Survived Bombing in World War II*. Oxford University Press.
Taberner, S., & Berger, K. (2009). *Germans as Victims in the Literary Fiction of the Berlin Republic*. Boydell & Brewer.
Taylor, J., & Davidson, M. (2012). *Bomber Crew*. Hachette UK.
Tello, V. (2022). Counter-memory and and–and: Aesthetics and temporalities for living together. *Memory Studies*, 15(2), 390–401. https://doi.org/10.1177/1750698019876002
The Book Thief. (2013). [Film] Dir. B. Percival, 20th Century Fox.
The Boy in the Striped Pyjamas. (2008). [Film] Dir. M. Herman, Walt Disney Studios.
The Keeper. (2018). [Film] Dir. M. Rosenmüller, Zephyr Films.
The Local. (2018, November 6). Why Cold War spy station Teufelsberg is now a protected historical site. *The Local*. https://www.thelocal.de/20181106/former-cold-war-listening-sta-
The Reader (2008), [Film] Dir. S. Daldry, The Weinstein Company.

The Telegraph. (2015). *Dresden: Then and now photographs of city razed in Allied firestorm. The Telegraph*. Retrieved February 15, 2022, from https://www.telegraph.co.uk/news/worldnews/europe/germany/11409209/Dresden-Then-and-now-photographs-of-city-razed-in-Allied-firestorm.html

The Times. (1944, January 31). Wiping out German war industries. *The Times*, 5.

Thelen, D. (1995). History after the Enola Gay controversy: An introduction. *The Journal of American History*, 82(3), 1029–35. https://doi.org/10.2307/2945110

Tien, J., & Florence, E. (2022). Geology as somatechnics: Re-imagining human and technology entanglements in geologies of the future. *Somatechnics: Journal of Bodies – Technologies – Power*, 11(4).

Till, K. E. (2004). Emplacing memory through the city: The new Berlin. *GHI Bulletin*, 35(Fall), 73–83.

Till, K. E. (2005). *The New Berlin: Memory, Politics, Place*. University of Minnesota Press.

Till, K. E. (2012). Wounded cities: Memory-work and a place-based ethics of care. *Political Geography*, 31(1), 3–14.

Tota, A.L. & Hagen, T. (2015), Introduction: Memory work–naming pasts, transforming futures. In *Routledge International Handbook of Memory Studies*, 23–8, Routledge.

United States Holocaust Memorial Museum (n.d.),

US Holocaust Memorial Museum (n.d.). Berlin. *Holocaust Encyclopaedia*. [Online]. https://encyclopedia.ushmm.org/content/en/article/berlin

Valjavec, M. B., Zorn, M., & Ribeiro, D. (2018). Mapping war Geoheritage: Recognising Geomorphological traces of War. *Open Geosciences*, 10(1), 385–94. https://doi.org/10.1515/geo-2018-0030

Valkyrie. (2008). [Film] Dir. B. Singer, MGM Distribution Co.

Vermeulen, P. (2017). Creaturely memory: Shakespeare, the Anthropocene and the new Nomos of the Earth. *Parallax*, 23(4), 384–97. https://doi.org/10.1080/13534645.2017.1374508

Virilio, P. (1989). *War and Cinema: The Logistics of Perception*. Verso.

Volčič, Z. (2007). Yugo-nostalgia: Cultural memory and media in the former Yugoslavia. *Critical Studies in Media Communication*, 24(1), 21–38.

Vonnegut, K. (2000). *Slaughterhouse-Five, or The Children's Crusade, a Duty-Dance with Death*. Vintage Random House.

Vuolteenaho, J. (2017). *Critical Toponymies: The Contested Politics of Place Naming*. Routledge.

Wagner, M. (2017). 'Blood and soil': Protesters chant Nazi slogan in Charlottesville. *Journal of Australian Studies* 81, 121–34.

Ware, S. A. (2004). Contemporary anti-memorials and national identity in the Victorian landscape. *Journal of Australian Studies*, 81, 121–34.

Washburn, W. E. (1995). The Smithsonian and the Enola Gay. *The National Interest*, 40, 40–9.

Weil, K. (2017). Matters of memory and creaturely concerns: A response to Pieter Vermeulen. *Parallax*, 23(4), 398–402. https://doi.org/10.1080/13534645.2017.1374509

Werrell, K. P. (1986). The strategic bombing of Germany in World War II: Costs and accomplishments. *The Journal of American History*, 73(3), 702–13. https://doi.org/10.2307/1902984

Wessolek, G., & Toland, A. (2017a). 'Devil in the sand': The case of the Teufelsberg Berlin and its cultural evidence. *19th EGU General Assembly, EGU2017, proceedings from the Conference*, 23–8 April, 2017, Vienna, Austria., p.18996

Where Hands Touch (2018), [Film] A. Asante, Shear Entertainment.

Whyte, K. (2018). Critical investigations of resilience: A brief introduction to Indigenous environmental studies & sciences. *Daedalus*, 147(2), 136–47. https://doi.org/10.1162/DAED_a_00497

Widmann, T. (2020, September 17). Playing memories? Digital games as memory media [Blog]. *Digital Holocaust Memory*. https://reframe.sussex.ac.uk/digitalholocaustmemory/2020/09/17/playing-memories-digital-games-as-memory-media/

Wieviorka, A. (2000). *From survivor to witness: Voices from the Shoah*. In J. Winter & E. Sivan, (Eds.) *War and Remembrance in the 20th Century*, Cambridge University Press.

Wigley, M. (2002). Insecurity by design. In M. Sorkin & S. Zukin (Eds.), *After the World Trade Centre: Rethinking New York City*, 69–86, Routledge.

Williamson, L. A. (2010). Bush's mythic America: A critique of the rhetoric of war. *Southern Communication Journal*, 75(3), 215–31.

Wilson, M. G. (2013). Sheets of past: Reading the image in W. G. Sebald's *Austerlitz*. *Contemporary Literature*, 54(1), 49–76.

Winter, J. (2006). *Remembering War: The Great War Between Memory and History in the Twentieth Century*. Yale University Press.

Woodward, C. (2001). *In Ruins*. Chatto & Windus.

Wright, J. (2017). *Darkest Hour*. Focus Features.

Yad, Vashem. (n.d.). *Transports to Extinction: Holocaust (Shoah) Deportation Database*. Yad Vashem – The World Holocaust Remembrance Center [Online]. https://deportation.yadvashem.org/index.html?language=en&itemId=10583375&ind=7

Young, J. (1993). *The Texture of Memory: Holocaust Memorials and Meaning*. Yale University Press.

Young, J. E. (1992). The counter-monument: Memory against itself in Germany today. *Critical Inquiry*, 18(2), 267–96.

Young, M. (1996). Dangerous history: Vietnam and the "Good War". In E. T. Linenthal & T. Engelhardt (Eds.) *History Wars: The Enola Gay The Enola Gay and Other Battles for the American Past*, Basic Books.

Yusoff, K. (2013). Geologic life: Prehistory, climate, futures in the Anthropocene. *Environment and Planning D: Society and Space*, 31(5), 779–95. https://doi.org/10.1068/d11512

Yusoff, K. (2018). *A Billion Black Anthropocenes or None*. University of Minnesota Press.

Zalasiewicz, J., & Zalasiewicz, M. (2015). Battle scars. *New Scientist*, 225(3014), 36–9. https://doi.org/10.1016/S0262-4079(15)30036-1

Zalasiewicz, J., Williams, M., Waters, C. N., Barnosky, A. D., Palmesino, J., Rönnskog, A.-S., Edgeworth, M., Neal, C., Cearreta, A., Ellis, E. C., Grinevald, J., Ha, P., Sul, J. A., Jeandel, C., Leinfelder, R., McNeill, O., … Wolfe, A. P. (2016). Scale and diversity of the physical technosphere: A geological perspective. *The Anthropocene Review*, 4(1), 9–22.

Zehfuss, M. (2007). *Wounds of Memory: The Politics of War in Germany*. Cambridge University Press.

Zill, R. (2011). "A true witness of transience": Berlin's Kaiser-Wilhelm-Gedächtniskirche and the symbolic use of architectural fragments in modernity. *European Review of History: Revue Européenne d'histoire*, 18(5–6), 811–27.

Zinn, H. (1997). The bombing of Royan. In H. Zinn (Ed.), *The Zinn Reader: Writings on Disobedience and Democracy*, 267–80, Seven Stories Press.

Index

Abel, S. 205, 208
accountability 10, 14, 49, 110, 124, 126, 131, 155, 212, 221–2
  and agency 77, 212
  dispersed model of 124–5, 127, 136–41, 222
  distributed 131–3
  networked model 141–53, 223
actants 14, 64, 67–8, 87, 125–7, 129, 133, 135–7, 142, 155, 173, 198, 210
  assemblage of 126, 129, 135, 143, 155
  human and non-human 14, 67, 126, 142–3, 146
  Teufelsberg as 77
actor network theory 64, 131
Adey, P. 144, 152, 161, 163, 170, 179–80, 182
aerial archaeology 182
aerial attacks/bombing 4, 29, 73, 83, 87–8, 106, 138, 143, 152, 159–68, 170, 180–1, 183, 211. *See also* area bombing
  artillery and 75
  and objective safety 30
aerial bomber and surface 180
aerial gaze 163, 182
aerial photography 14, 16, 77, 88, 90–4, 147, 155, 157, 170, 176–9, 184, 218–20
  and aerial bombing 159–63
  aerial mastery 160, 178–9
  in cultural memory 163–8
  and photogrammetry 182
  Topography of Terror 158–60
  visibility 179
aerial targeting 144, 163, 170, 182
agency 64, 77, 125–6, 129–30, 133, 136, 138, 143, 154–5, 184, 209
  of actant 64
  distributed/dispersed 132, 136, 141, 222
  materials with (*see* materials with agency)
  networked model 77, 141, 212

Alaimo, S. 141, 203
Allied bombing/Allied bombing campaigns 2, 8, 19, 33, 73, 75, 84, 97, 120, 127, 148, 150, 198–9, 201
  accounts from airforce veterans 28, 31, 215
  casualty estimates 3, 22, 31, 33, 124, 166, 219, 221
  damage estimates 2, 20, 75, 78, 124, 127–8, 221
  description of aftermaths 131, 169, 203
  description of effects 5, 10, 19, 29–30, 35, 127, 135, 148, 168, 216–18
  kill chains 138, 143–4
  operations at air bases in the UK 135
Allies 1, 4–5, 8, 15, 16, 20–1, 36, 39, 42, 73, 94, 98, 124, 128, 143–4, 146, 150, 163, 165, 167–8, 174, 188, 198, 215, 217, 221, 223–4, 226 n.1, 230 n.11, 231 n.14
  absolute/moral righteousness 41, 45
  chains of command 165
  destruction 230 n.6
  historical responsibility of 54
  Nazi Germany *vs.* 10
  post-war cultures of 28
  self-image 25
Alone in Berlin (2016) 43
Amad, P. 161, 165, 170, 184, 230 n.4
  cinema's military hardwiring 162
American air force (USAAF) 3, 32, 34, 132, 134, 143, 167
American Civil War 6
American international Echelon spy network 96
American national identity 39, 41, 217
American National Security Agency (NSA) 76, 95–6, 117
Anders 223–4
Anderson, B. 103–4, 106, 152, 180, 202
Anders, W. 230 n.12

Anglo-American 16–17
  war mythologies 33, 38
Anglo-American memory cultures 8, 10,
    12, 14–16, 21, 24, 29, 45, 69,
    71–2, 74, 86, 97–8, 102, 110–11,
    113, 121, 124, 126–7, 149, 154,
    157–60, 166, 174, 179, 184, 187,
    197, 201–2, 211, 226 n.3
  area bombing 12, 19–20, 26–8, 48, 111,
    121, 124, 126, 172, 211, 216, 218
  moral righteousness 38–9, 45
  Second World War 10, 19, 34, 72, 86,
    94, 106, 123, 154, 216
  underpins and structures negotiations
    221
Anglosphere 25, 40, 143, 153, 164, 166,
  169, 179
Anhalter Bahnhof 13–15, 67, 71, 74–5,
  81–2, 98, 110–11, 118, 124, 126,
  145–8, 151–3, 155, 194, 219,
  223–5, 227 n.1, 231 n.15
  deportations 111, 118, 120, 122, 148,
    153, 228 n.7, 229 n.9
  haunting 117, 121
  history 117
  remains 117, 231 n.15
  ruins of 112–13
  S-Bahn station 81–3, 117, 147, 151, 153
  transience of 113
Anthropocene 15, 50, 66, 77, 187–8, 204–5
  ground zero/golden spike 204–5, 231
    n.2
  Teufelsberg as site (*see* Teufelsberg, as
    site of Anthropocene)
Anthropocene Working Group (AWG)
  204–5
anthropocentrism 73
Anthropogenic geology 206, 209
anthrozone 209–10
Arc de Triomphe, Paris 82
archaeology (archaeological) 13, 50, 98,
    106, 111, 123, 187–90, 195
  aerial 182
  dig/digging 81, 98, 102–6, 187, 191,
    202
  geology and 205–6
  listening station 116
  remnants 190, 192, 195–6, 201
  revelatory potential of 103
archeo-sphere 209

area bombing 3–5, 12–13, 16, 21, 45, 51–3,
    93, 94, 98, 118, 120, 123, 127–8,
    133, 152, 166, 211, 221
  Anglo-American memory of 12,
    19–20, 26–8, 48, 111, 121, 124,
    126, 172, 211, 216, 218
  campaigns 10, 12, 34, 40, 74, 222, 229
    n.4
  cultural memory of 20, 23, 45, 57, 69,
    73, 75, 85–6, 89, 98, 106, 111,
    121, 126, 155, 183, 201, 216–18
  effects 35, 135, 184, 216
  and German victimhood debate 9,
    21–5
  legitimate targets 145
  networked accountability 141–53
  space, memories 53–5
  victims of 9–10, 12, 16, 23–5, 29–30,
    51–2, 117–21, 129, 139–41, 154,
    165, 168–71, 201, 217–19, 221,
    223, 226 n.2, 228 n.1, 231 n.1
Arendt, H. 145
Arnold-de-Simine, S. 113, 120
Arthur 'Bomber' Harris memorial 28, 74
Assmann, A. 11, 53–4
  heterogeneous forms of memory 54
  normative framework 54
authenticity 61–2, 190, 192
authentic traces 61

Barad, K., material-discursive 85
Battle of Britain 37
Bauman, Z. 145
Bell, D. S. 41
Benjamin, W. 100, 114, 191
  Angel of History 98
  optical unconscious 111
  poetic thinking 87
Bennett, J. 14, 58, 64, 67, 69, 77, 116, 125,
    129, 131, 135, 136, 141, 144–5,
    153, 222, 228 n.3
  'The Agency of Assemblages and the
    North American Blackout' 126
  billiard-ball causality 135–7, 224
  efficient causality 136–7
  emergent causality 132, 137
  human and non-human matter 133–4
  impersonal affect 64
  Latourian approach 131
  theory of distributive agency 131

thing power 64, 142
Vibrant Matter 65, 68, 126
Berger, K. 11
Berlin Airlift 79
Berliner Schloss 74
Berlin Wall 60, 80–1, 83, 96, 104, 139
Beshty, W. 194–5
Biddle, D. 152
Bielenberg, C. 148
Binns, D. 36
Bishop, R. 180
Black Lives Matter movement 6, 44, 47, 72
  Edward Colston statue 6, 216
  removal of statues 6, 47
  slave trade history 6, 47, 216
  Winston Churchill statue, protecting 6–7, 216
Black, M. 121, 228 n.6
blackouts 126, 131, 133–4
Blitz Myth 34–7, 73–4, 113–14, 124
blue marble effect 230 n.12
bodies and bodily violence 15, 137, 159, 167–77, 184, 187, 202–3, 211
  rubble generated 173
  and scale of 174–7
  sensory violence 14, 170, 177
Böll, H. 231 n.3
Bomber Command 31, 33, 74, 134–5, 143, 164, 167, 224, 229 n.2, 230 n.3
bombing(s) 4–5, 13, 23, 28, 33, 41, 90, 102, 122, 124, 127, 129, 134, 141, 144, 148–9, 155, 158–9, 168–9, 175, 184, 187, 206, 219, 224–5. *See also* area bombing
  of German cities 2, 21, 26, 39, 133, 169, 198, 218
    Baghdad 102
    Berlin 1–3, 5, 8–9, 13–14, 28, 45, 173–4
    Cologne 173, 198
    Dresden 21, 32, 102, 132, 150, 154, 173–4, 198
    Hamburg 30, 102, 169, 173–4, 198
    Leipzig 173
    Munich 173
    Stuttgart 173
  Hiroshima 6–8, 28, 169, 217
  raids 1, 3, 21–2, 24, 31, 40, 81, 107, 112, 122, 135, 148, 169, 198, 229 n.9

scale 2, 4, 33–4, 146, 158, 174–7, 211–12, 219–20
spike 209
Bond, L. 56, 58
Brenner, H. 150
Brexit 37–8
  referendum 36, 44
Brian, A. M., post-race 42
British Royal Air Force (RAF) 3, 30–1, 38, 122, 134, 143, 167, 219
burial and digging 80, 83, 98, 103–4, 121, 123, 201
  aerials and 179–83
  and forgetting 197
  non-linear histories 107–10
  rhetorical uses of 104–7

Calder, A. 35–6
  self-image of Britain 35
Captain America comics 41–2
Captain America: The First Avenger. (2011) 42
Cartwright, L. 90
cause and effect, linear model 16, 77, 132, 134–8, 141, 143, 212, 218, 223–5
Cavicchi, J. 190, 196, 199
Charlwood, D. 167, 230 n.8
  No Moon Tonight 152
Chauvin, D. 6
Checkpoint Charlie 81
Childers, T. 30
Christchurch Greyfriars 74, 113
Churchill, W. 149, 216
Clark, L. B. 112
Cocroft, W. D. 116
Cold War 2, 27, 36, 42, 51, 60, 76, 81, 96, 102, 116, 146, 159, 215
  era memorials 74
  hyper-surveillance culture 102
  politics and memory cultures 81, 104, 148, 191–2
  spy station, ruins 77, 98, 110–11
Cole, T. 129, 130, 137
collective memories 33, 41, 56, 59, 164
Colston, E., statue toppling 6–8, 11, 216
commemoration 37, 62, 190
communication
  culture as 55, 57
  idealist/transmission model of 57, 60
communicative texts 25, 48, 57, 85

Confino, A. 62
Connelly, M. 29, 32, 38, 229 n.3
contemporary archaeology 196
Copley, C. 195
Corsico 119
cosmopolitan memory 56
counter-memory/counter-memory texts 55–6, 60
Craps, S. 56, 58
Crouch, T. 221
Crownshaw, R. 50
Crutzen, P. J. 204
cultural communicative practices 18, 55–6, 61, 88
cultural currency 197
cultural geography 48, 55, 61–3, 70
cultural landscape 18, 60, 205
cultural memory 5, 9, 11–12, 20–1, 25, 28, 34, 40, 45, 47–8, 51, 53, 55, 69, 72–3, 77, 86, 88, 97–8, 102, 106, 122, 126, 136, 141, 184, 211, 216, 229 n.9, 231 n.1
   aerial photography 163–8
   Anglo-American (*see* Anglo-American memory cultures)
   civilian deaths and destruction 5, 8–10, 25, 28, 45, 98, 134, 139, 174, 213, 221
   and cultural geography 63
   culture in 55–9
   entangling 8–9, 77, 89, 103, 110, 146, 155, 187, 210
   key functions of 8
   and national identity 8
   negotiation and re-formulation 70, 84, 90, 190
   visual culture and 164
curated ruins 228 n.3
Czaplicka, J. 190

D'Amato, T. 231 n.1
The Dam Busters (1955) 31–2, 168
Daniell, R. 65
Darian-Smith, K. 51–2. *See also* memory, work
dark tourism 62–3
data collection 71, 89
   notebooks 91–2
   photographs 90–1, 93

Davis, R. G. 142, 166, 226 n.1
Deleuze, G. 131
Dellenbaugh-Losse, M. 59
Dempsey, A. M. 120
denazification 81, 148, 159
der Historikerstreit 22. *See also* German Historian's Debate
designed memory sites 61
DeSilvey, C. 91
Deutsche Bahn, A. G. 83, 146, 153
Dickinson, R. E. 128
Diefendorf, J. M. 78, 173
digital memory 50
Dillon, B. 111
distributed accountability 131–3, 153
   historical responsibility 136–41
distributed agency 132, 136, 222
diversity of German experience, films 43
The Documentation Centre for Displacement, Expulsion, Reconciliation 227 n.1
dominant memory 56, 127, 132, 137, 154, 166, 203, 220
Driscoll, K. 65, 139–40, 227 n.1
   political violence 129
drone cultures 162–3
drone warfare 144, 158, 170
Drozdzewski, D. 63
Dunkirk 36–7
Dunkirk (2017) 36, 42

East Germany 75, 79
economy of violence 127, 130
eco-services 208
Edensor, T. 59, 114, 120
   spatialisation of memory 60
Edgeworth, M. 209, 212
efficient causality 136–7
Eichmann, A., trial of 52
Elżanowski, J. 164, 196–7, 200–1, 203, 207
Enola Gay controversy 7–9, 31, 169, 216–17, 221
Enola Gay exhibition 30, 217
entanglement/entangled memory 49, 68–9, 73, 77, 86, 89, 98, 103, 110, 121–2, 146, 177–83, 187, 203, 208–9, 210, 212
Erll, A.
   implicit collective memory 56

travelling memory 56
Essen, RAF attack on 79
European civilians 183
European fascism 40
Euro-scepticism 8, 72
expanded network 133–6, 143, 184, 222

Fallada, H., *Jeder stirbt für sich allein/ Every man dies alone* 43
Fischel, J. 24
Floyd, G. 6
forensic traces of violence 15, 77, 186–7, 213
   human remains 198–203
   pile of remnants 188–9
   rhetorical uses of remnants 190–5
   waste 195–8
Forest, B. 58
Foucault, M. 12, 58, 67, 69, 72, 86–7, 98, 100, 123
   effective history 72
   genealogy 12, 26–7, 44, 69, 107
   A History of Sexuality 58
   history of the present 26–7, 49, 123
   knowledge as perspective 72–3, 87
   power 26, 44, 58, 67–8
Franklin, S. 37
Freeman, L. A. 65
Fresh Kills 196–7, 199, 201
Friedrich, J. 35, 127, 168–9, 170, 198, 228 n.1, 230 n.11
   alternative history of bombings 24
   Der Brand/The Fire 19, 24, 29–30, 102
Friedrich the Great 99–100
Fullbrook, M. 60–1

games and gamification 50
Geisen, B. 105
genocide 25, 48, 66, 98, 100, 126, 129–31
   and ethnic cleansing 52
   machine, Nazis' terror and 2, 148, 150, 152, 223–4
   perpetrators 10
geology (geological) 187, 204–6, 210
   anthropogenic 206
   and archaeology 205
   epoch 204–5
   forces 209, 211–12
   and humans 208

German Historian's Debate 22, 81, 226 n.2, 228 n.1
German perspectives 4, 9–10, 57, 154
German victimhood debate 4, 9–11, 20, 22–4, 27, 45, 53, 55, 72, 106, 168–9, 201, 226 n.2, 227 n.1, 229 n.4
   and air war memory 27
   area bombing and 21–5
   German perspectives 10
   and historical responsibility 23, 25, 27
   memory of 52
ghosts 114, 116–22, 202, 225
Gleis 17 memorial 13, 71, 75, 82–3, 126, 145–7, 151, 153, 155, 201, 223, 228 n.7, 229 n.9
Goebbels 81
Goehring, C. 230 n.5
Golanska, D. 68, 73, 85–6, 89, 177, 230 n.13
   collision approach 49, 70, 86
Goldstein, C. S. 28–9, 39–40, 227 n.3
   silence 38
   truism 35
Gonzalex-Rubial 103
good story 36, 41, 215, 221
   Brexit 37–8
   Second World War 41
good war 5, 39–40, 43, 113, 216
Gordon, A. 13, 120
   ghostly matter 187
Graham, S. 205–6
   manufactured ground 206
Grant, S.-M., militarised commemorative culture 217
Grayling, A. C. 226 n.1
Great Acceleration 205
Gregory, D. 129–30, 138, 144–5, 161, 165, 169, 183–4, 211, 226 n.1, 229 n.6
   kill chain 143
Grillplatz 79
Groehler, O. 226 n.2
Grosse Hamburger Strasse Memorial Cemetery 13, 74, 83, 118, 120, 122, 147, 151, 201
Grosser Bunkerberg 79
ground zero/golden spike (Anthropocene) 204–5, 209, 231 n.2
Grunewald 81–3, 97, 99–100, 102, 145, 151, 153, 208

The Guardian 33
Guattari, F., assemblages 131
Gulf Wars 36, 39, 162

Habermas, J. 226 n.2
Hagen, T. 49
Hake, S., fascist imaginary 43–4
Halbwachs, M. 50
Hamilton, P. 51–2. *See also* memory, work
Haraway, D.
　naturecultures 85
　semiotic-discursive 85
Harris, A. 137, 219, 229 n.3
Hart, L. 152
Harwit, M. 7, 221
haunting 14, 77, 103, 114, 117, 120, 124, 135, 187, 201–2, 223, 225, 228 n.2
　and buried history 201
　and time 120–3
hegemonic institutions 58
Heimat 100, 102
Hewer, C. J. 33–4, 174
Hiroshima, atomic bomb on 6–8, 28, 169, 217
Hitchens, C. 41
Hitler, A. 19, 42, 82, 97, 99, 112–13, 136–7, 148, 192, 224, 227 n.4
Hoelscher, S. 22, 57
Hollman, T. 199
Hollywood war films 17, 28, 31, 36, 39, 42–3, 68, 227 n.3
　othering of Nazi 44
Holocaust 4, 9–10, 12–13, 23–5, 38–41, 48, 51, 54–5, 77, 82, 101, 104–5, 111, 117, 121–2, 124, 126–7, 129–30, 145–8, 150–3, 155, 171, 173–4, 183, 201, 216, 221–2, 224–5, 227, 228 n.1, 229 n.4, 229 n.8
　denial 5, 24, 52, 231 n.14
　monstrosity of 51
　victim narratives 20, 48
　victims and survivors 11, 23–4, 52–3, 216, 221, 225, 231 n.14
Holocene 204, 209
Homo sapiens 210
Hughes, H. 218
human remains 15, 50, 77, 187, 196–203, 210
humans and planet 187, 204, 206–7, 210
Huyssen, A. 101–2

Illustrated London News 32
immigration 44
Imperial Germany, Romantic forests 102
Indigenous and First Nations People 210
Industrial Revolution 205, 231 n.2
Ingold, T. 59, 92
interdisciplinary approach 47–8, 69, 84, 93
internal globalization 56
International Space Station orbits 2
Iron Curtain 42, 51, 191
Irving, D. 22
Islamophobia 52, 101

Jackson, M. 87
Japan 204, 215. *See also* Hiroshima, atomic bomb on
　imperialism 40
　Japanese victims 7, 9, 11, 216
　nuclear destruction 28
Jewish memorial cemetery 13–14, 71, 74–5, 83–4, 110, 118–19, 121, 124, 147, 151, 225
Johnson, B. 6, 10, 37–8, 58
Jordan, J. A. 151

Kaiser Wilhelm Memorial Church 74–5, 111, 223, 228 n.2
Kaplan, C. 87–8
Kassel 128
Kelsey, D. 42
Kennedy, R. 86, 179
Kettenacker, L. 9
Kleiner Bunkerberg 79
Klemperer, V. 150
Knittel, S. C. 65, 227 n.1
Kolk, H. A. 114
Korean war 21
Korte, B. 37

Ladd, B. 65, 114, 189
Lammert, W. 83
Landsberg, A.
　brainwashing model 57
　prosthetic memory 56–7
Latour, B. 64, 67, 125. *See also* actants
Leave and Remain campaigns 37

Lebensraum 100
Lederer, C. 76
legitimate target 22, 126–7, 145, 150–3, 155, 163, 223
Lekan, T. M. 100, 102
Le May, C. 215, 217, 222
Levy, D. 52, 56
Lewis, T. 91
Lipstadt, D., immoral equivalency 24
London Blitz 73–4, 113–14, 124
Los Angeles Times 217
Lowe, K. 33, 166–7
Luftwaffe 33, 42, 177, 224
Lynch, D. 76, 101

Mangold, E. B. 230 n.5
Marschall, S. 62
mass graves 5, 10, 12, 20, 25, 35, 40, 45, 54, 83, 118, 120, 127, 135, 137, 141–2, 159, 168, 201
  civilian causalities 3–5, 8, 22, 28, 33, 124, 166
Massol, C. de 211
materiality of sites 14, 48–9, 61–4, 66, 68–70, 73, 86, 91, 177, 222
materials with agency
  memory and new materialism 65
  posthuman memory studies 66–8
  vibrant materiality 64–5
material violence 14, 67, 155, 159, 172, 197, 219
material witness 15, 60, 190, 195
Matheson, N. 161
McNamara, R. 215, 222
McRae, L., official order 55
meaning-making 67, 84
Memorial for Murdered Jews of Europe 119
memorialization 47, 61, 197, 202
memorials and monuments 59–61, 63, 74, 201
memory 5, 14, 47, 49–50, 52, 68, 105, 121, 123, 211, 216
  Anthropocene 210–13
  and architecture 59
  boom 51
  on cultural scale 53, 56
  and cultural texts 55, 57, 164
  and culture 48

decoupling 50
entangled (*see* entanglement/entangled memory)
industry 50
and mass trauma 51–3
and place 48, 59–63
work 51–3, 58, 148
memory studies 48, 56, 69, 227 n.1
  and cultural geography 48, 63
  field of 51
  and German history 25
  and the Holocaust 9–13, 23, 38, 51–3, 201, 216
  and mass trauma 51–3
  and new materialism 12, 48, 55, 64–5, 72, 211, 230 n.9
  and posthumanism 66–8, 70, 85
  short history of 49–51
  space for area bombing 53–5
  third wave 56
  victim accounts 12, 23, 139–41, 154, 168, 221, 226 n.2
Mendelssohn, M. 83
Merill 182–3
Micieli-Voutsinas, J. 190, 196, 199
militarized perception 162
military-scientific objectivity/rationality 28–9, 89
Ministry of Information 164
Mitchell, B. 163
mnemonic movement 58, 86, 183
model of destruction, Cologne 21
Moeller, R. G. 3, 23, 107, 150, 154
moonscape 178
Moorhead, A. 21
morale bombing. *See* area bombing
morality 26, 28, 31, 41, 43, 44, 122, 127, 144, 221
Morris, B. 84
Moshenska, G. 166
Müller, H. 118
Munich 78–9

Nagasaki, bombing of 169, 217
Nash, H. 143
Nasty Girl controversy 105
national identity, German 101
National Socialism 62, 105
nations' cultural heritage 47

Nazis/Nazi Germany 4, 23, 41–2, 44, 53, 55, 100, 104, 118–19, 121, 135–6, 152, 163, 168, 194, 221, 223, 227 n.4
  vs. Allies 10, 127
  brutality and expansionism 32
  comedy 227 n.4
  crimes against humanity 38–9, 149
  criminality 40
  enemies of Nazism 81
  fascism 25
  genocidal regime 24–5, 98, 126, 142, 222
  genocide machine 2, 148, 150, 152, 223
  immorality 40, 221
  Nazi Reich 97
  perpetrators 10, 129, 142
  persecution 81, 129
  problem of forests and 98–103
  war crimes/atrocities 16, 41, 98, 107, 110, 122, 149, 218, 223, 231 n.4
  warmongering 34
Neiman, S. 7
neo-fascism 72, 101, 107
neo-Nazism 26, 43, 52, 101, 110
networked accountability 136, 141–2, 223
  conceptual distances 142–8
  legitimate targets 150–3
  retribution and justice 148–50
Neue Wache 74–5
new materialism 63–5, 68
Niederkirchnerstraße 81, 104–5
Nienass, B. 65
Nietzsche, F. 26
night-time bombing 161, 226 n.1
9/11 attacks 66–7, 88, 130, 196–7, 199–200
Noakes, L. 8, 40
nonhuman violence 133, 135, 152, 154, 207, 211, 213, 222
Nora, P. 50–1
  lieux de mémoire project 65
nostalgic moral certainty 39–41

objective distance, perpetrators 14, 16, 198, 218–20
objectivity of the world 87
official memory 60, 169, 191–2
Olick, J. 52
Operation Thunderclap 166

Overy, R. 198
oxidization and gravity 67

palimpsests 76, 92–3, 123
Pattinson, J. 8, 40
People's War 31
perpetrators/perpetrator perspectives 9–12, 23, 48, 52–4, 129, 139, 141, 154, 166, 168
  Allies as 221
  categories 140
  German perspectives 57, 154
  history 106
  moral framework 221–3
  of Nazi crimes and atrocities 10, 129, 142
  objective distance of 16, 218–20
  studies 140
  victim and 11–12, 16, 139–41, 154, 159, 165, 168, 218, 221
photographic truth 90
place, memory and 57, 59–61, 67, 69, 85–6
  cultural memory and geography 61–3
  cultural role and function 61
political and cultural potency 22
political and sociological disciplines 50
Portelli, A. 19, 165–6, 174
posthuman memory studies 66–8
post-war memory cultures 21–2, 27–8, 31, 45, 52–3
post-war narratives 17, 31
post-war remembering/forgetting 15, 80, 105
Puff, H. 196

racial purity and timeless mysticism 100
racism 47, 102
Radstone, S. 86
reluctant defenders of freedom 35–6
remembering, cultural 11, 13–14, 18, 25, 45, 53, 56, 61, 65, 67, 77, 84, 106, 137, 157, 159, 177, 180–1, 192, 225
The Research and Experiments Department of the Ministry of Home Security 30, 134
revisionism 9, 25, 29, 53, 110, 145, 168, 201, 217–18
  historical 5, 12, 45, 110

Reynolds, D. 36, 39–40
Richardson, M., everyday militarisms 162
Rigney, A. 85
Rixdorfer Höhe 79
Romanticism and Romantic nationalism 97, 99–100
Rothberg, M. 140–1
  Multidirectional Memory: Remembering the Holocaust in the Age of Decolonization 56, 229 n.4
Roth, M. S. 69
rubble 1, 5, 8, 70, 75–6, 78–9, 96–8, 109, 125–6, 128, 138, 155, 172–3, 181–2, 188, 195–6, 207, 209, 230 n.14
  Gestapo 104
  as hidden beneath 106
  9/11 terrorist attacks 66–7, 130, 196, 199
  and post-war memory 80, 173
  salvage 78
ruderal ecologies 206–7, 231 n.2
ruins 13, 32, 50, 60–1, 82, 96, 103, 110, 120, 124, 175
  aestheticization 116
  of Cold War spy station 77, 98
  curated 228 n.3
  haunted 114–20
  iconography of 111–14
  in post-war Europe 196
  'Thousand Year Reich' 82, 99
Ryan, J. F. 33–4, 174

Scandura, J. 199
Schofield, J. 116
Schuttberge 195
Schutzstaffel (SS) 81
Schwab, E. 194–5
Schwerbelastungskörper 14–15, 71, 74–5, 82, 186, 192–5
  ground level at 194
  interior 193
Sebald, W. G. 23–4, 92, 106, 119, 142, 149, 168–70, 173
  Austerlitz 119
  battle of annihilation 21
  On the Natural History of Destruction 4
  'On air war and literature' 4

total destruction 174
Second World War films 28–9, 37. *See also specific films*
Secret State Police Office (Gestapo) 81
self-reflexive method 8, 84–5
sense-making processes 62–3, 70, 91–2
sensory and experiential realities 16, 218
Silesian War 99
site identification 73–5
site of analysis 71, 74, 77, 93, 111
site of Anthropocene 15, 77, 187–8, 203–6, 208, 210. *See also* Teufelsberg, as site of Anthropocene
sites of memory 14, 55, 60–1, 63, 69–70, 85–6, 126, 176
  Berlin as 216
  materiality of 68, 70
  as texts 69
sites of violence 14, 77, 168, 218
social and digital media 50
Sontag, S. 90–1
Soviet Union, fall 76
Soviet War Memorial, Treptow Park 74
Spaatz, C. 137
Speer, A. 75, 79, 97, 99–100, 112–13, 180
  'Germania' 82, 192
  neo-classical and neo-Romantic architecture 97
  theory of ruination 79, 97–100, 123
Spender, S. 100–1
Spinoza, B., affective bodies 131
Stahl, R. 162–4
Stande Null (Zero Hour) 173
Steinbach, perpetrator history 106
St Giles Cripplegate 74, 113
strata 95, 97, 102, 121, 123, 223–4
Stuckey, M. E., homogenizing effect of mythology 39
Sturken, M. 57, 66–7, 90, 200
Suberamanian, M. 205
Sumartojo, S. 62
survivor objects 7, 67
Sznaider, N. 56

Taberner, S. 11
taboo 23, 107
technosphere 205
Tello, V. 55
Teltow Plateau 75, 95, 108, 175, 182

terror bombing. *See* area bombing
Teufelsberg 1–5, 8, 13, 68–9, 71–8, 84,
    88–9, 93–5, 106, 136, 143, 153,
    157, 180, 183–4, 219, 225, 227
    n.5. *See also Trümmerberge*
  abandoned spy station 115
  archaeological dig 102–3, 202
  bodily/sensory violence of bombings
    14–15, 157–8, 168, 171–7, 184,
    220
  entanglement 211–12
  forest at 99, 108–9, 172, 186, 190
  as haunted ruins 13, 124
  human remains 77, 198–203, 210
  mode of being 203
  NSA listening station 76, 95–6, 115–16
  remnants/ruins 77, 94, 104, 108,
    111–13, 115, 139, 186, 188–9,
    194, 213
  rubble and stones 2, 128–9, 172, 186–8,
    197, 200, 207, 222
  as site of Anthropocene 203–6
    assemblages 208–10
    bombing memory 210–13
    violences 206–7
  spy station 96, 101, 111, 115–16, 176,
    194, 225, 227 n.4
  strata of history 97–8, 121, 224
  vibrant materiality 125, 137, 141, 155,
    198
  vibrant matter 153, 155
thanatourism 62
Thelen, D. 217
theory of ruination 79, 97–100, 123
Till, K. E. 58, 62, 104, 107, 114, 119, 191
  transgenerational phantoms 110
Toland, A. 108, 205, 208
Topography of Terror 13–15, 60, 62, 71,
    75, 80–1, 98, 104–7, 109, 123,
    126, 144, 146, 148, 150–2,
    158–60, 164, 167–8, 170, 175,
    177–9, 184, 186, 189–91, 195,
    219–20, 224, 227 n.1
  documentation centre 80–1, 148–50,
    175, 189, 191
  Historical Site Tour 178
  materiality 177
  open spaces at 171
  remnants/ruins 15, 104–5, 148, 190–2

  signage at 149
Tota, A. L. 49
total war 22, 150, 163, 223
trans-Atlantic slave trade 6
traumatic memory cultures 68
Trümmerberge 1, 13, 15, 72, 74, 78–80,
    94, 107, 109–10, 115, 138, 140,
    143, 157–8, 171, 174–5, 177–8,
    182–4, 186, 195, 197, 219–20,
    225
  in Berlin 1, 13, 72, 74, 78, 80, 107, 110,
    143, 171, 175, 225
  creation 143, 182
  Dorferblick 74, 79
  human remains 201–3
  Humbolt Flaktower/hill 74, 79
  Insulaner 74, 79
  Marienhöhe 74, 79, 158
  Prenzlauerberg Volkspark 74, 79, 186
  remnants 15, 107, 188
  rubble 181–2
  Volkspark Friedrichshain 74, 79, 186
  Volkspark Hasenheide 74, 79–80, 140
Trümmerfrauen 79, 135, 189
Trump, D. 36, 43–4, 72

UK 6, 20, 177
  British slave trade 6
  historical foundations of 20
unification, German 97, 100
United States 44, 217, 226
  Confederate statues, removal 7
  historical foundations of 20
  transnational cultures of 34
United States Strategic Bombing Survey 30
urban and cultural landscape, Berlin 60

Valjavec, M. B. 204
Vergangeheitswebelantung 51
Vermeulen, P. 56, 58, 66
veterans' perspectives 31–2, 217–18
vibrant materiality 64–5, 68, 70, 125, 137,
    141, 198, 222
vibrant matter 65, 67, 126, 129, 153, 155
victors 4, 17, 191, 215
Vietnam War 21, 226 n.1
Vinitzky-Seroussi, V. 52
violence 8, 12, 14–15, 29, 40, 61, 71, 78,
    80, 83–4, 123–4, 127, 130, 132,

		138, 144, 146, 151, 153, 157, 167, 178, 184, 202, 213, 217, 219, 222, 230 n.10
	of aerial bombing 77, 107, 152
	Anthropocene 206–7
	of area bombing 20, 122, 223
	bodily and sensory 14–15, 129, 137, 159, 168–77, 184, 187, 202, 211
	and brutality of war 29
	economy of 127, 130
	European colonization 129
	forensic traces (*see* forensic traces of violence)
	geopolitical system of 140
	Islamophobia and racial 52
	material witnesses 15, 67, 219
	violent epistemologies 163
	visceral 30, 155, 169, 177, 202, 219
Virilio, P., war and cinema 161–2
virtual and augmented reality 50
visitors and sites 8, 15, 48–9, 63, 68–70, 72, 81–2, 84, 95, 159, 179, 184, 195, 218, 229 n.1
Vonnegut, K., *Slaughterhouse Five* 22, 132–3

Ware, S. A. 59

warfare 31, 88, 144, 161–4, 169–70, 182, 204
war memory
	history of present of 25–7, 49
	Second World War 10, 53–4
War on Terror 36, 88
waste 195–8, 201
Wessolek, G. 108, 205, 208
Whitehead, M. 144, 161, 163, 170, 179–80
Widmann, T. 41
Wiel, K. 66
Wigley, M. 127, 130
Wilhemstraße 167
Williams, A. J. 144, 161, 163, 170, 179–80
Williamson, L. A. 35
	Yankee ingenuity 34
Wilson, M. G. 92
Winston Churchill statue, protecting 6–7, 216
Woodward, C. 112

Zalasiewicz, J. 209, 211
Zalasiewicz, M. 209
Zehfuss, M. 10, 20
Zeller, T. 102
Zinn, H. 138

www.ingramcontent.com/pod-product-compliance
Lightning Source LLC
Chambersburg PA
CBHW071816300426
44116CB00009B/1336